Praise for *Outlaw Christian*

What impresses me most abou███is remarkable book is its absolute clarity. You don't have to be ████gian to understand this book; you don't have to be a Chris██████ just have to be a thoughtful and open-minded human be███████ants to have a richer, deeper, more meaningful life. Jacqu████sie not only tells us what we need to do, but she also illustr█████we need to do with marvelous examples from her life, her te███████g, and the lives and experiences of her students. The final chapter on hope is absolutely stunning in its concreteness. If Sir Thomas More was "the man for all seasons," then this is "the book for all seasons." A life changing book.

—TONY ABBOTT, PROFESSOR EMERITUS OF ENGLISH, DAVIDSON
COLLEGE, AUTHOR OF *THE ANGEL DIALOGUES*; AND WINNER
OF THE 2015 NORTH CAROLINA AWARD IN LITERATURE

Reading *Outlaw Christian* was like having a late-night conversation with a dear friend. The experience is filled with deep confessions, refreshing honesty, and new grace. I hope readers take away the same thing I did—a rekindled love for the God who finds us and frees us.

—SARAH THEBARGE, AUTHOR OF *THE INVISIBLE GIRLS*

While this is a Christian book, its gifts are available to anyone who has ever wrestled with the seemingly impossible task of making sense of suffering, loss, evil, inequity, and loneliness—including atheists like me. Reading Dr. Bussie's call to reject clichés and sit with uncertainty, I found myself hoping this book makes its way into the hands of every Christian who has ever had their questions or pain shut down by a platitude or an easy answer.

—CHRIS STEDMAN, AUTHOR OF *FAITHEIST* AND EXECUTIVE
DIRECTOR OF THE YALE HUMANIST COMMUNITY

I served as a parish pastor for twenty-five years. Walking with my people in times of crisis and deep pain I came to realize that some of their deepest struggles were not about loss nor about making sense out of what had happened, but find⬛g the space within themselves and within their faith commun⬛ ⬛o speak honestly and openly about their doubt and anger ⬛ ⬛God. Now Jacqueline Bussie, a theologian of t⬛e church, ⬛ ⬛r experience and gives voice to all who have been ⬛aught i⬛ ⬛ef that doubt is faithlessness and anger toward God is blas⬛ ⬛uite the opposite, Dr. Bussie argues, doubt and anger are rea⬛ ⬛ions of a living faith. *Outlaw Christian* might break the rules, bu⬛ it opens up the possibility of deeper faith.

—Rev. Elizabeth A. Eaton, presiding bishop, Evangelical Lutheran Church in America

There's nothing fluffy about this book. It is raw, sassy, and from the heart. Bussie reminds us that God is not scared of our doubts, fears, and darkness—God even experienced them in Jesus. This is a fresh invitation to the faith for skeptics, doubters, seekers, and even folks who like that old-time-religion. Become an outlaw Christian. God likes holy rebels.

—Shane Claiborne, author of *The Irresistible Revolution*, *Jesus for President*, and *Executing Grace*

Dr. Jacqueline Bussie has written this book for those Christians who crave the honest Gospel, stripped of deceptive prettiness and unreal promises; one that acknowledges our pain, welcomes our doubts, legitimizes our anger and insists that only when we are able to witness to the entire truth of our lives can we truly understand what the Good News means for us and for the world. *Outlaw Christian* invites us to step out of bounds again and again in search of an authentic faith with the end result being that we encounter our most authentic self.

—Paul Raushenbush, *Huffington Post* executive editor of Global Spirituality and Religion

To my students—past, present, and future

Outlaw Christian

Outlaw Christian

Finding Authentic Faith by
Breaking the "Rules"

JACQUELINE A. BUSSIE

NELSON
BOOKS

An Imprint of Thomas Nelson

Published in Nashville, Tennessee, by Nelson Books, an imprint of Thomas Nelson. Nelson Books and Thomas Nelson are registered trademarks of HarperCollins Christian Publishing, Inc.

Published in association with the literary agency of Daniel Literary Group, Brentwood, TN 37027.

Thomas Nelson titles may be purchased in bulk for educational, business, fund-raising, or sales promotional use. For information, please e-mail SpecialMarkets@ThomasNelson.com.

Some names and identifying details have been changed to protect the privacy of individuals.

Unless otherwise noted, Scripture quotations are taken from New Revised Standard Version Bible. Copyright © 1989 National Council of the Churches of Christ in the United States of America. Used by permission. All rights reserved.

Scripture quotations marked NIV are from the Holy Bible, New International Version*, NIV*. Copyright © 1973, 1978, 1984, 2011 by Biblica, Inc.* Used by permission of Zondervan. All rights reserved worldwide. www.zondervan.com. The "NIV" and "New International Version" are trademarks registered in the United States Patent and Trademark Office by Biblica, Inc.*

Any Internet addresses, phone numbers, or company or product information printed in this book are offered as a resource and are not intended in any way to be or to imply an endorsement by Thomas Nelson, nor does Thomas Nelson vouch for the existence, content, or services of these sites, phone numbers, companies, or products beyond the life of this book.

ISBN 978-0-7180-7665-8 (eBook)

Library of Congress Cataloging-in-Publication Data

Names: Bussie, Jacqueline Aileen.
Title: Outlaw Christian : finding authentic faith by breaking the rules / Jacqueline A. Bussie.
Description: Nashville : Thomas Nelson, 2016. | Includes bibliographical references.
Identifiers: LCCN 2015036333 | ISBN 9780718076641
Subjects: LCSH: Christian life.
Classification: LCC BV4501.3 .B897 2016 | DDC 248.4--dc23 LC record available at http://lccn.loc.gov/2015036333

Printed in the United States of America

16 17 18 19 20   RRD   10 9 8 7 6 5 4 3 2 1

Contents

Contents

Outlaw Christianity: (noun)

1. a new, life-giving faith for those who ache for a more authentic relationship with God and other people by no longer having to hide their doubt, anger, grief, scars, or questions

2. an honest, outside-the-law faith for those seeking a hope that really speaks to the world's hurt

Chapter One

Tired of Dishonesty?

Become an Outlaw Christian

> *When the man saw that he did not prevail against*
> *Jacob, he struck him on the hip socket; and Jacob's*
> *hip was put out of joint as he wrestled with him.*
> *Then he said, "Let me go, for the day is breaking." But*
> *Jacob said, "I will not let you go, unless you bless me."*
>
> —GENESIS 32:25–26

My mother was my best friend, until the day she forgot who I was. On that day, my own mom looked at me with kind eyes and asked, "Who are you? Are you my mom?" For the next sixteen years, early-onset Alzheimer's made sure my mother had no idea who anyone was, let alone me. On most days, this made me feel like one of the outcasts in ancient India whom the gods required to crawl backward out of the room, broom in hand, sweeping away her own footprints behind her. Parts of myself began to disappear, destined for the dust heap.

Watching the person I loved best in the world die made me realize that nearly everything I as a Christian had ever learned about suffering and evil was a crock, with a lot of pious clichés about "God's plan" and "God needing another angel" thrown in. I wrestled with this conclusion for years, but in the end it won out. All the so-called answers that I had been taught about suffering and sacrifice and salvation, when replayed in my sleepless head after a day of changing my mom's Depends, stung like a splash of bleach in my eyes. Words that once consoled made God feel further away than ever. I found myself asking, "Why didn't anyone ever tell me this is what life and love really feel like?" To make matters worse, all my family members splintered in their grief, and no one ever really talked about how much it hurt to lose my mother. Not talking about the hard stuff was nothing new, though. In the house where I grew up, pain was an invisible queen whom our silence kept on the throne. Fortunately, in the home where I live now, she no longer reigns.

When I was younger, before my mom got sick, I was completely in love with God. If you had known me then, you would have guessed I would grow up to be a religion professor. I often daydreamed about how it would be when I'd next see God's face, because I never doubted there would be a next time. I looked forward to it the way later in life I would look forward to seeing the person I was in love with, with cartwheels in my chest. I did not understand yet that my privilege was what made loving God feel so easy and natural, the same way red raspberries follow white blossoms on the summer vine. My vines had not yet suffered disease or drought, and I had not yet learned to pay attention to the vines of those persons who had suffered all that and more. As it turned out, my friends and their survivor-vines with their impossible fruit had everything to teach me. This book exists because of them.

As I became an adult who lived eyes-wide-open to the suffering of others, my love for God evolved. The way I grew to love God came to feel a lot like the way I felt back in high school when I fell in love with one of my best friends. He did not love me back, not "that way," he claimed as he broke the news that night in his Honda Civic and I hid my wet eyes behind my hands. From that day on, my best friend, though I still loved him with all of my heart, was a constant disappointment. Even looking at him hurt. His presence stung of loneliness, though of course his absence was even worse. I was a disappointment to him too, no doubt, because though he loved me, he recognized that in my eyes his love did not go far enough. Time with him was something I desperately longed for, but when I got it, my joy was so mixed up with longing that I felt like I was at the beach—my favorite place—but was being forced to eat sand. If you have ever loved someone who did not love you back, you know exactly what I mean. Everyone can connect to a story of unrequited love. But the weird thing is that no one ever wants to talk openly about the fact that for big chunks of our lives, millions of us feel this way about God.

In my journey toward becoming a more authentic person, I came to realize I was not like most other religious folks I knew. For one, I never outgrew the longing to talk about the stuff that hurts us most. I came to believe all of this secret keeping and soul hiding was, in the words of my hip nephew, cray-cray (read: crazy). For another, I had more in common with my atheist friends than with many of my Christian ones, though I myself was a Christian and not an atheist. I remember in college discovering the atheist whom Christians love to hate, the "God is dead" philosopher Friedrich Nietzsche. I stumbled upon a sentence that made me stop short in which Nietzsche argued that although Christians want to claim Christ redeemed the world, a simple glance at the world and all its death headlines should be enough to tell us that Christ could only be said to have failed.

I stared at those words for a long time, hating how much they wrapped words around an unnamed fear that surfaced in my gut whenever I watched cable news or listened to my high school friend Mary Beth explain that she put a deadbolt on her bedroom door to stop her brother from "messing with" her. I began to suspect that perhaps Nietzsche, whom most forget was the son of a Lutheran pastor, was an atheist because he was as disappointed by God as I was sometimes. We both were confused by what looked like unkept promises. Secretly, part of me admired and was fascinated by Nietzsche's audacious authenticity, though I almost never admitted this to any of my conservative Christian friends and family, let alone to myself.

Unlike some of the atheists I knew, however, I didn't want to let go of God or my faith. Okay, that's not totally true. Some days I did want to throw God out like a used sweater that no longer fit, was irretrievably retro, and had holes in the elbows and stains down the front. But this sweater somehow kept reappearing in my closet, messing with my style. I couldn't ever completely break up with and let go of God even when I wanted to, or maybe closer to the truth, God wouldn't let *me* go or break up with me. For whatever reason, unlike my atheist friends, *I wanted God back.* Some of the Christians I knew admitted to sometimes feeling far from God like I did, but they had been taught to fear talking about it. Unlike them, I didn't want to accept God under the usual laws of dishonesty, silence, intimidation, and fear. About the time my mom was diagnosed with her illness, I decided to go to graduate school in religion. I wanted to become a theologian and a professor of religion in order to reclaim what I had lost as best I could.

And so, today, I am a Christian, but a strange one—one who sometimes finds herself closer kin to Buddhists, atheists, and agnostics than Christians. I am a teacher of religion, but probably unlike any you have ever met. No question or doubt is ever out of bounds in my classes. A religion major who was taking his fifth course with me once blew my mind when he raised his hand mid-class and declared, "You are the only person who ever tells us the truth about anything." Though I doubt I am the *only* one, since then, many other people in my life have said something similar. Apparently I am willing to go places that most other religious folks are unwilling to go.

But let's face it, honest people are usually lawbreakers. No wonder most people turn tail and run from truth telling, for who wants to live inside the jail of other people's judgment? Once I realized this tough truth about honesty, so much about my life clicked. No wonder I am always in trouble. But also, no wonder I can always find joy.

Some years later, a dear friend was reading some of the early pages of this book when he exclaimed, "You know what you are? You're an outlaw Christian." As you can see, the name stuck. The novelist Reynolds Price coined the term, but I want to put my own spin on it.[1]

The name *outlaw Christian* describes the kind of Christian I am and the kind I'm setting myself free to become: namely, a follower of Jesus who no longer accepts cocky clichés, hackneyed hope, or snappy theodicies—defenses of God's goodness and power—that explain away evil and suffering with a theo-magical sleight of hand. An outlaw Christian doesn't condemn questions or discourage doubt. Instead, an outlaw Christian seeks to live an authentic life of faith and integrity, and chooses to defy the unwritten laws governing suffering, grief, and hope that our culture and our religious traditions have asked us to ingest.

The faith of an outlaw Christian is bold, outspoken, and active in a world of pain. On the one hand, I am tired of the Barbie-doll-smile kind of hope so many Christians embrace that refuses to get dirt under its fake fingernails in the struggle against the world's deep suffering and injustice. On the other hand, I am tired of why-bother-even-getting-out-of-bed despair—especially my own—which at times has preemptively broken up with hope and authentic living in order to avoid further disappointment and heartbreak. Neither path will do. The faith of an outlaw Christian laments, loves, laughs, longs, and lives, but the one thing it never does is lie . . . about anything.

These days I try to be an outlaw Christian who walks the tightrope between realism and hope, between the *Way Things Are* and the *Way We Long for Them to Be.* I am a person who lives in a house of longing—not for daydreams, but for revolutions. I call it revolutionary because my longing—for a world, for example, of more mercy, justice, presence, hope, and humanization—changes things. Most of all, it changes me—where I go, to whom I show love, whom I sit down beside, and what I do, say, want, and teach.

Perhaps at this moment you are asking yourself, "Why should I read a book like this?" Let me start by saying that this is the book I wished I could've read during times of struggle in my own life—struggles with meaning, doubt, love, despair, hope, God, and justice. If you are a person who does not have all the answers about faith and life but can't stop thinking about the questions even though they are hard, this book is for you. If you are a person who sometimes watches the news and wonders in the pit of your stomach what God could possibly be up to these days while the world cannonballs even deeper into greed, war, and violence, this book is for you. If you are a person who has ever loved someone, lost them, and then heard the hidden question *why* blacksmith your heart so hard it felt like your ears bled, this book was written with you at heart.

If you believe you could gain something by listening to a story from someone who does not have all the answers but has met a lot of amazing people, learned a lot of hope-giving things, and spent a lot of time reading, praying, and walking around in the labyrinth of life's big, messy questions, again, this book encourages you to read on. If you have ever courageously wondered what the meaning of all this working, laughing, and laboring is, this book in your hands urges you not to put it down. One of my favorite sayings is that there is only one real difference between the courageous and the non-courageous, and that is, the truly courageous hold on to courage for five minutes longer. This book wants your five minutes.

A second question you might have for me is: "Why did you write this book?" I have four answers. First, I wrote this book for the many people in my life whom I love and appreciate and to whom I realized I had so much to say that I had never said. For my two pastors, who when I was a preteen never shut me down when I asked all the prickly questions in Sunday school like, "Why was my cousin Denise born with brain damage?" "Why did God let my friend Sunny die when that drunk driver hit her car?" and "Can't God love people of other faiths enough to send them to heaven too?" For my friend Tara, who after her third miscarriage in a row composed piano music to replace the prayers she could not pray and asked me, "How do you pray when you don't know what to say?" For my student Leah, who came to me one day to tell me she had been raped by her brother and father since she was twelve-years-old, which caused her to feel so utterly abandoned by God she sobbed into her arm, "I mean, is God just an a****** or what?"[2] For my students' and my South African host mother who saw her family murdered right in front of her during Apartheid but nonetheless opened her heart and no-running-water home to us, and who one day asked, "Why didn't anyone ever warn me life could hurt this bad?" This book is for all these people I love, and for many more, including the people you love who are brave enough to ask you tough questions like these.

Second, I wrote this book for myself, because this book is the story of a wrestler wrestling. I wrestle every day to believe that God is love and that hope is more than just marshmallow armor in a world sworded with disaster, lovelessness, and despair. I'm too embarrassed to admit to you how old I was before I realized that my name, Jacqueline, is the female version of the name Jacob, the famous troublemaker and God-wrestler in the Bible. Let's just say I have accidentally but consummately lived into the name my parents gave me. Like Jacob in the Bible, I get hurt a lot of the time and walk away from my faith-wrestling matches with limps and scars. No good can come from pretending otherwise. But the more willing I am to talk about my tough time in the ring, the more willing other people are to show me their own bruises and out-of-joint hips. Such openness changes everything in a way I hope you will experience for yourself.

Third, I wrote this book because of the invisible outlaw creed that lies behind its pages—the beliefs I would be willing to bet my life on if it ever came down to it. My creed goes a little something like this: I believe in the value of bearing witness to the hope, pain, love, and loss that I have experienced in this life, and in the value of listening to you bear yours. I believe none of us can heal until we start telling one another the terrible truths that shape our deepest grief. I believe that our secrets, when kept secret, are killing us. I believe God is real but a mystery through and through, which makes God worth talking about and trying to understand better because maybe if we all share clues, God won't be unsolved forever. I believe God is hidden much of the time, and all the folks who tell you otherwise are either lying to protect you (or themselves) because the truth hurts too much to admit, or they are incapable of telling the truth because they have not yet suffered the kind of soul-crushing loss that makes God feel majorly MIA to the rest of us.

But I also believe God loves to be found the same way an old secret journal knows its ink is wasted until the moment someone blows the dust off the cover and reads the first page. I believe you, too, want to be found, want to be known by God and other people more than you feel you are known now. I believe I will grow if you share your story with me, and that you will grow if I tell you mine. I believe God will grow if God hears all of our stories, and if we demand God listen to them all, no exceptions. I believe that sharing despair has the power to wither despair on the vine. Likewise, I believe hope can bloom even in the desert of conflict and loss. I believe our stories are love's currency, and faith's too. They can make us rich or leave us poor, and if they go untold, the result is always poverty. I believe in the power of community to hold us when we can no longer hold ourselves. I believe community can form around anything we are brave enough to share with one another, even if all we share is loneliness and loss. I believe shared vulnerability has the power to change the color of the sky as well as the seasons. I believe it is possible to dress for the weather.

I believe living a whole-grain life of faith and doubt will feed our soul's hunger better than the junk food jelly-bean diet of piety and clichés most of us have been forced to swallow whole like a catechism capsule. I believe authenticity, wonder, questioning, and honesty are the nutrients we need to make our faith healthy and whole and genuinely our own at last. I believe that many of you reading this page are, like me, sick to death of malnourishment, lies, faith-clichés, unaccounted-for pain, and hope that is mocked.

Fourth and finally, I wrote this book to set the record straight on an important word: *theology*. The word literally means "the study of God," or "God-talk." What a terrible, disappointing definition. I suspect you think of theology as something abstract, academic, and disconnected—a lifeless project reserved for intellectuals, PhDs, or pastors. But the truth is, theology is not something only theologians do. Theology is something *every* person of faith does, whether we call it by this name or not. People of faith, like you and me, do theology every day whenever we fight for justice, pass a dying friend a cold glass of water, wonder what God is up to, and cry tears of joy when our child returns safe to our arms. In other words, we do theology whenever we laugh, live, love, and lament.

My new life-relevant definition of theology, then, is this: *theology is setting the wounds and joys of our own stories next to God's.* Theology is the messy and beautiful reconciliation we people of faith make every day between God's life and God's promises on the one hand, and CNN and our own diaries on the other. Theology, therefore, is faith trying to make sense of the world so we can live better within it. Theology and faith are best friends who hate to live apart.

In the words of teacher and theologian Rebecca Chopp, theology saves lives. I believe that (1) all of our lives, without exception, are worth saving, and (2) if we don't start right now giving one another straight talk about how and why, we might one day wake up to find we can no longer remember what it was we hoped to save. This book is a practical guide for saving lives and finding the joy, authenticity, hope, and redemption for which we all yearn. This a book about outlaw Christians and how outlaw Christianity can set us free to love the unlovable, speak the unspeakable, remember the unmemorable, believe the unbelievable, survive the un-survivable, and perhaps most important of all, hope the un-hopeable.

Chapter Two

Angry at the Almighty?

Tell God the Truth

> *I will not restrain my mouth;*
> *I will speak in the anguish of my spirit;*
> *I will complain in the bitterness of my soul.*
>
> —JOB 7:11

> *One of the profoundest forms of faithlessness is*
> *the unwillingness to acknowledge our inexplicable*
> *suffering and pain.*
>
> —PASTOR AND THEOLOGIAN STANLEY HAUERWAS

When someone starts to cry in front of you, what is the first thing they usually say? What is the first thing *you* say when your broken heart makes you cry in front of a friend? "I'm sorry," we all say. But why do we say this? Is our sadness wrong or mean or ugly or embarrassing? Is it a rudeness or a mistake, like backing our car into the neighbor's mailbox? Of course not. Then why do we think our grief always merits an apology? The last time my students and I discussed this craziness, we all vowed together, "We will no longer apologize for our tears." Apologizing for our humanness is just one example of the many everyday practices that wound our spiritual selves but that we don't think to question. This chapter invites you to start asking whether these behaviors and beliefs really fit you and your life of faith or not, or whether you are just going along with them because everybody else is and coaching you that you should be too. As my mother always loved to remind me, "Just because all of your friends are jumping off a bridge doesn't mean you should too."

Whether or not we are willing to admit it, we walk through the world with an onerous inheritance of faith-laws and spiritual dos and don'ts strapped to our back. These rules guide our religious thoughts and actions with an imperceptible force—the way Adam Smith declared the economy is guided by an invisible hand—with the major difference that religious rules are *waaaaaaaay* scarier, because they claim that God will no longer love you if you don't follow them.

When I lived in rural Japan for a year, I saw that many of the *obaasans* (grandmothers) walked around town terribly hunched over because of their years spent working in the rice fields, their backs forming a near-perfect yet painful-looking crescent moon. We are spiritual versions of the obaasans. Yet with each other's help, we can become the people God wants us to be—people who walk around with our backs straight and unburdened, heads held high as hope itself.

Contemporary Christianity's unwritten book that enchains us contains commonly accepted laws about what people of faith should believe, say, do, and feel about evil, suffering, sadness, grief, and hope. The author of this acceptability manual is anyone's guess. No doubt it is a complex combination of Western pop wisdom, American cultural tradition and norms, communal expectations, capitalist superpower values, and religious authorities' teachings. What I can say for sure is that odds are a million to one that you—like I once was—are its finest (though perhaps unwilling) practitioner. The good news is that you no longer have to be.

The time has long since passed for these unwritten rules to be debunked, challenged, and condemned the way the FDA banned the toxin Red Dye No. 2 in the '70s. It's time for Christians—and anyone else who wants to join us—to become outlaws, because these fabricated laws are killing us softly.

To understand the depth of the spiritual damage these unspoken laws cause, we need to get down to some straight talk about how these so-called laws command us to love, grieve, and just plain *live* in this world that on some days is more bewildering than a Tokyo street map. By exposing these "laws" as narratives of the lie, we will lay bare the violence they do to our lives and our relationships.[1] A parallel here would be the way the law told Jesus he could not work on the Sabbath, but Jesus went ahead and healed a man's hand and fed his disciples on the Sabbath anyway, by explaining that we should follow only laws that are life-giving and not life-destroying (Luke 6:9). In order to really follow Jesus, we must stop following laws that destroy life.

Law #1: Never get mad at God. Anger at the Almighty is blasphemy.

The day after the Haitian earthquake hit on January 12, 2010, almost every global newspaper in print and online portrayed images of the tragedy. I saw a photo online of a tiny little girl orphaned by the quake. Her face was turned up to the sky and her skinny brown arms were raised as high over her head as they could go, as if she were begging God to pick her up at the end of a too-long walk. I knew that even before the earthquake, Haiti was one of the poorest countries in the world. That night I tossed and turned for hours. When sleep finally came, I dreamed that the little girl from the photo was crying at the side of my bed while I slept, but my arms were paralyzed and I couldn't pick her up. This is a dream I have had many times since.

For many years, my military veteran cousin Diane was the only female lieutenant of the special victims unit in a small town in the upper Midwest. Not until she retired was she even able to share with me some of the sexual crimes of abuse, incest, and molestation she had investigated. One night, with a glass of merlot in her hand that she sipped like an honesty serum, Diane confessed, "The one that scarred me the most was when a six-month-old baby was brought in who had been perpetrated on." She went on to raise the question that beats at the heart of this book: "Why is it some people are served a s*** sandwich from the day they were born?" Listening to Diane that night made me think of the German word the psychologist William James once used to describe human life—*Zerrissenheit*, a word for which there is no English equivalent, but that is best translated "torn-to-pieces-hood." It also made me think of a line in a book I read by a Holocaust survivor: "God is on leave."[2]

"Why is the child crying?" In Alice Walker's novel *Possessing the Secret of Joy*, the father of a boy named Adam claims that this question about a child's tears is the fundamental question one must ask of the world.[3] Surely Walker is right that this question lies at the center of the universe, just as it lies in the lungs of anyone who purports to have faith in humanity and/or in a God of love. Surely Walker is also right that God— who else could the father of Adam symbolize, after all?—wants us to confront this hard question head-on. If we refuse to ask ourselves and God this tough question, or we refuse to hear the hard and horrible answers, then we build our faith, justice, and hope on a foundation of marshmallow fluff.

And I still haven't told you the whole truth. The truth is that each of these stories of children crying made me so mad at God that if I had met God at that particular moment, I would have screamed in the Divine's holy, hidden face. I even might have spit. Now, don't get me wrong; of course these stories made me just as furious with the human race and with myself and the ugly, complicit role I play in the whole mess of injustice. But I'd be lying if I didn't admit they also made me want to roar at God with my mother's response to my disastrous teenage choices, "Sweet mother of pearl, what could you possibly be thinking?"

Even as I type this, I can hear the fear of judgment swirl in my eardrums. I can hear the law whispering in my ear, "Don't tell anyone how you really feel." I can hear like it was yesterday the words my dad always used to forbid us from sharing family secrets: "Don't air our dirty laundry." Now that I have confessed this rage at God, what will you think of me? Will you write me off as an untrustworthy Christian thinker? Will you believe that I am a Christian who still loves God? Will I lose my job as a religion professor at a Christian college? Will my students tell one another not to take my classes because I will try to make them "lose their faith"? Will people at my church—who respected me before reading this—now sneer instead of smile when I walk down the aisle in my Sunday dress to take the bread and wine? Will God despise and reject me?

These worries frighten me, for sure, but they no longer clutch me in their stranglehold of silence and secrecy the way they once did. Why not? Because something frightens me far more: *living a life of faith that is fake and inauthentic.* Silence, like every form of dishonesty, is life-destroying. I am scared to death of getting to the end of my life and discovering that my faith was a charade and something I never really owned, like my dad's leased car that disappeared back to the dealer's lot one day when he could no longer afford the payments. In my experience, only faith that is unafraid to ask the toughest questions can survive the toughest times. After all, it doesn't take much pressure to schmear marshmallow fluff so thin that it dissolves into nothing but a sticky memory.

As director of my college's Forum on Faith and Life, I travel all the time to churches, colleges, and community centers to talk to wonderful people about the questions and issues that matter most in their lives. Though this society of ours is otherwise completely polarized, one question always elicits the same answer from audience members, whether they are Muslim or Christian, female or male, CEO or waiter, old or young, conservative or progressive. And that question is: "How do you feel when you read the news online or watch the news on NBC,

CBS, or FOX?" Sadly, I don't have to be in the room with you right now or even have ever met you to know your answer to this question. Overwhelmed, depressed, helpless, confused, bewildered, horrified, numb, afraid, dumbfounded, stunned. Am I close?

Does the massive amount of hatred, war, homicide, terror, and violence that we perpetrate against one another make you feel like you cannot even turn on the news because you know if you do, you will just want to stay in bed and never get up? Does your community offer you no authentic space in which to ask all the starving questions that gnaw away deep down inside of you like a hidden tapeworm—questions like, *Are you still there, God?* and *Why, God, why?* and *How much longer does evil get to win?* Has your anger at God led you to abandon your faith or merely go through the motions to please your family? Have you ever had angry thoughts toward God, even if only for a second, in a children's cancer ward, a nursing home, a housing project, a courtroom, or in front of images of dead bodies being pulled from a movie-theatre shooting massacre?

If you answered yes to any of the above, then the important thing to realize is: *you are not alone.* You feel alone, I know. I know this because I often feel the same way, but really, nothing could be further from the truth. *You feel alone not because you really are alone but because of the nasty, unwritten faith-law that demands we keep such "sinful" thoughts secret and hidden from each other.*

Almost everyone I talk to about this has experienced rage at God at some point, as well as feelings of torn-to-pieces-hood, though in most circles they won't admit it. But I have noticed something remarkable, which is that if and when a brave, vulnerable person takes the lead and speaks directly to what most befogs her soul about God and life, other folks eventually follow suit. When it comes to our faith, most of us reside in the safety of the say-what-the-teacher-wants-to-hear Sunday school comfort zone, rarely if ever wandering outside into the call-it-like-I-really-see-it danger zone. *The goal of our faith should never be comfortableness.* As for me and my theology, we want nothing more than to keep it real. Only that way can I rest assured my hope is real too. And honestly, what could be more important than that?

I teach a class in my college's religion department called "The Problem of Evil," and I can tell you that if you build a safe, get-real space for people to talk about the hard and messy stuff, and if you are willing to go first, then just like Kevin Costner says in the film *Field of Dreams*, they will come. "The Problem of Evil" is always a popular class with students because evil is the question mark inside our faith that is dying to escape the prison of shame and self-censorship and ask in an audacious voice, "When will this massacre-madness stop? Why can't God just show up already?"

Here again, though, we are up against the cultural norm that teaches us that anger—any and all anger—is bad, a sign of lost control. Of course anger can be ugly, unwarranted, and selfish, but it simply isn't true that this is always the case. A mile-wide difference exists between the abusive, angry husband who throws a plate at his wife because his dinner is cold and the twenty-something who is so outraged by society's neglect of the homeless that she opens a teen shelter in her neighborhood.

I love what the church father St. Augustine says about this, which is essentially that a simplistic understanding of anger is rubbish. Augustine writes, "Hope has two beautiful daughters. Their names are anger and courage; anger at the way things are, and courage to see that they do not remain the way they are."[4] In other words, anger is an essential element within hope, because hope is not possible unless you get sufficiently mad at the mess that made hope necessary in the first place. The kind of anger at God and at the world's current outrageous state of affairs that I am talking about gets born in hope's womb. It gets fertilized by the longing for a world better than ours—a longing God planted in us with that stunning line in the Scriptures that promises a world where every tear will be wiped from our eyes and death, mourning, crying, and pain will be no more (Revelation 21:4). In a nutshell, that is the world both my hope and my anger want.

Anger Is Honesty

"Honesty is always the best policy," my mom used to say. We want honesty from everyone in life, and therefore know we should return the favor, yet for some bizarre and unfathomable reason, we vigorously exempt God from our honesty-is-best policy. If our dishonesty hurts the people who love us, why do we believe our dishonesty doesn't hurt God? Can you name one time in your life when burying your deepest anger and never, ever naming it to anyone made all the pain and hurt go away? Did your silence make everything fine again between you and the person who hurt you? If this doesn't work in our relationships with each other, how much less does it work in our ⟨relationships w⟩ith God? As they say in Alcoholics Anonymous, ⟨what we⟩ don't talk about and are *afraid* to talk about con⟨trols us more than⟩ we can't even guess. As for me and the people I know, we can't let go of our anger until we expose it to the air. Wounds kept under a bandage too long begin to fester.

Now just to be clear, I am not talking about being angry at God as a permanent state of being, nor am I saying fury should be the only way we relate to God when bad things happen. What I am saying is that for many of us, anger happens sometimes, and repressing or ignoring it not only makes you dishonest, it toxifies your gut.

When I was at my lowest point of depression during my mother's illness, I ended up weighing eighty-seven pounds and wasting away in a dark apartment, nibbling daily on a diet of lies and loneliness. I broke up with my boyfriend and returned none of my friends's phone calls. I became a master of self-sabotage, ensuring, as the saying goes, that I received not the love I craved but the love I felt I deserved . . . which was no love at all.

When I finally got help, a wise counselor taught me something I had never heard: *depression is anger turned inward*. In other words, I was taking all the fury I felt at God out on myself. The truth was I was livid with God for the fact that everyone in the entire world had become a total stranger to my Alzheimer's-ridden mother. Even the sight of her own family's faces could not console or comfort her; she was on board that *Titanic* alone. More than anything in the world, I just wanted her to have a hand to hold while the ship went down. That she was robbed of that one small thing felt like nothing I could really name, but the word *cruelty* came closest to the mark.

My counselor had me write, and then burn over a candle, a letter to God spilling my guts. I'm pretty sure the words *I hate you* were in there somewhere, but confusingly, *I love you* was the very page on which they were written. That was the summer I learned the hard way that all the anger at God you bottle up inside your soul finds a way out some way, somehow, usually exploding like a shaken-up Coke not in the face of the God you are actually mad at but instead in your own. Letting God have it in that long-overdue letter didn't change my life overnight, but I recognize now it was a crucial first step toward healing. Honesty set me free from having to live the rest of my life underwater.

When need be, outlaw Christians give voice to our anger at God. Most of us resist the freedom that comes with speaking the truth about our anger and our hurt, in that same weird way that even though we know darn well throwing up will make us feel better, we still fight giving in to the heaves. As my mother always said to me when the stomach flu drove me to my knees, "Just let it all out, I promise you'll feel better."

The point of all this is, God is a real friend, not a Facebook friend. God is interested in *way* more than your smiley, sunny pictures of your kids at their soccer game and your dog in his Santa hat, or for that matter your rant-post about the long line at Starbucks this morning. God wants the *whole* you. God wants a real conversation, not just a 140-character tweet or status update. God wants to sit with you, even if sometimes you just have to throw it all up. God wants to know *everything that is really going on with you,* all of your deepest thoughts and fears and idiosyncrasies and worries. "Just let it all out, I promise you'll feel better."

I have decided—as would be the case with any other friend I truly love—that not telling God what's on my heart feels like badmouthing God inside the closet of my mind. Therefore, on this page and in writing: *I am coming out of the closet as a*

Christian who is, some of the time, very pissed off at God. Okay, a lot of the time. God already knows this anyway, I imagine, because as Psalm 44:21 says, God knows the secrets of our hearts. So I guess the only person for whom this was really a secret was you. Oh yeah . . . and me, for a really, really long time.

Biblical Outlaws

By now I hope you are asking, "How do I know that it's okay for us to be upset with God, to tell God how we really feel?" "For the Bible tells me so," as the line in that old Sunday school song goes. For most of us, the Bible has become like an uncle who is always around but whom we have learned to ignore. We assume we already know everything he's going to say, or worse, we fear that what he's going to say will condemn half the people we love to hell. The Bible (and Uncle Bob) becomes incapable of surprising us. Because our minds are already filled with a messy and complicated set of assumptions and biases, when we actually do read the Bible, we oftentimes shape what we actually read to fit the "laws" we already know. At other times, we simply ignore the parts of the Bible that defy the laws or our expectations. Nowhere is this problem more evident than in our mistaken assumptions regarding what the Bible says about the value of anger at God and genuine questioning of the Divine.

I know this is true because I read the Bible for myself, and the Bible's pages actually overflow with admirable spiritual outlaws like Job, the psalmist, and Qoheleth (the writer of Ecclesiastes who is typically called "the Teacher" in most translations). Only the truly brave would want to meet these dudes alone on a dusty Wild West road, because one encounter with them will scare the wits out of what you think is true about how a faithful person relates to God. Yet I have met amazing people in real life who have followed in these outlaws' footsteps, which means that you and I can too. To do so, we need at last to be ourselves, rather than the people others want or expect us to be.

The Psalmist

First, let's take a look at what the writer of the Psalms has to say.

> *Because of you we are being killed all day long,*
> *and accounted as sheep for the slaughter.*
>
> *Rouse yourself! Why do you sleep, O Lord?*
> *Awake, do not cast us off forever!*
> *Why do you hide your face?*
> *Why do you forget our affliction and oppression?*
> *(44: 22–24)*

Here, the psalmist accuses God of not only forgetting and hiding from the Divine's own people but also slaughtering them. The psalmist is hopping mad at the world's out-of-control suffering.

Qoheleth

Second, the teacher Qoheleth launches some pretty scathing critiques about the world's immense pain and God's fairness:

Again I saw all the oppressions that are practiced under the sun. Look, the tears of the oppressed—with no one to comfort them! . . . And I thought the dead, who have already died, more fortunate than the living, who are still alive; but better than both is the one who has not yet been, and has not seen the evil deeds that are done under the sun. (Ecclesiastes 4:1–3)

Translation: "We're better off dead," says Qoheleth the outlaw right to God's face, or "We're better off never having been born." Qoheleth tells God he thinks it's downright evil that God creates human beings only one day to kill us all off:

All this I laid to heart, examining it all, how the righteous and the wise and their deeds are in the hand of God; whether it is love or hate one does not know. Everything that confronts them is vanity, since the same fate comes to all, to the righteous and the wicked, to the good and the evil. . . . This is an evil in all that happens under the sun, that the same fate comes to everyone. (Ecclesiastes 9:1–3)

The flabbergasting fact remains that Ecclesiastes is one of the Bible's books of *wisdom*, and the Bible calls Qoheleth our Teacher.

Job

Third and lastly, the book of Job provides the most interesting outlaw case of all. As you know, the book is about a righteous man named Job who loses everything all because Satan bets God that he can make Job sin against God if he does this to him. Satan snatches everything away from Job, including his health, possessions, and innocent wife and kids. Job laments his torn-to-pieces-hood and hurls angry questions at a God who appears guilty of reckless endangerment. Job's friends come to visit him and offer him the standard stale religious explanations for why Job is suffering—"God is punishing you for your sin. God is teaching you to be a better person. God will use your trials to purify and strengthen your faith. Everything happens for a reason. God has a plan, yada-yada-yada." At the end of the book, God appears in a whirlwind and refuses to answer any of Job's questions, suggesting that since Job was not there when the Almighty created the world, he could not possibly understand why the world works the way it does.

Take out the Bible and read aloud a few passages from Job. Try to start fresh. Erase from your mind all you have heard and been taught about the book, and really *read* it, the curious way you would read a message in a bottle that the ocean washed up to your feet. The first time I read the book of Job this way, I was as stunned as if my great-granny had gotten up out of her front porch rocking chair and started doing handsprings.

For starters, Job wants to take God to court for being an abusive parent. Job believes he would undoubtedly win if only he could get a judge to preside over the case:

> *Oh, that I knew where I might find him,*
> *that I might come even to his dwelling!*
> *I would lay my case before him,*
> *and fill my mouth with arguments. . . .*
> *There an upright person could reason with him,*
> *and I should be acquitted forever by my judge.*
> *(23:3–4, 7)*

In chapter 6, Job asks God to just go ahead and kill him now rather than continue to torture him:

> *O that I might have my request,*
> > *and that God would grant my desire;*
> *that it would please God to crush me,*
> > *that he would let loose his hand and cut me off! . . .*
> *And what is my end, that I should be patient? (vv. 8–9, 11)*

A few chapters later, an unreserved Job accuses God of cruelty:

> *Bold as a lion you hunt me;*
> > *you repeat your exploits against me . . .*
> > *you bring fresh troops against me.*
> *Why did you bring me forth from the womb? (10:16–18)*

And finally, Job accuses God of being unjust and unloving:

> *God has put me in the wrong,*
> > *and closed his net around me.*
> *Even when I cry out, "Violence!" I am not answered;*
> > *I call aloud, but there is no justice.*
> *He has walled up my way so that I cannot pass . . .*
> *He breaks me down on every side, and I am gone,*
> > *he has uprooted my hope like a tree. (19:6–8, 10)*

Translating Job's Bible-speak into modern-day, twenty-first-century lingo helps us rediscover how astonishing his claims really are. So here goes: "God, I hate my life. The world you have created is totally unjust and it sucks"; "God, you hate me"; "I wish I had never been born"; "God, you masochist, you created me just to torture me"; "Just kill me now and get it over with already, it's what you will do in the end anyway"; and "God, you treat human beings like a lion who savagely shreds his prey in his teeth, like a serial killer treats the victim he is slashing open with his knife." If you ever heard someone in real life say these things to God, no matter what they said later or earlier, would you ever in a million years describe such a person as "patient"?

The Patience of Job

Haven't you heard folks use the expression "the patience of Job," as in "That person is so amazing, they must have the patience of Job"? I can think of a lot of other words to describe a person who would say this stuff—such as *irate, outraged, incredulous,* or *pissed off*—but *patient* would never, ever be one of the attributes that would come to mind. At the end of the book, yes, Job does repent in dust and ashes (42:6). (Christians love to repeat that part, ignoring all the rest.) So in the end, we could claim Job is humbled, humiliated, and maybe repentant, but patient? *Seriously?* A patient person would not need to repent before God, as he would only have been waiting—patiently!—for God's righteousness to appear all along.

Can a couple of verses of purported patience really trump thirty-seven *chapters* of vehement impatience? Thirty-seven chapters of comments like, "The earth is given into the hand of the wicked; he [God] covers the eyes of its judges—if it is not he, who then is it?" (9:24), and "He snatches away; who can stop him? Who will say to him, 'What are you doing?'" (9:12). Job is the only one with sufficient courage to ask, "God, what in the world are you doing?"

Ironically, in jarring contrast to the bizarre and never-questioned colloquialism "the patience of Job," Job flat-out rejects patience as either a spiritual virtue or an authentic option for a faithful outlaw like himself. In Job 21:4 (and elsewhere), Job explicitly describes himself as impatient (!):

> *As for me, is my complaint addressed to mortals?*
> *Why should I not be impatient? . . .*
> *Why do the wicked live on,*
> *reach old age, and grow mighty in power? . . .*
> *Their houses are safe from fear,*
> *and no rod of God is upon them. (vv. 4, 7, 9)*

Even though we modern readers for some zany reason want to believe Job is patient, this passage reveals that Job himself harbors no such preposterous self-delusions. But it's a fascinating question: How did we ever come up with a description of Job that is the antithesis of the person the Bible portrays him to be? Why do we insist on giving Job a label that he himself specifically rejects? Furthermore, why would it be wrong to be impatient for healing, for justice, for liberation, or for a sight of God's face? As if in anticipation of our interpretive missteps, Job utters a sentence of uncanny foreshadowing, "I know I am not what I am thought to be" (9:35).

Obviously, the unwritten faith-law stated at the beginning of this chapter—*Never get mad at God and don't argue with the Almighty*—is at work in all its painful weirdness here. Because of Law #1, we are uncomfortable with a biblical faith-hero who is an outlaw, who questions God and calls God out on the dumb-founding, cruel massiveness of human suffering. And so, rather than challenge the law and become outlaws ourselves, we create our own Disney version of Job to uphold the law's pharaoh-like power. In other words, rather than change ourselves (too hard and costly!), we change Job (much easier and cheap!).

For example, in media mogul Arianna Huffington's recent bestseller *Thrive*, she perpetuates the pop-culture Job by claiming that in the midst of all the horrible things that befell him, all Job said was: "The Lord gave and the Lord has taken away. Blessed be the name of the Lord praised."[5] Well, Arianna is right. Job does say those words, but only in chapter *1*, before he is inflicted with boils all over his body and watches his whole family die. In the forty other chapters that Arianna ignores, virtually everything Job says negates this platitude with a vengeance.

Rooted in our American desire to tattoo meaning onto suffering's back no matter the cost, we create Fantasy Job. Airbrushed Job. Job 2.0. *Job is patient with God, not angry. Job praises God even in the midst of his most terrible suffering, and so should you.* We whitewash Job, re-spin his story of ache and anguish in a coating of Splenda so artificial and chemical-sweet, many of us cannot even bear the taste of it on our tongues. As a friend of mine likes to say about death-by-chocolate desserts, the first two bites are amazing, but all the rest are sugar-nasty.

I love how the real Job—not the sugar-nasty version—speaks exactly what is on his heart. "I will not restrain my mouth; I will speak in the anguish of my spirit; I will complain in the bitterness of my soul" (7:11). Sometimes I use these words as a necessary preface to my prayers, which are just honest conversations with God about all the junk in life I just don't understand. Every time I say these startling verses out loud, I feel their audacity coursing through my bloodstream like a bracing shot of bourbon. Try saying them yourself. How do they make you feel? Whiny? Guilty? Liberated?

If you feel guilty or ungrateful saying such words yourself, consider this: (SPOILER ALERT!) *in a shocking twist at the end, God affirms all Job has said.* While we expect that God would be furious with the things Job has said, and side with Job's friends who all take the party line and offer traditional explanations for suffering, this does not happen. Instead, when God finally appears in the whirlwind at the end of the book, God sides with Job and discredits all the bland, cliché justifications the friends have offered (and that we ourselves have heard a million times from our Christian friends).

> The LORD said to Eliphaz the Temanite: "My wrath is kindled against you and against your two friends; for you have not spoken of me what is right, as my servant Job has. Now therefore . . . my servant Job shall pray for you, for I will accept his prayer not to deal with you according to your folly." (42:7–8)

WHAT?!?

Claiming that Job deserved all the suffering he received or that God allowed him to suffer so that his faith would grow stronger is *folly*, or foolishness, even to God?

Though God during the whirlwind diatribe expresses frustration with Job's audacity, in the end God seems to respect Job's chutzpah more than the friends' tired and threadbare rationalizations of suffering. God is not mad at Job; instead, in the book's final verses, God gives Job back everything he had twofold.[6] God somehow, someway, shockingly champions Job's anger as "right speech," as an acceptable way to speak with God. But most people ignore all this and persist in the mistaken notion that the book of Job teaches you not to stand up to God, but instead to be patient and keep your lowlife human mouth shut because the big powerful God-in-the-sky created the world and you didn't, thank you very much. Some people can love a God like that and at times I respect and even envy those who can, but I myself just can't do it. I know I can't, because I've tried and I nearly died. Never forget that if you can't love a keep-your-mouth-shut God either, then you are not alone. Some people in the Bible like Job are standing behind you, saying, "Yeah, I've got your back."

In the end, I have nothing but respect for Job's honesty, though at first what he says hurts God and me both to have to hear. Job's words are a theological Brillo Pad that scrapes away centuries of caked-on crusty crap. Biblical scholars will of course remind us that the final version of the book of Job that is in the Bible today is the composite result of several different writers and editors, which can account for inconsistencies in the text's message. While true, the end product is what eventually passed muster, and what astonishes me is that the wild story as we have it is actually in the Bible. But I suspect I know at least one good reason why it is there, and that is . . . *to set the hurting Job-like part of ourselves free.* Job, an outlaw, teaches us we don't have to Disney-fy our feelings or faith.

Job told God exactly how furious he felt and God did not run away from him, shouting, "Traitor!" or "Sinner!" Instead, *God showed up.* When I yell at God, I secretly want this more than anything. Most people who are really angry at God just want God to come back home already, and stop being a runaway. Though God's whirlwind explanation to Job might fail to satisfy, the fact remains that *God rewards Job's honesty with presence.* Hiding Job's wounds under a cotton-candy robe of denial robs the story of all its hope. It makes most people believe God is a big bully in the sky whom you better never stand up to on the playground unless you want the snot kicked out of you. But the liberating truth is that ultimately, God doesn't intimidate; God authenticates. What God authenticates is your heartrending struggle to be in relationship with Love even when it feels like Love has left you.

This makes the book of Job one of the most uplifting books in the entire Bible, especially for outlaw Christians, who have figured out that they couldn't hide their real selves from God even if they wanted to. God in Job's story makes me believe that God's whole self will show up if my whole self shows up. No mask necessary. God's jaw-dropping verdict that Job speaks rightly makes my own cries to God feel legit and heard. In the words of Elie Wiesel, Holocaust survivor, Nobel Peace Prize winner, and one of my spiritual heroes, "[Job's] ordeal concerns all humanity. Did he ever lose his faith? If so, he rediscovered it within his rebellion. He demonstrated that faith is essential to rebellion, and that hope is possible beyond despair."[7]

As an outlaw Christian set free for honesty, I feel like I no longer need to censor the things my heart longs to say to God. I have the right, as a person in a loving relationship with God, to demand that God show Love's face in the midst of deep suffering. As Wiesel explains, "God likes those who have the courage to stand up to him."[8]

If you feel so moved, put down this book right now. Find a safe place to shout. What do you want to scream at God about or even with God about? What in your life or our world makes you angriest at God? Write God a letter, say it out loud, or fill in the blanks right here:

_____

_____

_____

Wherever people in the world follow Job's lead, they have it out with God. In the book *Holy the Firm*, Annie Dillard shares that one Sunday, her pastor was in the middle of a long intercessory prayer filled with the usual requests—comfort and justice for the oppressed, wisdom for world leaders, hope and mercy and healing for the sick and grieving. Suddenly he stopped and shouted in frustration, "Lord, we bring you these same petitions every week!" After a deep breath, the pastor continued his prayer. Because the pastor went off script and let his prayer become a protest, Dillard decides that she "likes him very much."[9] Provoked by God's promises, have you ever let your prayers become protests?[10] Do you secretly respect and like people who do? Do you wish you were one of them?

Or does all of this talk of getting angry with God make you uncomfortable? It's okay either way, because the path of the outlaw Christian is not for everyone. It's only for those who need it. The other day my friend Caryn said to me that the relationship of every married couple should remain a mystery to everyone who is not the couple themselves. I admire Caryn for this acceptance. I, on the other hand, for no good reason other than nosiness, am always trying to figure out the dynamics of my friends' relationships.

My friends Pam and Jim argue a lot. Whenever my husband and I walk into their house, accusations tart the air like a recently cut grapefruit. Pam and Jim have no qualms about cutting loose into serious disagreements right in front of us. In the car on the way home, my husband and I usually rehash the tension of the visit. "Could you believe it when he said _____? And she was like _____?" (No, in case you are wondering, I am *not* proud that we do this.) When Pam and Jim first got together thirteen years and three happy children ago, I worried that they might not last. Obviously I am an idiot.

I see now that I was a total hypocrite not to realize that my relationship with God is a lot like Pam and Jim's. There is much confusion, arguing, misunderstanding, jealousy, and name-calling, as well as endless bewilderment and interrogation about motives, intention, absences, and whereabouts. Seen through the eyes of an outsider, it's not always pretty. Some of my friends think God and I are constantly on the cusp of divorce, but in truth, God and I both would laugh at such a suggestion. To these friends, doomsday seems nigh only because, like Pam and Jim (and Job), I choose not to hide God's and my arguments and mutual bewilderments from them. I am unafraid to let our dirty laundry hang on the line, because my mother taught me that when everything else has failed, very often the sun can take the stains out.

Arguments and anger are only half of the truth between God and me. Late at night, when all the guests have backed out of the driveway and God and I are alone, we share a tenderness that would baffle anyone who had seen us at each other's throats a few short hours ago. I don't understand my relationship with God, but what I do understand is that we are a braid, God and I. The apostle Paul is right, we are all working out our salvation with fear and trembling (Philippians 2:12). The greatest gift we can give one another, therefore, is to let each other work out our relationships with God without the judgments that usually follow a visit to one another's houses.

As long as we are talking to God, even if we are arguing, complaining, lamenting, and questioning, then we are still in relationship. Any kind of communication is still relating, and is not the same as shutting out or shutting down. In other words, anger means that if God happens to show up, we will still answer the door, if for no other reason than to finish telling God off.

Everybody forgets about Job's wife, but in the story she (not Job) is the one who divorces God. Perhaps she is in the story to teach us the difference between cursing and questioning, between doubting and dying, between walking out and staying, even if staying means staying angry. "Curse God, and die," Job's wife says to him (2:9), and that is exactly what she does. But Job refuses to take her advice. Job is pissed off at God beyond belief, yes, but he keeps pounding on God's door with both fists. Outlaw Christians are like Job, not Job's wife.

As Elie Wiesel reminds us, "The opposite of love is not hate, it is indifference."[11] Love and hate are blood brothers, and not from different families or castes like we are taught to believe. In my view, all hate is just endless disappointment and frustration at finding a cold stone or a callus where love once was or should have been.

When I listen to friends who are really upset with God because of some injustice sewn deep into the world's microfiber, instead of accusing them of a weak or "lost" faith, I suspect they love God pretty deeply (unless they tell me otherwise). I believe this because no one makes us angrier than those we love best. If someone cuts us off in traffic and doesn't apologize, we're enraged for what—five or ten minutes? But if parents or siblings don't love us the way they should even for a day, we can be enraged and wounded for a lifetime. Why? Because we love them and expect them to love us back. Our anger is just a mask we wear to hide the embarrassing fact that our reckless love, going ninety miles an hour, crashed head-on into a steel guardrail of disappointment and thwart.

In like fashion, we do not divorce God just because we express anger or confusion about what God could possibly be up to. The psalmist, for example, is furious with God in that passage where he shouts, "Why do you sleep, O Lord? . . . Why do you hide your face? Why do you forget our affliction?" (Psalm 44:23–24). But at the end of the psalm, he pleads, "Rise up, come to our help. Redeem us for the sake of your steadfast love" (v. 26). Almost all of the psalms end on some note of reassurance like this, with the psalmist's reassertion that God will really hear his cries. We, on the other hand, mistake anger for endings. This error results from pop culture, not biblical wisdom. We need not mourn honesty or even conflict, both signs of a relationship's vitality. Instead, we need only mourn divorce, a relationship's death.

I have several atheist friends who have "broken up" with God—all for very good reasons, mind you. In nearly every case, the breakup involved ugly arguments over evil and suffering. When I was younger, this terrified me and I fretted over whether I could continue being friends with both them and God at the same time. Thankfully, I have grown up. Maturity means that in a situation of divorce between persons whom I love, I do not have to pick a side and be friends with only one of the partners. Nowadays, when my friends who have let God go (or feel let go by God) want to mourn, I mourn with them. I couldn't let go of God if I wanted to (at times I've tried)—but in such a broken world, and given the horrific, specific ways the world has torn certain people to pieces that I have not had to endure, I totally can see why they would. I mean, who am I kidding not to admit this? The important thing, as I see it, is not to let go of anyone's hand no matter what road they are walking down.

I hope I have given you reason enough to see why Law #1—*never get mad or argue with God*—is a lie. A life-sucking narrative of the lie you should consider breaking without shame or secrecy, especially if you are the kind of person who has already broken it a thousand tiny times within the recesses of your mind. Because hope is anger's mother, if you start breaking this law, I promise you will encounter hope along the road and she will never leave your side. Also, airing your authentic tears, concerns, and emotions in the sunlight rather than hiding them or apologizing for their existence will restore your humanity. As the theologian Jürgen Moltmann has said, "God is waiting for human human beings."[12]

Chapter Three

Doubting Your Faith?
Learn to Lament

> *Sometimes I think it is my mission to bring faith to the faithless, and doubt to the faithful.*
> —PAUL TILLICH

> *Life is doubt, and faith without doubt is nothing but death.*
> —MIGUEL DE UNAMUNO

> *Don't expect faith to clear things up for you. It is trust, not certainty.*
> —FLANNERY O'CONNOR

Law #2: Don't doubt. Doubt is faith's opposite, and is therefore sinful.

It's late in the holiday season of 2012, and a popular weekly magazine lies on the desk in front of me. On its cover are twenty gorgeous, smiling six-year-olds. One of them stands next to a car where he has scrawled *I Love You* in the frost with his unmittened index finger. For one innocent second I ask myself, "Why is this issue of the magazine featuring children?" Just as quickly I remember the answer that dislocates my heart: a twenty-year-old walked into their school last week and shot them. I stare at their faces for a long time and think of that moment in the gospel of Matthew when Jesus cries from the cross, "My God, my God, why have you forsaken me?" (27:46). My fingers fumble for the cell phone beside me and look up *forsake* in the online dictionary. *Forsake*: "to give up or leave someone entirely; to renounce or turn away from someone or something entirely." Synonyms: *abandon, leave, forget, ignore, neglect, maroon, quit, strand, discard, desert, ditch, dump.*

If you are anything like me, then you have grown up believing that doubting or questioning God's presence, goodness, power, or justice is sinful and shameful. If doubt is the terrible sin we have always been taught to believe it is, then the dictionary definition of forsake suggests that the greatest sinner in the Bible is none other than Jesus himself. But of course, Christians do not consider Jesus a sinner or a blasphemer. So how can we explain that in Matthew 27:46, Jesus accuses God of not simply abandoning him but having ditched him *entirely*? Is doubt about God's presence and love, especially in times of deep suffering and loss, sinful? Who is right, Jesus, or the faith-laws that we have been taught? I don't know about you, but I would place my bet on Jesus every time.

In the Gospels, over and over again Jesus takes religious folks' teaching and flips it on its head. Though many of us today consider Jesus a gentle teacher of self-evident truths, the truth is that Jesus is and was revolutionary, radical, and extremist. The words *radical* and *extremist* get a bad rap because we wrongly associate them only with violence. But as Rev. Martin Luther King Jr. said in his "Letter from a Birmingham Jail,"

> Was not Jesus an extremist for love: "Love your enemies, bless them that curse you, do good to them that hate you, and pray for them which despitefully use you, and persecute you." Was not Amos an extremist for justice: "Let justice roll down like waters and righteousness like an ever-flowing stream." Was not Paul an extremist for the Christian gospel: "I bear in my body the marks of the Lord Jesus." . . . The question is *not* whether we will be extremists, but what kind of extremists we will be. Will we be extremists for hate or for love? Will we be extremists for the preservation of injustice or for the extension of justice?[1]

Dr. King, following Jesus' example, stated that he was a radical for love. So when I use the word *radical*, I am using the term according to its actual definition—getting back to or coming from our roots, like its related word (and root vegetable), *radish*. For Jesus, the root vegetables of our faith in God are love and nonviolence and radical hospitality, but our world is so broken and banged up that only so-called radicals practice these beautiful basics with any regularity. Consider the revolutionary moment when Jesus straight-up criticized and corrected the Bible as well as popular culture when he said to the masses, "You have heard that it was said, 'An eye for an eye and a tooth for a tooth.' But I say to you . . . if anyone strikes you on the right cheek, turn the other also" (Matthew 5:38–39).

With this outrageous encouragement to the people to go against good common sense *and* everything they have been taught by society and religious circles, Jesus turns outlaw . . . literally. To realize this, you have to recognize that "an eye for an eye" is in quotes here because Jesus was quoting (and rejecting) not only the law of the Jewish religious authorities of his day, as recorded in the Bible (Leviticus 24:19–21), but also the secular Babylonian law, as recorded in Hammurabi's Code, which prescribes exactly the same get-even style of justice. Jesus goes rogue like this again and again in the Gospels, as in the well-known passage where he says, "You have heard that it was said, 'You shall love your neighbor and hate your enemy.' But I say to you, Love your enemies and pray for those who persecute you" (Matthew 5:43–44).

When you grasp how countercultural and counter-religious Jesus' revolutionary claims were in his own day, then you comprehend why both the Romans and the religious folks alike wanted him dead. Their law condemned him to death because he rejected much of it, choosing to operate beyond its constricting boundaries. If Jesus were with us today, I suspect that he might weigh in with similar revolutionary advice about doubt: *You have no doubt heard it said, "Doubt is the opposite of faith and a sin." But I say to you, this is a bold-faced lie.*

The other day in one of my theology classes, a student raised her hand and said, "I don't go to church anymore. I have a lot of doubts about God and the Bible and the awful ways religious people act. I know that makes me a bad Christian, so I've just stopped going." If I had eaten a tootsie roll every time someone has said something like this to me, then every tooth in my mouth would have a cavity. It is ingrained in us to equate doubt with failure and wrongness. As a result, most people's faith withers on the vine the moment it encounters doubt. What remains is a wasteland of dead undergrowth that never sees the light of day.

My particular stripe of Christianity is Lutheran, and one of the things I most admire about my tradition is that our founder, Martin Luther, was a huge doubter and questioner. Therefore technically, to be true to itself, our tradition should embrace doubt and questions. But all I can tell you is this: I work with young people every day—many of them Lutheran—and almost all of them think doubt is not only horribly wrong and shameful, but also that it is the opposite of faith. The message is not getting through.

Instead of condemning doubt, we should listen to Christian thinker Paul Tillich, who in *Dynamics of Faith* said, "Doubt is a necessary element in [faith]. . . . Living faith includes . . . doubt about itself . . . and the risk of courage."[2] Tillich was a German pastor who, after his mom died of cancer when he was only seventeen, joined the army as a military chaplain during World War I. One of his jobs during the war was to drag dead and maimed bodies from the trenches back to base camp. I teach my students that all theology grows out of a context and that this context matters. In my mind, these facts about Tillich make him the kind of guy you need to listen to when he talks about things like courage, risk, and doubt.

In the quote above, Tillich is not talking about radical doubt or metaphysical doubt, the kind that doubts everything, doubts even doubt itself like a graduate school philosophy class chasing its own tail. No, he is talking about the kind of doubt that asks the question, How do I know what I know and how do I know what's true? The fancy term for this is *epistemological doubt*, but it's something that careful and thoughtful people practice every day whether or not they have ever heard this fancy term. This kind of doubt asks practical, helpful questions such as, How do I know if I'm on the right track with the way I live? Are the things I believe true? Are they right? Are they good? Are they making the world a better place? How do I know if I am doing God's will or not?

Yet when I say the word *doubt* in a religion class or in church, people usually assume I am talking exclusively about disbelief, or more specifically, unbelief in God. It's true, of course, that some people doubt the existence of God. But we tend to overemphasize this either/or struggle as the only kind of doubt there is. One reason for this is because our culture loves to dichotomize everything into either/ors—as in the famous line, "Either you are for us or against us." Another reason is our fascination with European-inspired philosophy, which obsesses about the question of God's existence.

But here's the dirty secret I'll bet you already have figured out: on the ground and in the trenches, most people's concerns about God stretch far beyond mere existence. Most people's primary question is not, is God real or does God exist? Instead, they puzzle over questions such as, does God care? Is God good and just? Will God answer my prayers? Will God answer yours? Does God love me, love all of us?

C. S. Lewis, in *A Grief Observed*, the book he wrote after the death of his wife, wrestled terribly with feelings of God's cruelty and absence: "Not that I am (I think) in much danger of ceasing to believe in God. The real danger is of coming to believe such dreadful things about Him. The conclusion I dread is not

'So there's no God after all,' but 'So this is what God's really like. Deceive yourself no longer.'"[3] Tellingly, C. S. Lewis was so afraid that Christians would judge and condemn these outlaw comments in *A Grief Observed* that he originally published the book under a false name. Yet today, when I ask people what book has best helped them through loss, guess what book they most often mention? Yep, you betcha, as the saying goes in Fargo, *A Grief Observed*.

If God posted status updates on Facebook or tweeted on Twitter, what would the posts say God is up to right now? Does God hear the child crying? Does God cry too when we do? Many people deep down also want to ask God nettlesome questions like Job, the psalmist, C. S. Lewis, and Jesus did. Questions like, *How long, Lord, how long? Why do the wicked prosper? Will this pain ever end?* and *Are you here, God, or have you ditched us?* These questions are faith's heartbeat. We have submerged them down deep inside of ourselves, so far it often takes a stethoscope to hear them, but they are still there. Beating.

What Is Doubt?

Doubt gives birth to questions. By doubt, I mean the uncertainty that plagues all human actions and thoughts and renders them ambiguous. By doubt, I mean residing in the uncomfortable state of the not-sure, the maybe, the possible, and the I-have-no-clue-why. Doubt often stabs us in the dark with thoughts of *not-good-enough* and *not-smart-enough*. Doubt acknowledges the reality of our insecurity and signals its arrival with *or not* wonderments. Does God care about us or not? Does God have a plan or not? Does prayer change the world or not? Am I loved or not? Will I ever make a difference or not? Will the world ever live up to our dreams or not? "Or not" is the house doubt has built, and all of us live there sometimes. This is all Paul Tillich is trying to say when he suggests that doubt is an essential element within a faith that is alive.

All of these God-questions—which are theology's gift and task and therefore all of our responsibility—are like seagrass pushing their roots down into the sand. Seagrass, which grows only a couple of feet high on the shore, has invisible roots that wind down forty feet deep into the sand. Without doubt, our faith is shallow and rootless. We fail to go down deep. Doubt is a sign of a healthy and deep-rooted faith, though most of us are taught to believe the opposite.

Why do the faith-laws prohibit doubt? Probably because doubt is a confession of our uncertainty. Uncertainty is shameful—a sign of ignorance. Ignorance is weakness, and all weakness is bad. Therefore, doubt is shameful and weak. We learn to hide shameful things we do not like about ourselves. Therefore, we must hide any doubts that arise during our quest to live, die, and love one another as faithful human beings. Certainty, on the other hand, makes us feel comfortable, fearless, in control, and self-sufficient. Unfortunately, no such certainty exists, and these feelings are illusions.

In our culture's wisdom, uncertainty is not for grown-ups or for the healthy and respected. Our culture teaches us that pesky why-asking belongs in the nursing home or kindergarten. In the Alzheimer's ward, my mom always asked, "Why am I here? Why can't I go home?" Mikey, a great kid I used to babysit, always asked me an endless string of why questions, such as, "Why do the ants live in the dirt? Why do I have to go to bed? Why do the clouds move?" Sometimes Mikey drove me nuts. But maybe the reason we adults get so frustrated with kids' questions is because they are still trying to make sense of this crazy world, whereas most of us have given up.

After all, doubt in the form of curiosity and a longing-down-to-the-bones to understand is what makes children ask questions. Deep down, maybe adults envy children for their endless ability to care and to keep asking why, even though we never give them an answer that satisfies and we ourselves stopped asking long ago. Children are brave enough to ask questions for which no answer is possible because for them, *not* to ask such questions is impossible. Eventually, the world coaxes this skill out of children. Kids learn that burying their doubt underground grants them a passport to the life of adults, who live largely as frauds.

The other day my friend Maggie's son said, "Mom, why do adults lie all the time? Whenever people ask you how are you, you always say 'fine' even when you are not." Have you ever con-sidered the possibility that when Jesus says we should become as little children, he means that in order to speak rightly of the world, we, like children, must have the guts to ask why over and over again? "Truly I tell you, unless you change and become like children, you will never enter the kingdom of heaven," Jesus said (Matthew 18:3). "Let the little children come to me, and do not stop them; for it is to such as these that the kingdom of heaven belongs" (Matthew 19:14). I believe Jesus at least in part here means we should become people who are unafraid to ask why-questions of the world, because, when asked with a genuine yearning in the heart, these questions are a subversive means of calling the world out on its trauma and terror.

Audacious why-asking birthmarks the new revolutionary

humility of the outlaw Christian. Why do CEOs in the United States make 369 times the salary of their average employees? Why does a child in the world die every five seconds of starvation while half the kids in my neighborhood are obese? Why is our country so polarized that our political leaders on both sides do nothing but filibuster each other and shut down the government when they don't get their way? Why do our leaders put politics over people without regard for the most vulnerable among us—even though we know full well Jesus said that whatever we do for the least of these, we do for him?

Outlaw Christians ask these questions because we don't believe the world should look the way it does. We doubt the world's justice and God's in-controlness of a world so out of control. In such a situation of suffering, greed, and inequality, we *should* be curious, unafraid to ask *why* all the time. When Jesus gets upset and knocks over the money changers' tables in the temple, he claims that the religious folks have turned the house of prayer into a "den of robbers" by making profits off of selling sacrifices to the poor (Matthew 21:12–16). No doubt at the root of Jesus' action is the question: Why are we allowing the rich to exploit the poor in the name of God? Such doubt gives new life to faith, because it makes us rise up, push for change, and knock over tables of injustice.

The Problem with Certainty

Isn't certainty grand—the domain of professors, politicians, pundits, and even the prayerful? Consider how certainty wins accolades in our culture. Only politicians who speak with absolute certainty win elections and respect amid the shrapnel of our broken and bipartisan political war zone. Have you ever known a politician who, when asked a question, answered, "I'm not sure"? If they did, I bet they lost the next election. Yet none of us actually believe that any one person knows all the answers to the world's problems, do we?

I once saw a US president being interviewed at the end of an eight-year term. The journalist asked him if he felt he had made any mistakes during his time in office. No, he answered, not a single one. Some people in the audience cheered. I sobbed, and for some strange reason thought of a strategy used by beauty pageant contestants—Vaseline on the teeth to make them shine and force the lips into a petroleum smile. Our twisted yearning for doubt-free leaders encourages politicians and CEOs to become unctuous (read: oily) con artists in order to please us. We traffic in certainty porn.

And yet, though you were probably schooled never to admit this, have you ever respected somebody for being willing to answer a hard question with a raw "I just don't know"? Have you ever learned more from someone's uncertainty than from their certainty, like the daughter in one of Alice Walker's novels who says, "Yes, Mother, I can see you are flawed. You have not hidden it. That is your greatest gift to me"?[4] I bet you know several people in your life who boldly refused to get their passport to fraudulence and you respect and love them for it—even if you don't quite realize this is why or agree with them on everything.

The ambivalence of doubt unsettles us. On the plus side, doubt is astonishingly honest. On the minus, it is honest vis-à-vis attributes we do not want to accept—namely, our limits, incompleteness, and perpetual uncertainty.

But wasn't the French historian Voltaire right when he said, "Doubt is an uncomfortable condition, but certainty is a ridiculous one"?[5] Isn't uncertainty just plain human? Theologian Reinhold Niebuhr explains that we are finite beings who always yearn for the infinite. We hate this tension. Let's face it, finitude sucks. Who wants limits? I love nothing more than when people reach beyond their limits, like the paraplegic athletes in the documentary *Murderball*, who developed the awesome sport of wheelchair rugby. But believing we are infinite and not finite is a dangerous lie that leads to really bad decision making—such as driving after one too many drinks.

What I want to propose is that maybe cherishing certainty is like eating chocolate cake, drinking red wine, or playing *Guitar Hero*. In moderation: fine. In excess or as an absolute rule to be done in all times and places: damaging, toxic, and a form of thievery toward the people you love.

Why Doubt Is Good

How can doubt, rooted as it is in uncertainty, be a good thing, or at the very least an acceptable thing? For starters, we should acknowledge and name the doubt within us because, much like snot and passing gas, doubt is natural and human— that is to say, embarrassing and unwelcome but real and impossible to be healthy without, much as we want to pretend otherwise. But more than just natural, doubt is also necessary, healthy, and good for our faith-life. I want to let you in on six ways I have discovered that doubt functions as a robust spiritual virtue, rather than faith's wimpy opposite.

Doubt Acknowledges Ambiguity

First, doubt acknowledges that the world is an absurdly ambiguous place, and that authentic faith must therefore wrestle with ambiguity and its very real arms. *Ambiguity* comes from the Latin word *ambi*, meaning "both," and *agere*, meaning "to drive, lead, or act." *Ambiguity* literally means, then, "to drive both ways," and in common usage means "having multiple meanings or interpretations, being uncertain and difficult to comprehend." Doubt painfully reminds us that our entire lives are shot through with ambiguity. For example, the sun, which feels so magnificent as it caresses your face, gives you cancer while doing so. Our beautiful country, which was built on the backs of slaves, exalts freedom more than any other value. The famous pastor and Nazi resister Dietrich Bonhoeffer observed that the very same God who loves us also demands that we live in the world as if there were no God at all, "The God who is with us is the God who forsakes us . . . Before God and with God we live without God."[6] The people who love us best also hurt us the most. All this is ambiguity par excellence, and when I put it in these concrete terms, you can see how ambiguity splits hearts in half.

The world today drives our hearts in both directions— toward hope and despair, often at the same time. Some days I am so confused, I don't even know which way to turn and still be a person of integrity. I don't even know how to pray in a way that won't make God look guilty of neglect or favoritism. For example, I want more than anything to express gratitude to God for the food on my plate, but what does my well-intended prayer of thanks for food imply for those kids in the world who die of starvation every five seconds? For if I thank someone for a gift, doesn't my thank-you imply that they are (at least in part) responsible for the gift? But if God is the one responsible (at least in part) for my having plenty of nourishing food to eat, isn't God also responsible (at least in part) for the fact that some people do *not* have food to eat and die of starvation? If we understand food and good health to be gifts from God, doesn't this dangerously imply that God has withheld these gifts or allowed them to be withheld from those who don't possess them? Of course I believe gratitude to be one of the greatest virtues we Christians should cultivate in life, but how can my prayer have it both ways?

When I was a kid, I was told to "thank God for our food." I came to believe that food dropped straight out of the sky from God's bountiful hands onto my Scooby-Doo plate. Even though my own family included farmers and truck drivers, I was never taught in my prayers to thank alongside God the farmers who grew the food, the underpaid migrant workers who picked it, the truck drivers who drove it to our state, the minimum wage–earning shelf-stockers and cashiers who sold it to us at the grocery store, or even my own mother who slaved over the stove every night cooking it for the five of us.

Recently I came across a Zen prayer that Thich Nhat Hanh, a Buddhist monk, recites prior to eating: "In this plate of food, I see the entire universe supporting my existence."[7] I like Hanh's meditation a lot because the wording allows me to include God in my gratitude without excluding gratitude to all the unseen human beings who also had a hand in the gift of the food in front of me. It's a perfect example of how learning from another religious tradition helps me be a better Christian. Jesus commands us to love one another as he loves us, and let's face it, though no one intended it that way, many of the prayers I grew up praying were downright unloving.

The worst perhaps is the Johnny Appleseed prayer song, which I loved growing up. "Oh, the Lord is good to me / and so I thank the Lord! / For giving me the things I need / the sun and the rain and the apple seed. / The Lord is good to me." I know this song is genuinely well-intentioned. But I for one can't sing it or hear it without wincing at the memory of me as a kid belting out, "Oh, the Lord is good to *me!*" as if I were especially chosen by God to get to eat my mac and cheese, never considering that if that were true, the implication would be that millions of people starving across the globe should be singing, "Oh, the Lord is horrible to me."

These days, when I ponder the #blessed phenomenon, I wonder: Aren't a lot of the material things I call God-given "blessings" just human-given privileges in disguise (many of which are tangled up in sinful systems of injustice)? And doesn't the use of the word *blessing* in such situations give a phony God-stamp-of-approval to unjust systems in the world that allow me to have ridiculously Costco-stocked shelves while others have nothing? If we believe God blesses us with food, does that mean we believe those who don't have it are "unblessed" in some way? Of course I don't believe this, which is why even though I believe myself to be incredibly blessed, blessing-language and #blessed make me as jittery as a cat at the vet.

Do you see how hard it can be to live eyes-wide-open to the world's ambiguity? As Elie Wiesel said in an interview, "Ambiguity is the name of our sickness, of everybody's sickness. What are we looking for in life, in existence, in history, in our own being? For the One to do away with ambiguity."[8] One of the things I most look forward to about Redemption is an end to this plague of ambiguity—the ugly, maggoty side that for now seems to hide inside of everything good.

Doubt Admits Paradox as the Truth About the World

Second, as I wrote in my first book, *The Laughter of the Oppressed*, the paradox at the heart of faith is: God is good, and life can be horror. How I wish it were not so, but how profoundly I have found both assertions to be true. For what is faith if not trust in a God of love and justice and mercy and compassion, trust in the God who sets prisoners free and loves each one of us—as St. Augustine says—as if there were only one of us? And what is our cable news reality if not a litany of horrors—child molestation, sexting politicians, suicide bombings, babies in dumpsters, prisoners of war, and tsunamis?

What is to be done with a world as wrecked and redeemed as this one? Each story—the gospel's promises and CBS News' sadness—makes us doubt the truth of the other. But the outlaw Christian holds on to the truth of both, refusing to choose between them. It's not an either/or, but a both/and. The outlaw Christian recognizes that in a world as broken as ours, no one will take our message of hope seriously unless we have first taken hurt and heartbrokenness seriously.

An authentic faith must incorporate this paradox into the very folds of its skin. An outlaw faith does not decide between the narratives of promise and presence, and terror and absence, though it knows, of course, on which hand hope must place all bets. Although I pray and trust that I will one day stand across from the God of love who will teach me a perfect understanding of why there is so much pain in the world, for now, that is not the case. In this life, my faith walks the daily tightrope between disappointment and anticipation, lament and hope. Outlaws don't choose between love of human beings and the love of God. Outlaws are not afraid to accept paradox as the tough truth about the world and our faith because as the wise writer G. K. Chesterton once said, paradox is "truth standing on her head to attract attention."[9]

For all these reasons, doubt is best thought of not as the opposite of faith but as a point on the same continuum. When I teach Paul Tillich, I illustrate that the faithful person rides as if on a pendulum—swinging back and forth between the poles of absolute doubt/uncertainty and absolute faith/certainty. Most people are in different places on this continuum depending on the day and the hour and the moment you choose to ask them. They might respond very differently after a funeral than they would after a wedding, for example. Only jumping off the pendulum and abandoning the swing all together is the opposite of faith, not doubt, as the faith-laws would have us falsely believe.

The pastor Reinhold Niebuhr, whom I have already mentioned, has an amazing definition of love: love is the "impossible possibility."[10] Likewise, I want to define faith as the uncertain certainty. Faith is unlovable love, distrustful trust, and disbelieving belief. If faith were not these things, then there would be no difference between having faith in God and accepting verifiable facts like the sky is blue and Obama is the first African American US president. Remember Hebrews 11:1, "Now faith is the assurance of things hoped for, the conviction of things not seen." Because of this "not seen" part, hope creates a space for doubt to squirrel its way into faith's attic.

Catholic novelist Walker Percy applauds doubt in the midst of faith as a form of authenticity. He portrays many of his novel's hero-protagonists as what I call unbelieving believers. The protagonist Will Barrett of *The Second Coming*, for example, asserts, "Is there another way? People either believe everything or they believe nothing. People like the Christians or Californians believe anything, everything. People like . . . the professors and scientists believe nothing. . . . The rest of my life . . . shall be devoted to a search for the third alternative, a *tertium quid*—if there is one."[11] A faith that asks questions from the depths of doubt's wellspring—especially questions about God's presence and justice in the world—is the third alternative, the route of the outlaw.

One of my all-time favorite writers, Dorothee Soelle, followed this path. Though a devout Jesus-loving Christian, she once oddly described herself as a believing atheist. What are these wise people trying to say to us? They are trying to say: *Courageously accept doubt and uncertainty as essential elements in faith. Do not fear paradox, because sometimes paradox is just real life.*

My best friend Julia recently found out that her friend Erica had been diagnosed with leukemia. To help give her some rest, Julia took Erica's son, Ian, along with her family on vacation to the beach. Julia said she and the kids had a fantastic time on the trip. However, she said she also felt her eyes tear up whenever she looked at Ian throwing the Frisbee and laughing, because she knew what grief lay ahead for him. Seeing her sadness, Julia's husband tried to reassure her—"It could be worse," he said. "At least Ian is old enough that he will always remember his mom and has had her with him during the most impressionable parts of his life." Julia didn't disagree with anything her husband said but she was not consoled in the least—which was why she called me to talk about it.

I said to her, "I hear you." The problem with "it could be worse" logic is, of course, that it also could be better—for certainly millions of people get to spend half a century with their mothers before they die, unlike Ian. I then said to Julia, "You do not have to choose, you know. The vacation can be both beautiful and bitter for you. We think everything has to be either/or, but sometimes this is just a lie."

Julia caught her breath for a minute and said, "Thank you for giving me permission to feel all the things I really feel." The both/and. Let's not make each other choose anymore between gratitude and grief. They are, and always have been, the closest of sisters. The poet Kahlil Gibran said it best: "When you are sorrowful look again in your heart and you shall see that in truth you are weeping for that which has been your delight."[12]

Doubt Signals Authenticity

A third way doubt can be good for our faith-life is that doubt can help put us in an authentic relationship with God. Within the Jewish sect of Hasidism, of which Elie Wiesel is a member, doubt is considered a spiritual virtue. To have doubt means to understand God rightly—that is, as the Divine Infinite and Complete who can never fully be understood by the finite, incomplete human person. To the Hasidim (people who practice Hasidism), doubt is the way we respect God and show how the real God surpasses all we could ever say about the Infinite. We can learn much from this attitude. The poet John Keats also argues for a reconsideration of doubt as a strength when he discusses what he terms "negative capability," that is, the capacity to exist in "uncertainties, mysteries, doubts."[13]

Doubt, in other words, makes us open and receptive, especially to letting God tell us who Love is rather than assuming we already know all there is to know about Her. Doubt accepts God as both Mystery and Someone We Can Know. When we are confident and secure, we are open to only one thing: ourselves. Doubt, however, opens us up to more than ourselves as a source of knowledge and life-giving insight. If God is real and is bigger than we are, then radical openness to God can be seen as a positive attribute tied to right understanding and humility. Doubt is a sign of remembering the real mysteriousness of God and our own inability to fully know such a God, just as we do not fully know ourselves or each other. Remember 1 Corinthians 13:12: "For now we see in a mirror, dimly, but then we will see face to face. Now I know only in part; then I will know fully, even as I have been fully known."

A good example of this is the disciple named Thomas, who speaks twice in the Gospels. A lot of Christians give Thomas— whom many call "doubting Thomas"—a bad rap, not so much because of what the Gospels say about him, but because of the faith-law that gives doubt a bad rap. In the gospel of John, when Jesus appears to the disciples after his resurrection, no one recognizes Jesus right away. Mary Magdalene, the first to glimpse Jesus at the tomb, mistakes Jesus for the gardener. When Jesus appears later to the male disciples, they don't recognize him either until Jesus "showed them his hands and his side" (John 20:20). But Thomas wasn't there for this; so when the disciples tell him about these incredible visits from Jesus, he says he won't believe that they "have seen the Lord" until he sees "the mark of the nails in his hands," puts his "finger in the mark of the nails," and puts his "hand in his side" (John 20:25). When Jesus shows up again, he addresses Thomas first thing by saying, "Put your finger here and see my hands. Reach out your hand and put it in my side." Thomas does this and then cries out, "My Lord and my God!" (vv. 27–28).

What outlaw Christians notice in this story is *not* the one and only line we are taught to notice—Jesus' command, "Do not doubt but believe" (v. 27). First, we notice that everyone else in the story fails to recognize Jesus also, but for some strange reason, only poor Thomas gets labeled "doubter." This suggests the "doubting Thomas" interpretation is an unfair reading that probably misses the point. Second, while everyone else in the story seems to have forgotten Jesus' suffering in light of his glorious resurrection, there is only one person who remembers it—and asks about it.

Thomas, in other words, is the only person who remembers Jesus' whole story—all the hurt, and the hope too. Thomas believes redemption is more than just an erasure of pain. For him, redemption involves the way people live on *in spite of* the fact that they still carry scars on their skin. Thomas expects scars. If the guy in front of him doesn't have scars, Thomas will know he can't be the Jesus he knew—because the real Jesus suffered something awful. Thomas is the only one in the room brave enough to remember that a friend's painful wounds still remain without having to be shown them first.

This radical new reading of Thomas helps us make sense of why in the only other Bible story (John 11) in which Thomas speaks, he is beyond a shadow of a doubt—pun intended!—portrayed not as a faithless loser but as the bravest, most loving, authentic friend Jesus has. When Lazarus dies and Mary and Martha beg Jesus to come back to them in Judea, the disciples try to talk Jesus out of it by saying, "The Jews were just now trying to stone you, and are you going there again?" But Thomas—and *only Thomas*—pipes up and says, "Let us also go, that we may die with him" (John 11:7–16). All the other disciples fear for Jesus' life and their own, but Thomas is willing to die along-side Jesus.

It's so sad that we label Thomas "doubting Thomas," but ignore the fact that he is also "willing-to-die-with-Jesus Thomas." What is the ironic point of the story? Could it be that scar-sharing is the solid foundation for any authentic friendship? That no one really knows who we are until we are brave enough to show our scars to them? That the people who have put their fingers and eyes on our scars and still stick with us anyway are the people who understand best how to love us? Thomas's story teaches us all of these lessons and more. Those people in your life who accept and name suffering for the wounding thing it actually is are the only friends who can ever override the fear of walking with you down all life's paths of pain. Only people who believe your wounds are real in the first place can ever imagine placing their wounds next to yours.

Doubt Breeds Creativity and Openness

Fourth, doubt can put us in right relationship with the world by helping us become creative and receptive to people, places, and presence. Doubt opens us up to the marvelous possibilities of one another and the world. As such, doubt stimulates our creativity.

People who doubt are seekers. Certainty's pitfall is that it can close us off from the views of other people, sometimes even to the point of being unable to listen to them. Which kind of person would you rather talk to—a person who thinks they know everything and has nothing to learn, or a person who thinks they know many things, but not everything, and might have something to learn from you? A doubting person is a seeker, and they do the latter. As my mother used to advise me and my siblings during our cranky teen years, "Why don't we all try to be more like the person we'd like to be around?"

Have you ever tried to have a discussion with someone who was absolutely certain about their views on a certain political or social issue—say abortion or capital punishment? Did they listen to you or understand your position? Sadly, I think we all know the answer. The law of our land demands that we despise and dismiss those with whom we disagree.

Outlaw Christians live differently. We do not buy into the legacies of hate and conflict that are killing us. Outlaw Christians live by two important truths: (1) Understanding and agreement are not the same thing. I can understand you even though I disagree with you, even though the law of our culture teaches us that this is impossible. And (2) because I am a broken person, my views and my actions may very well be wrong. Outlaw Christians live by love, and as we said, love is the impossible possibility. We also live by a humbling confession of doubt, which whispers in our ear at every turn, "You could be wrong, so you'd better listen up."

Christian ethics is the hardest class for me to teach. Years ago I began starting every class session with two exercises: first, a prayer that I would be able to love my students no matter what views they held, and that they would recognize that I loved them this way; and second, a reminder that no matter how strongly I felt about all the issues at hand, it was indeed possible—though I hated to admit it—that I could be wrong. For me this was a practical and painful application of the biblical teaching, "All have sinned and fall short of the glory of God" (Romans 3:23).

Living out my vocation in accordance with these two principles does not mean that I gave up trying to teach my students anything nor that I became a relativist who accepted everything they said as fine and true and equally valid.[14] It does not mean that I gave up being a person with strong convictions and serious values. Ironically, on the contrary, it meant anything but. What living out of a place of doubt does mean is that I became a teacher whom most students trusted. My classroom became a place where tears, laughter, and the sharing of scars were regular occurrences. Living into my doubt meant being able to listen to and learn from my students in a way I never had before. My own small flicker of doubt enabled me to become a person who understood that other people have convictions just as deep as mine, and therefore we'd better figure out a way to live together. Sometimes my students' deep convictions changed or nuanced my own opinions. But even when my mind did not change, my personhood changed dramatically. Doubt helped me become a person who can hear other people without my usual earplugs of defensiveness.

I once had a student in my Christian theology class named Jessica who was an atheist. Throughout the term, I shared with the class some of my own doubts and struggles of faith rather than keep them hidden. At course's end, Jessica wrote me a short letter. She told me that I was the only Christian she had ever met who admitted to having doubts about God's goodness and power because of how sad suffering in the world made me. She confessed that she was an atheist largely because she had watched her brother struggle with bipolar disorder all of his adult life. She wrote that when she had children someday, even though she herself would probably still not be a Christian, she would teach her children my doubt-is-not-the-opposite-of-faith theology, so that they could consider a new way of being Christian. Jessica's note reminded me that in this world of fake IDs, synthetic boobs, faux diamonds, pretend smiles, spray tans, and phony-everything-you-can-think-of, doubt is one of the few things that remains authentic. And authenticity attracts.

Doubt Builds Community and Interconnectedness

Fifth, and related to what we said above, doubt helps us build community based on the gift foundation of trust. Doubt is healthy because doubt is a confession. It says, "I do not know everything. You hold insights I need. God and you both have things you have not yet shown me, but maybe someday will if I am lucky and listen closely enough." In this way, doubt helps us build authentic relationships with each other.

Doubt teaches us the truth about our radical interconnectedness. We believe fiercely in our own independence—even allocate national holidays in celebration of it—but in reality, independence is a lie. Interdependence is the truth about humanity. Would any of us have survived a day of our infancy without our parents' love and care? Did we grow all or any of the food we ate in the last year? Wise people throughout history have tried to make us doubt our self-sufficiency and instead grasp the profound truth of our interdependence. The apostle Paul said in Romans, "We, who are many, are one body" (12:5). Similarly, South African archbishop and priest Desmond Tutu asserted that the concept *ubuntu*, a word for which there is no English equivalent (how telling!), is the real truth about human life. Tutu defined ubuntu like this: "*Ubuntu* . . . speaks of the very essence of being human. . . . It is to say, 'My humanity is caught up, is inextricably bound up, in yours.' We belong in a bundle of life. We say, 'A person is a person through other persons.' It is not, 'I think therefore I am.' It says rather: 'I am human because I belong. I participate. I share.'"[15] Doubt teaches us not I think, therefore I am, but instead, you are, therefore I am. Ubuntu.

It's true that the experience of doubt hurts and humbles. Terribly. It's best to be honest about this. However, in learning to live with doubt, we learn to cultivate other important virtues, such as trust. Trust is the only thing that can patch the rip doubt leaves in our spiritual socks. In the face of doubt you can't just profess, claim, assert, or shout louder, the way we Americans tend to do when we want to win arguments. If doubt is the shampoo, trust is the conditioner. Trust stops the breakage, the harshness and stripping-bare that doubt can cause. Doubt in myself can translate into trust in you. Doubt says, "I am broken and incomplete. I am not whole. Can you put me back together?" By posing the questions certainty ignores, doubt trusts that if we put our partial answers next to one another, we are closer to an answer than we were before. And even when that is not true, we are still closer to one another.

Doubting yourself can be a positive thing sometimes, provided you don't let it immobilize you. Think of a time you doubted yourself and had difficulty making a decision or reaching clarity on an issue. Did you talk to friends and loved ones about it? When doubt drives us into a friend's arms, we realize: doubt is *need*. "I am not enough on my own!" it shouts. This is the dirty secret behind why we, citizens of a nation that worships independence, despise doubt. Who wants to admit they are not enough? Who wants to admit need?

However, think about this in reverse. How do you feel when a friend calls you up in her darkest hour? When your brother asks you to come sit at his bedside during surgery? When your daughter cries and cries until you—only you—take her in your comforting arms? A lot of us love to feel needed by others in this way. Your day claims a worth it did not seem to have before the phone rang, before you and you alone were able to make the child's tears subside.

Do you prefer talking to people who ask you questions, or to people who go on and on about themselves, never asking you a thing? As a teacher, I know students who ask questions are always the best students. Similarly, what do you think of friends who come to you for advice when they are burdened with their own doubt about what they should do? Friends who seek your help about things are clearly friends who trust, respect, and value you. This kind of need for one another, motivated by compassion and agape, opens us up to ubuntu. Doubt helps us see our interdependence for what it is: the truth about our lives. *We need each other. I need you. You need me.*

Doubt Drives Activism

Sixth and finally, another way doubt can be spiritually good for us is by helping us build an authentic relationship with ourselves. Here, doubt can serve as a form of self-critique and much needed self-suspicion—a recognition of our real state of brokenness. Let's say I give money to a favorite nonprofit organization, such as Habitat for Humanity. This makes me feel good as well as look good in the eyes of others. We are taught to stop our thinking at this point. But doubt leads me to ask tough, self-examining questions, such as, is giving money to charity doing

ve the neighbor, or am I just using it as an excuse
serve at the local homeless shelter myself? Does my
do anything to change the massive system of injustice
a.   verty that leads to homeless families in the first place?
Doubt leads me to ask myself, "Why am I so uncomfortable
when I pass that homeless veteran on Main Street?" Is it because
I know it's absurd and unfair that I live in a cozy three-bedroom
house where most nights of the year all of the beds are unslept in
except one? We avoid questions for two reasons. We either don't
have the answers or we don't like the answer we suspect deep
down is true. This is why doubt just might be a good thing after
all. It can help protect us from our own self-deception. It awakens curiosity instead of resignation to ignorance. Doubt is an
alarm clock that awakens us from the lies we have been telling
ourselves about ourselves in order to be able to sleep in peace.

The opposite of doubt is not faith but resignation and its
favorite cloak, passivity. People who accept the status quo are
those who do not doubt that everything in the world is just
as it should be—that all is according to "God's perfect plan."
People who doubt, on the other hand, ask tough questions of
themselves and of people in power, and these questions drive
their activism. Doubt helps get us up off our duffs and get *doing*.
Outlaw Christians could also be called "doubtlaw" Christians.

In this way, doubt is an expression of what I called in the first
chapter *revolutionary longing* and is therefore a way of following
Jesus, who teaches us to long for justice. Though we yearn for an
ultimate divine answer to our doubt-driven questions, we also
act now in such a way as to make our questions someday unnec-
essary. We ask, "Does our community really value justice?" and
"Why does the gap between the rich and poor grow daily in

our country?" The urgency of these questions often drives us to serve at the local food pantry, to participate in protests, and to push for social change. If you let the horse of your doubt gallop free, where would it take you? What kind of work would it lead you to do?

If faith is just spitting out creeds and perfect beliefs, then surely a laser printer or an ATM would do a better job at having faith than we do. But God claims to want faith from *us*, so it must be more than a business transaction, more than the mere spewing out of inputted facts and right answers. Faith must be about us, must involve us in all of our wild humanness. It must be something we do, embody, strive for—something we paradoxically receive yet practice. The Christian writer and pastor Frederick Buechner says doubt is essential because without it, there is no room for you.[16] I think he is right. In your relationship with God and with other people, will you let your doubt make space for you?

Law #3: Never question.

Sarah Stillman, an investigative journalist for *The New Yorker*, once shared a great story at a human rights conference. One Sunday, a Sunday school teacher was reading to a class of five- and six-year-olds from an illustrated children's Bible. The day's lesson was from the book of Genesis, chapters 6–9, the story of Noah and the ark. The teacher showed pictures of Noah putting his entire family and two of each animal, male and female, in the ark so that their lives would be spared when God destroyed the world by a flood. She read, "All human beings; everything on dry land in whose nostrils was the breath of life died. He blotted out every living thing that was on the face of the ground, human beings and animals and creeping things and birds of the air. . . . Only Noah was left, and those that were with him in the ark" (Genesis 7:21–23).

The teacher ended the story with the happy Bible illustration depicting the ark, the rainbow, the saved animals, and a beaming Noah on deck holding a dove. But one little boy pointed at the open page's colorful drawing and said with great conviction, "That's a lie. Where are all the dead bodies?" Even a child can recognize when hope is built on a foundation as flimsy as a denial of death. Was this little boy's raw honesty what Jesus had in mind in Matthew 18:3? "Truly I tell you, unless you change and become like children, you will never enter the kingdom of heaven."

How many of us have heard the story of Noah's ark a thousand times and yet never questioned its justice? Never asked why with the flood, God killed innocent babies, children, and animals who could not yet have been responsible for the world's violence that God so abhorred? Have we asked about those dead bodies? Have we ever asked "Why?" or "Where did they go?" Or do we pretend like their corpses didn't exist? Who is this God of the Bible, anyway? If the president of another country decided to nuke all of the United States into oblivion because a lot of American politicians were corrupt and had done horrible, violent things to people in that country, I bet most of the world would deem that person a homicidal dictator with absolutely no sense of justice. Fortunately for God, because Law #2 declares the Divine too supreme to be questioned, many Christians hold God to a far lower standard than they hold any human being. But my friend Vanessa, who is an outlaw pastor, once confided in me that she considers the flood the first Holocaust.

One of my favorite theologians and pastors, Dietrich Bonhoeffer, suffered imprisonment and death at the hands of the Nazis during the Holocaust for having participated in a resistance movement against Hitler and the Third Reich. In his prison cell, Bonhoeffer wrote that the most valuable thing about suffering was that it had taught him, a man of privilege, to see the world "from below, from the perspective of the outcast, the suspects, the maltreated, the powerless, the oppressed, the reviled—in short, from the perspective of those who suffer."[17] In other words, Bonhoeffer learned to see the world from the perspective of the dead bodies, which in his day were dead Jewish brothers and sisters.

Asking prohibited questions from "below" made Bonhoeffer an outlaw, and the law quite literally executed him for it. There are buckets of subversive questions that people in power would rather we not ask, but Bonhoeffer shows us that this tough-question-asking perspective is absolutely essential to the life of the true Christian who loves her neighbor as herself. Bonhoeffer's life also reveals that living outside the law will probably get us in trouble, in more ways than one. In contrast, some Christians would rather have the dead bodies airbrushed right out of the picture, because faith is safer that way. Faith, however, was never meant to be safe. It was meant to be sincere.

"The Good News?!?"

I met another outlaw just the other day at my college's daily chapel service. On this particular day, Brittney, a senior student, had volunteered to read the assigned gospel passage. In Lutheran services, at the end of the reading of the gospel—a word that in the biblical Greek literally means "good news"—the reader usually exclaims, "The good news!" or "The word of the Lord!" The congregation then replies, "Thanks be to God."

Now, I honestly don't know whether Brittney had previewed the reading before she stepped up to the podium to read, but given what happened next, I suspect she was reading the verses cold turkey. Brittney began to read the gospel of Matthew's parable of the talents, in which Jesus compares the kingdom of God in this story to a master who entrusts three slaves with portions of his property (talents) while he is away. All was well until Brittney read aloud the parable's unusual ending:

> Then the one who had received the one talent also came forward, saying, "Master, I knew that you were a harsh man, reaping where you did not sow, and gathering where you did not scatter seed; so I was afraid, and I went and hid your talent in the ground. Here you have what is yours." But his master replied, "You wicked and lazy slave! You knew, did you, that I reap where I did not sow, and gather where I did not scatter? Then you ought to have invested my money with the bankers, and on my return I would have received what was my own with interest. So take the talent from him, and give it to the one with the ten talents. For to all those who have, more will be given, and they will have an abundance; but from those who have nothing, even what they have will be taken away. As for this worthless slave, throw him into the outer darkness, where there will be weeping and gnashing of teeth." (Matthew 25:24–30)

When Brittney finished these words, she was *supposed* to assert, "The good news!" But instead, she asked a question,

"The . . . good . . . news?" And then, as if that weren't enough, Brittney did the unthinkable. She chuckled. Out loud. It was more of a snort-laugh, really, the kind we let out when we're incredulous, or when we realize we've been had. Clearly, much like the little boy in the Sunday school class, this twenty-something was not buying what she perceived this Bible story to be selling. Rather than betray herself, she questioned the unquestionable. She could not even pretend, for the sake of pious propriety, that the idea that the poor, who already have nothing, will one day lose everything, could ever be considered *good news.*

And the best part is, a second impossible thing happened once she did this. Once Brittney laughed, *most people in the chapel laughed too.* Her question had opened the door for us to openly admit, through our laughter, that the parable was baffling, even disturbing. None of us understood its byzantine logic, but we never would have admitted this without her courage. Brittney proved Bob Dylan right: honesty means living outside the law.

And honestly, for many of you, the Bible is a text that has hurt you or been used by other people to hurt you for your whole life. It's high time we all come out of the closet with the passages in the Bible that we find utterly baffling, irrelevant, or even cruel. Top on my list would be Deuteronomy 13:

> If anyone secretly entices you—even if it is your brother, your father's son or your mother's son, or your own son or daughter, or the wife you embrace, or your most intimate friend—saying, "Let us go worship other gods," . . . you must not yield to or heed any such persons. Show them no pity or

compassion and do not shield them. But you shall surely kill them; your own hand shall be first against them to execute them, and afterwards the hand of all the people. Stone them to death for trying to turn you away from the LORD your God. (vv. 6, 8–10)

It cuts my heart to the quick to realize that so many Christians I know can quote passages in the sacred texts of other religions that they find weird or offensive or violent, but when they are asked what passages in the Bible they would use those same adjectives for, they either gasp in horror at the blasphemy of the question or simply can't think of a single one. Yes, I completely agree that it is dangerous to let people and communities decide which parts of the Bible still apply to their lives or not. But isn't it more dangerous to pretend like this is not happening already (compare the Amish to the Episcopalians!) and to not let anyone talk within the church about their struggles to interpret how the Bible should apply to their lives?

One of the best interfaith studies class sessions I ever taught was the day everyone had to say one thing about their own religious tradition or its sacred texts that they found troubling. It was as if I had given colored paint for the first time to people who had only ever sketched in charcoal. A lot of my students tell me that through my classes they find a way to be Christian again, which might sound counterintuitive to you since I am one of the faith's toughest critics. But maybe people respect honesty way more than you or I give them credit for. When we don't let people within Christianity critique Christianity or talk about the stuff within it that baffles or hurts them, they will just walk away. I know, because every year my classes are filled with young people who have done that very thing.

Mother Teresa, Outlaw Christian?

The notion that people with authentic faith do not question the Bible or God's goodness and justice is very ingrained within us. I am sure you consider Mother Teresa a paragon of faith, a perfect follower of Jesus who gave up her privileged life in Europe and moved to Calcutta, India, to care for the poorest of the world's poor. But do you know that even Mother Teresa radically questioned God and was filled with doubts? You perhaps do not know this, because Mother Teresa's private journals and letters went unpublished until 2007, a decade after her death, when finally they were released in *Come Be My Light: The Private Writings of the Saint of Calcutta* (and made into the film *The Letters* in 2015). Mother Teresa herself expressed a fear of the letters ever being made public. This reminds me of C. S. Lewis's fear of publishing *A Grief Observed* under his real name. It saddens me that we kept Mother Teresa's letters secret for so long, especially when I think of the many people I've known in life who would have been comforted to know that even Mother Teresa asked the very same questions their souls couldn't escape asking.

That Mother Teresa and the church kept her letters concealed for her entire life testifies to the radical power of the unwritten faith-laws. My heart broke to discover inside the book's pages that Mother Teresa was an outlaw Christian, and an immensely lonely one. Given her important position in the global church, she was not permitted—nor would she permit herself—to go public with her true self.

This was not the Mother Teresa I had ever learned about in Sunday school. On every page, Mother Teresa's streetwise, in-the-trenches faith battles it out with the prescribed unwritten faith-laws. Her tough questions make me love her for her courage, but tragically, she condemns herself for "breaking" the faith-law that forbids questioning God. Check out this heartbreaking sentence she wrote, for example, in which she cruelly censors her own overflowing-with-questions heart: "How long will our Lord stay away? . . . Where is my faith? . . . My God—how painful is this unknown pain. . . . So many unanswered questions live within me—I am afraid to uncover them—because of the blasphemy."[18] The entire book is filled with gut-wrenching passages just like this.

Mother Teresa, like so many of us, struggled down deep in her soul with the realization that she was living outside the law in her secret heart. Because every day she wiped the sweaty brows of hundreds of children who were dying for lack of food or antibiotics, God sometimes felt like a distant mystery to her—but she knew she was not allowed to say so. Indeed, in an article entitled "Mother Teresa Is a Fraud," the popular atheist website anamericanatheist.org once quoted this book specifically as proof that Mother Teresa was a "fraud," and not a true Christian at all.[19] We should notice here that the unwritten laws of Christianity are so powerful and pervasive that even atheists who don't buy anything else Christianity is selling still buy the faith-law that says "real" Christians don't doubt or question God. Wow. Seriously?

And the worst part is, a big part of the reason Mother Teresa wouldn't let herself express her true feelings was probably because of people like me. We onlookers labeled her as a saint and forced her to live inside the tiny box of our expectations.

For how do most Christians define a saint? Most Christians define a saint as a person whose faith is perfectly obedient to God, in spite of the fact that the apostle Paul used the term in reference to *all* believers.[20] I used to define a saint as a perfect person, but I no longer can and I no longer do. As an outlaw Christian, I instead define a saint as a person whose faith is perfectly honest with God. In other words, saints refuse to lie, even when everyone else is doing it and urging them to lie too. Maybe saints aren't holier than the rest of us, just more honest. Maybe honesty is a huge part of holiness.

In my mind, Mother Teresa's secret letters prove she is more of a saint than ever. She ran her Home for the Dying and Destitute and did God's work of loving the poor with her own two hands even when she feared God no longer lived in the house with any of them. How many of us would persist in doing backbreaking, self-depleting work if we believed the Boss had left the building and was no longer keeping tabs? I am sad to say I would not. But the hypocrite in me knows I'd better start trying to become the kind of person who would, because that is the only kind of person I would want to hire.

Have you ever asked grievous, searching questions like Mother Teresa? If you ever summoned up the courage to do so, how did people around you—friends, parents, teachers, pastors, priests—respond? Did they make you feel chastised, guilty, or unhealthy? Did people of faith accuse you of backsliding or becoming an atheist? Or did they make you feel that your questions were legitimate? No matter what anyone has ever said or will say to you, never forget this book's set-you-free declaration: all of your questions are legit, and you are well within your rights to ask them. Moreover, to ask them may well have the surprising effect of drawing you closer to God, rather than pushing you further and further away.

You are perhaps wondering how I know this. And once again, my answer is the Bible. We have already seen that some of our favorite spiritual outlaws like Jesus and Job are positively fearless when it comes to posing questions to the Divine, and they are lifted up in the Bible as wise but tough acts to follow. But the psalmist, whom we have not yet discussed in much detail, rivals both Job and Qoheleth in his question-asking. For the psalmist, the real truth appears the reverse of Mother Teresa's conclusion: *not* questioning God on all matters of evil, suffering, death, and justice is the true blasphemy.

The Psalms: Questioning Par Excellence

The poignant words of the psalmist and Job suggest that not to question God is to have an inauthentic relationship with God. To *not* ask God why the child is dying, or why evil appears to be winning the day again, is irresponsible and disingenuous—an act of self-blinding in the manner of Oedipus. Consider the following powerful verses in which the psalmist literally demands that God answer his questions.

> *Why, O Lord, do you stand far off?*
> > *Why do you hide yourself in times of trouble?*
> *(Psalm 10:1)*

and

> *How long, O Lord? Will you forget me forever?*
> *How long will you hide your face from me?*

How long must I bear pain in my soul,
and have sorrow in my heart all day long?
How long shall my enemy be exalted over me?
Consider and answer me, O LORD my God! (Psalm 13:1–3)

And finally:

O LORD, how long shall the wicked,
how long shall the wicked exult? (Psalm 94:3)

When my mother, who sang in the church choir her entire life and loved God with every part of herself, was dying in a nursing home and could no longer speak or swallow on her own, I often took out the Bible and read the Psalms aloud to her in her bed. Once, and I will never forget it, I read Psalm 10 to her, and the words, "Why, O LORD, do you stand far off?" made tears no one could explain fall down her cheeks like rivers.

Would anyone call out the psalmist, whom many believe to be David, as a sinner and blasphemer for asking these hard questions of God and God's justice? Would anyone claim that David, whose very name means *God's beloved*, just needs to try harder and stop writing these silly missives to God? Would anyone ask him, "Hey, David, why don't you stop whining and move on already?" If not, then why do we apply this exact criticism to ourselves? Why did Mother Teresa condemn herself for asking God almost word for word the same questions that the psalmist asked? Why are we letting these laws suck the life out of us? Why are we letting these laws crush us into silent compliance, so that we each feel we are floating in the ocean on a solitary raft of our own sadness and bewilderment?

Do we really believe that God is like the worst kind of parent, who, when their young child asks them why-questions, simply replies, "Just shut up, why don't you?" When did honesty with God become heresy?

Honesty can't be heresy, because the Bible's consummate question asker is . . . drum roll please . . . *none other than Jesus himself.* The greatest and toughest question ever asked of God in the Scriptures is the one Jesus asks in Matthew 27:46, which I mentioned at the beginning of this chapter. Jesus—an innocent man suffering from his culture's version of capital punishment—hurled the question heavenward as he hung on the cross, "My God, my God, why have you forsaken me?" And though most people don't remember it, in asking this question, Jesus was quoting the psalmist, who already had asked it hundreds of years earlier in Psalm 22. Jesus felt justified in speaking the anguish in his heart because the outlaw psalmist had already paved the way for that kind of honest relationship with God. If we want to take seriously the charge to be followers of Jesus, we had better learn from his example. It is Christ-like for anyone held in suffering's clutches to ask why the Divine has abandoned us and let us slide into the depths of each other's crazy cruelty.

In my view, theological reflection upon all of these conveniently ignored biblical passages in the Psalms and Job and the gospel of Matthew bears an uplifting message. And that message is: *God is not afraid of your questions.* You should not be afraid of your own earnest questions either. Ask away. Here is where Judaism, Jesus' own religious tradition, can be a massive, life-saving help to Christians. In Judaism, questioning God and wrestling with these questions lies at the center of the practice of faith, not on the sidelines. Within Judaism, the Genesis story of Jacob wrestling the angel all night long beside the Jabbok is the metaphor for the life of faith, which wrestles with God until dawn on every shore of river-soaked suffering. Jacob wins, as the story goes, but he walks away with a limp and a new name, Israel—symbolizing that every Jewish person is Jacob and therefore a wrestler. In Judaism, not only is God cool with your questions, but God also *wants* to hear them. They are a sign you are taking the covenant seriously and are in the relationship for the long haul, rather than merely hitchhiking across town on God's flatbed.

This brash refusal to fear either the wrestling match or the subsequent limp is one of the things I love best about Judaism. How well my Jewish brothers and sisters ask God and one another the questions we Christians find intimidating, if not terrifying! As Nicole Krauss has written, "When a Jew prays, he is asking God a question that has no end."[21] Elie Wiesel adds, "I am asking the questions from within faith, not outside faith. If I didn't believe, what would be the problem? But if you believe, then you have painful questions."[22] In my experience, all people of faith have painful questions, it's just that Christians are largely taught to repress them and feel ashamed of them.

Elie Wiesel: Rebel Believer

Obviously, Elie Wiesel has had a huge influence on my spiritual life. I still remember reading him for the first time during my first year of college. My professor taught us that Wiesel was so angry at God over the Holocaust that he wrote a book in which he put God on trial, and God received the verdict of guilty. I couldn't believe my ears. I had grown up in the South, the deep, deep South, and let me tell you, nobody but nobody I had ever known dared talk that way about the Lord Almighty. In class we read the book *Night*, Wiesel's memoir of his time spent in Auschwitz, where nearly his entire family was murdered by the Nazis. I will never forget the afternoon when I read the haunting scene in which Wiesel was forced to witness the hanging of a child in the camp. Wiesel boldly asked, *Where is God?*[23] I sat on my bed and crinkled the page-edges of Wiesel's book into yellow-brown waves with my tears. *Where is God now?* When I finished, I knew I would never be the same person again. Elie Wiesel taught me *it is okay to ask.*

I grew up to write my own books, and—no surprise—the first one is largely about Elie Wiesel. Every year now, I teach Wiesel's work to my own students. But when I teach Wiesel, I never cease to be shocked by the vast number of students who assume that—because Wiesel is openly angry at God and asks such thorny questions—of course he has "lost his faith." Wiesel, however, is well known as a practicing Jew who, as I learned when I recently had dinner with him, still keeps kosher, meaning he lives out his faith even to the point that it determines how and what he eats. He has not lost his faith at all, yet my students assume he has because he consistently violates laws #1 and #2 in his writing.

Responding to people who presume he has lost his faith, Wiesel remarks, "The revolt of the believer is not that of the renegade, the two do not speak in the name of the same anguish."[24] I love this quote. Believers possess an anguish that rebels do not—the anguish that not only are they suffering deeply but also that the God who claims to love them is *doing nothing to stop it*. Only someone who still loves God rebels *against God*; everyone else just rebels. Orphans can't rebel against a parent they don't have.

But the weird question remains, why do we confuse anguish and lament with unfaithfulness and disobedience? How did dissent come to mean disbelief? Perhaps our culture confuses these categories in order to foster patriotism and obedience, for many claim that to criticize our country and its actions means that we are "un-American" and do not share its "values." My husband and I once criticized a certain aspect of US foreign policy in front of a family member, to which she responded *tout de suite* with the mantra, "Well, if you hate it so much, why don't you just leave?" I responded by saying that I love my country the way I love my family: instead of traipsing out the door the instant things get real and disagreements break out, I want to stay and try to work it out.

With God and country, we are taught to accept and obey rather than question and reflect. But such thinking is wrongheaded. I subscribe instead to the saying attributed to Founding Father Thomas Jefferson: dissent is the highest form of patriotism. Really, anything or anyone whom you love merits your thoughtful questioning. And anyone who claims to love you back owes you thoughtful listening to your point of view. Think about it. If someone you loved was behaving strangely or in a way that hurt themselves and others, wouldn't you ask them, "Hey, what's going on with you?" If the person you love became a mystery to you, wouldn't you ask them, "Hey, I don't understand you. Why are you acting this way?" Would you seriously just let them walk off barefoot into a blizzard without a word or a question? While it's true that they might not answer you honestly or at all, isn't the right thing to do to still ask? To not ask these questions would be dysfunctional—to pretend that nothing is wrong when actually you feel crazy with confusion.

For a lot of people on their faith journey, God seems to act like a teenager. Withdrawn, confusing, and poker-faced. Always staying out past curfew. Vague on details and impossibly evasive with answers, especially to questions such as *Where have you been?* and *What have you been up to?* and *Why can't we just sit down and talk?* Because these are normal, loving questions for a person to ask who is in a healthy relationship, I do not judge people who ask questions like these—even when the person they ask them of is God.

Looking back, I can see now that Elie Wiesel galvanized my faith into a life of questioning, because he was bold enough to ask God all of his. Wiesel set me free to be the real me; he let my outlaw self out into the wild. Because of him, I don't have to lie to myself anymore about who I really am or what my relationship with God feels like, especially on the bad days, the days when I fear we might be beyond redemption.

When I was a kid, I kept all of my secret worries and questions about God locked away in my diary. Now I openly write and talk about them with amazing people who are equally honest. They always give me the courage to unfold a little bit more of my genuine self out into the fresh air where it can breathe on its own. The good news is that when I do this, I discover that other people have their own news of liberation and redemption to add to the daily news . . . but I never knew this when we were all afraid to talk about it with each other.

I know you've discovered the same thing when you gave this kind of radical honesty a try. I've also found that I am not as alone in my feelings as I thought I was. Though I no longer expect any answers to most of the questions I have for God, I ask them anyway. Not asking them feels irresponsible and unloving toward God, feels passive-aggressive like the way we love to tell everyone *except* the person we're actually upset with how upset we are with that person. As an outlaw Christian, I have kissed passive-aggressiveness good-bye. I tell it straight.

Because of Wiesel, Job, Jesus, the psalmist, and all the other spiritual outlaws I have encountered in life, nowadays I believe not only that lament is okay, but also that I am *supposed* to give voice to the sheer anguish I often feel in the face of what appears to be overwhelming evidence of God's absence. Every time I stare at the age-enhanced photos of missing children at the post office, I feel like I am looking at God's face too. God should have a Missing Person postcard, because an invisible card like that is already branded on the heart of people everywhere who suffer for reasons they do not understand. As Buechner once said, God is "of all missing persons the most missed."[25]

Actor Cory Monteith

Once when I was channel-surfing, I stumbled upon an episode of *Inside the Actors Studio* where the host James Lipton was interviewing the actors from the hit show *Glee*. Lipton asked the actors what they hoped God would say to them if they ever made it to the gates of heaven. As a religion professor and theologian, I was interested in how the pop stars would respond to this intriguing invitation to "do" theology in public. When it was actor Cory Monteith's turn, his face turned thoughtful, disappointed, and grim, and he said that if he ever met God, he hoped God would say, "Sorry I haven't been around. There's a good explanation."

I saw in Monteith in that moment a kindred spirit—an outlaw. Behind all the success and wealth was a man who experienced God as the worst kind of deadbeat dad and absentee adult, but who also hoped beyond hope he would one day hear an explanation from none other than God's own mouth. Monteith's eyes showed me how much it pained him to admit this insecurity aloud on national TV. I remember saying a silent prayer that he had someone in his private life who would let him be an outlaw and with whom he could share the source of his secret grief. In my experience, if you dig down deep enough, folks who make pointed comments about God being off-duty almost always have a very specific experience of suffering in mind, and nine times out of ten it is something terrible that has happened to them.

Less than a year later, I awoke to the news headline that Monteith, age thirty-one, had died of a lethal dose of heroin and alcohol. All I could think of when I heard the news was the haunting apology Monteith one day hoped to hear from God, "Sorry I was never around." Everyone else seems to have forgotten the actor ever said this, but I still pray with all I've got that Corey got his face-to-face, as well as an explanation.

Lament

We can see now that having it out with God is normal, healthy, and functional within a loving relationship with God, but did you know that the Bible even has a specific name for this behavior? *Lament*. Lament is the biblical word-name for having it out with God. It is a liberating practice found in the Bible, but long since forgotten or ignored. A major reason I am still a Christian is because ironically, the very same God we sometimes experience as the most missed of missing persons provides us with a spiritual practice designed specifically to bring our authentic selves out of hiding. Lament is when we— *together in community*—do these three things: ask questions about death's overwhelmingness, express doubt regarding what God is up to in a world of suffering and evil, and grieve God's missingness. Lament is the God-given spiritual practice that serves all of these purposes at once.

Lament creates a space for Christians to come together to say to God's face that we miss Love and that the world's pain is breaking our hearts. The precise origin of the word *lament* is unknown. The first root—*la*—in many languages means sadness or tears, as in the French word *larmes*, meaning "tears in our eyes." The second root, *ment*, may share a root with the English word *mantra*, meaning thought or idea. For these reasons, I define a lament as a thought-tear, or a tear-thought. A lament is a tear put into words.

The Bible has an entire book called Lamentations. The book contains the poignant collective voice of the Jewish people as they cried out to God after the destruction of Jerusalem. Consider for example Lamentations 5:20–21: "Why have you forgotten us completely? Why have you forsaken us these many days? Restore us to yourself, O LORD, that we may be restored; renew our days as of old." Also:

> Look, O LORD, and see
> how worthless I have become.
> Is it nothing to you, all you who pass by?
> Look and see

> *if there is any sorrow like my sorrow,*
>   *which was brought upon me,*
> *which the LORD inflicted*
>   *on the day of his fierce anger.*
> *From on high he sent fire;*
>   *it went deep into my bones; . . .*
> *he has left me stunned,*
>   *faint all day long. (1:11–13)*

In Lamentations, all the people's hope is in God, but so is all their sorrow. This is a paradox for sure, but it is the very truth a lament invites us to tell.

But biblical laments do not occur only in the book labeled Lamentations. No, they are everywhere. The prophet Jeremiah instructs us: "Teach your daughters how to wail; teach one another a lament. Death has climbed in through our windows" (Jeremiah 9:20–21 NIV). The psalmist—a lamenter par excellence—echoes Jeremiah: "Record my misery; list my tears on your scroll" (Psalm 56:8 NIV). The morning after the Newtown massacre at Sandy Hook Elementary, I found my mind saying over and over again in my head like a mantra, *Death has climbed in through our windows. Record our lament.* I also found my soul looking everywhere for an authentic lament or a space to lament in, but regrettably I came up empty-handed. Are we doing what Jeremiah asked us to do as people of faith? Has anyone ever taught you how to lament? Are we teaching one another? Do we even know how to lament ourselves? Where do we let people record their laments? Do we list our tears on the scroll of Jesus' face? Where and when and how do we do this?

Oftentimes I worry that as a culture and even as a church

we have lost the biblical spiritual practice of lament. I remain unconvinced that we know how to lament authentically anymore in a way that moves beyond media spectacle. Personally, I lament the lost art of lament. The tell-it-like-it is theologian Walter Brueggemann said it best, "The lament psalms offer important resources for Christian faith and ministry, even though they have been largely purged from the life and liturgy of the church. Such purging attests to the alienation between the Bible and the Church."[26] In straight talk, Brueggemann argues here that we—the church—have lost touch with the biblical practice of lament, and this in turn has made a lot of folks lose touch with the church. Can we recover this aspect of our walk with God that the Bible so clearly portrays as essential?

In the excellent book *Raging with Compassion: Pastoral Responses to the Problem of Evil*, pastor John Swinton tells the story of a terrorist car bomb that went off in his neighborhood and killed many people. Swinton went to church the next day alongside all the other people in his town, all of them longing for and seeking some kind of healing and meaning. But nothing in the church service—not even the pastor's sermon—acknowledged the tragedy that had hit the town just the day prior. Swinton was crushed but realized something important: "As I reflected on the way in which my church worshipped . . . I suddenly understood clearly that there was no room in our liturgy for sadness, brokenness and questioning. We had much space for love, joy, praise and supplication, but it seemed that we viewed the acknowledgment of sadness and the tragic brokenness of our world as almost tantamount to faithlessness."[27] When we teach people that lament is wrong or sinful or blasphemous—as we do when we buy into law #2—then people come to our churches and are devastated by the disconnect with their everyday lives.

I can only imagine the vast number of people who would never go back to a place like Swinton's church, which didn't even try to speak, let alone minister, to their deepest need in their darkest hour. To return to such a place would be like returning to a hospital that had no beds or nurses or medicine the last time you visited. Would you go back for a second helping of the very same casserole that made you sick the first time around?

Christians are terrified and baffled by the latest polls that show a fast decline in numbers of people belonging to mainstream churches, yet I must confess that I am not surprised. I am not so arrogant as to claim to have a totalizing explanation or solution, but I think I know part of the reason. In a world that looks like the one we see on the news every day, a Christianity with no room for lament will surely doom itself to irrelevance. I have become an outlaw Christian to save this kind of Christianity from its own death. I want Christianity to live—abundantly—and to give us life too. Perhaps together we can help Christianity become relevant again to the real lives we live.

One of the questions I struggle with all the time is how to help our congregations and communities, our families and friends, recover the practice of lament as a legitimate response to evil and suffering. Life events such as cancer, 9/11, job loss, divorce, suicide, movie-theatre massacres, the Boston marathon bombing, school shootings, war, political polarization, inequity, or the death of a partner, parent, or child demand it. I have found one thing that works, and it's shockingly simple. All I do is create a safe space for people to lament, and I invite them into it.

I teach my students, for example, to repeat after me, "Lament is not faithlessness." To prove this point, I have students in my Problem of Evil class read the scriptural examples of outlaws like Jeremiah, the psalmist, and the writer of Lamentations. The students also read Swinton's book on lament, and then for their assignment, I give them a choice. I say, "You can write a regular paper on the reading, or you can get more creative—you can write your own lament." In a class of twenty young people between the ages of eighteen to twenty-two, guess how many chose to write their own lament? All of them. On a beautiful spring day a few years ago, my entire class (including me) sat together in a circle on the lawn—and we read our laments aloud. It was one of the best days I have ever experienced as a teacher. I highly recommend trying this one at home and writing your own.

To give you a model of what a twenty-first-century lament looks like, I want to share with you my student Elise's lament. Elise, our school's homecoming queen, had courageously told the class earlier in the term that she had suffered sexual trauma during her early formative years. When I asked Elise if I might include her lament in this book, she replied, "Yes, of course. I want to be a pastor someday, and that kind of honesty is important." I told her that I wished the world had more pastors like her. Elise is now in seminary on a full scholarship. Her lament lets all of her secret thoughts about God out of their cages as if they were tiny hummingbirds. May they set the questions and wonder inside of you free to fly as well, perhaps even back to God.

God,

There are many things I could rail at you for. I can't even speak to you most of the time because I'm too angry or confused. Think about the four thousand dead in Syria who wanted basic human freedoms. The thousands of children that die every day. The accidents and non-accidents, the murders, the crashes, the bad foreign policies. Civilian casualties. Profit-driven war. I could shake my fist at the sky for the growing demand for human slavery, cheap labor, sex slaves. Why are women treated the way we are? Why do you allow extreme hatred against people of color after hundreds of years of mistreatment? Why can't you change hearts?

Why are you allowing these things?

My cousin is dying of brain and lung cancer. She can't even string a sentence together anymore, but she remains faithful to you. Her children watch as her life slowly drains from her and stand helpless, hoping for a miracle to restore their mother.

My greatest lament is that I don't know how you work. Do you suffer with us, or was it only for that one moment in history, a blink of an eye when you were here and realized how awful we can be to each other and how hard life is just trying to get by on a daily basis?

Are you simply with us in spirit, like a regretful family member that simply can't make our piano recital?

Do you intervene? Do you reach down your mighty arm to change small outcomes here and there? Are you in control?

Is it you that turns the world and protects us?

I don't ever know what to say to you because I don't know who you are. What do you talk about with someone you feel like you barely know? Maybe I'm not trying hard enough, but lately trying to have a relationship with you is like trying to befriend my shadow. I feel as though I'm talking to myself, crying to myself, and eventually I just fall silent because it feels absurd and disturbing.

My heart is torn. Can I be mad at you when you don't intervene because it's not in your nature to? I wish you would just show up. Be present in my life. What am I missing?

I sit in comfort and in good physical health while I feel like the world around me is gasping for breath and for you. What have I done to set me apart? Will I be punished for the way I live now when it's over? I don't know what to say to you most of the time.

I don't want to have to scream to-do items at you and constantly petition for you to step in, step up, feed us, help us, lead us when I feel like so many of us just stare up at the sky, waiting for something better. Maybe you're lamenting, too. Maybe you do look around and simply shake your head and weep.

You know, you could have let us stay with you wherever you are. We could have stayed in the garden. Was it you that really killed all the firstborns? Did you send a flood? Did you take people out of bondage? If you can do all of those things, but can't prevent genocide, what do we need you for?

Do you love us? Are you all good all the time? My mom believes that and she could even say that to me at her father's funeral. My mother is good all of the time. She has been horribly mistreated her whole life by her parents and her heart is still open and innocent. She's a miracle, but what about all of the children in other places being beaten and raped right now? Where will they know love from?

We keep messing up. I keep hurting people and hurting myself and worrying myself to the edge of my sanity about the other things that are out of my control. For what? What is the purpose of our lives here? Do you watch us?

What am I doing here? If my vocation is simply to reach out to others, then I will do it. If you want me to change the way things are, I will try. But what will you do?

There will be generations and generations of people after me asking the same things about their own lives and what you are doing in it. After so many thousands of years hearing us, aren't you tired of all of this yet?

I want to be where you are. I want to hear what you have to say. I want to see all of my loved ones who have been lost to me here, perfectly restored. I want to wake up where you are and understand why.

Chapter Four

Sick of Hearing "God Has a Plan"?
Surprise! God Is Too

> *Miserable comforters are you all. Have windy*
> *words no limit?*
>
> —JOB IN JOB 16:2–3, SPEAKING TO HIS FRIENDS

> *My wrath is kindled against you and against your*
> *two friends; for you have not spoken of me what is*
> *right, as my servant Job has.*
>
> —GOD TO JOB'S FRIENDS IN JOB 42:7

Law #4: Always speak in clichés about suffering and evil.

Think for a minute about a time in your life when you suffered a terrible grief. What did other people, especially Christians, say to you in an attempt to comfort you? I can still remember the things well-meaning friends, colleagues, and church members repeated to me and my family. It took seventeen years for my mother to waste away in the memory-less wilderness of Alzheimer's disease, so believe me, I got an earful. In the beginning they said things such as, "God has a plan," "Let go and let God," "It was meant to be," "God is testing your faith," and "God never gives you more than you can handle." At the end, they switched to, "Everything happens for a reason," "God needed another angel," "God's ways are not our ways," "Time heals all wounds," "She's with God now," "She's in a better place," and "It was just her time." Like sprinklers left on during a hurricane, their words rained down on my already soaked face.

On my bad days, these people's pious phrases felt like 100-percent, pure, grade-A bull schmegeggy. On my best days, like 99 percent. I know these friends never intended to hurt my feelings. Nonetheless, like Job's friends in the Bible, my friends were miserable comforters—people whose mouths unwittingly cut a cruel north wind across my face.

But hidden behind that truth lies another. My friends' pious platitudes also shamed me. Their words made me think of all the times I had uttered similar things to someone in crisis, and how, because I was so focused on being an A+ Christian and giving them the "right" answer, I had ignored that subsequent look on their face of frostbite. I realized how easily clichés fall from your lips when you are not the one beaten up by sorrow. I learned the hard way how badly we need to start breaking this terrible law of speaking in suffering-clichés.

Have religious folks ever tossed clichés at you when you were grieving? If they did, then whether they knew it or not, those folks were doing theology by constructing a theodicy. *Theodicy* is a shiny twenty-five-cent vocabulary word with a very simple meaning. A theodicy is a justification of God's goodness, justice, and omnipotence in the face of the world's radical evil and suffering. As many have explained it, theodicy struggles to explain how all of the following three claims can be simultaneously true: first, that God is perfectly good, loving, and just; second, that God is all-powerful; and third, that evil and suffering exist in the world (in extraordinarily large quantities). Theodicy addresses the timeless quandary: How can we continue to believe in a God who is Love in a world where we experience so much evil and hurt?

For outlaw Christians who reimagine theology as placing the joys and wounds of our lives next to God's, theodicy matters. Theodicy lies at the center of a life of faith as it is really lived in a world of hurricanes, E. coli, cystic fibrosis, manic depression, and gang wars. How we think about theodicy directly affects how we will struggle to resist and alleviate evil and suffering. Every time we utter one of these oversimplified, hackneyed phrases that attempts to reconcile the three claims above, we fail to do our own hard thinking about the world's muddiest problems. We just regurgitate a pop theodicy that the faith-laws have taught us is the "right thing to say" in such a situation of loss. Theodicy is everywhere for those who have ears to hear.

It's kind of weird to me that whenever awful things happen, like tsunamis and school shootings, we Christians feel personally compelled to become God's public defender. Every time the cops click handcuffs around a perp's wrist on shows like *Law & Order*, they say, "If you cannot afford an attorney, then one will be appointed to you." That attorney, provided free by the state, is of course the public defender. Theodicy reminds me of this.

Every time dreadful, vile crap happens in the world, Christians speak as if they each received a letter in the mail written in God's own handwriting pleading:

> I need you to defend me. I can't afford anyone else.
>
> Sincerely,
>
> God

For most people, that is all that a theodicy is—a defense of God. I don't know why we feel so strongly that God needs us to rally to Justice's defense. But we sure must believe God needs defending in the public square and even in the courtroom of our own hearts because otherwise, theodicies wouldn't exist. Are we afraid that God will lose to the prosecution if we are not on the defense team? Do our theodicies overestimate ourselves and underestimate God? Many people define theodicy as "justifying the ways of God to humanity," but if anyone in the universe were big enough and smart enough to defend or justify themselves on their own and not need our help, wouldn't that person be God?

Our overuse of threadbare theodicies makes me think of the phrase from Shakespeare's *Hamlet*, "The lady protests too much, methinks."[1] If Christians run around defending at all costs God's absolute innocence and absolute in-controlness after every horrific event in the world, doesn't the strength of our protest come from the fact that deep down we know the evil in the world radically calls both of these things into question? After all, who needs a lawyer or a public defender? Only someone who, according to evidence, appears guilty enough to require a trial. Now, of course a trial does not at all mean that the accused person is actually guilty, but it does mean that the public needs to hear out the case from both sides.

In the courtroom case of theodicy, the person doing the accusing is the sufferer, God is the accused, and we religious folks are God's public defenders. In this self-appointed role, do we listen closely enough to what the suffering witnesses say about how they experience the world and God? Or do we leap prematurely to the role of public defender when we haven't even heard the prosecution's opening remarks, let alone the entire case? If the way we have completely rewritten Job in our minds is any example, I am not at all convinced that we practice deep listening to folks who are suffering and to what they have to teach us about God and grief and faith. When we do, their sobs drown out a lot of the trite answers we have heard our whole lives about why evil happens.

The real question about theodicies that I want to ask, therefore, is not, *are theodicies true?* But instead, *do theodicies comfort you in your darkest moments of grief?* When your friends, coworkers, and family members said these theodicies to you in the past, did their words make you feel better? Or did they just make you more miserable, further from God than ever? For many people, though they may never confess it, the answer is no, these pious clichés do not bring comfort. Outlaw Christians reflect thoughtfully about why theodicies so often fail to achieve the comfort they intend, and they seek alternatives to pious clichés.

Let's look at three popular clichés about suffering: "God never gives you more than you can handle;" "Suffering makes you and your faith stronger;" and "What doesn't kill you makes you stronger." All of these similar platitudes are in a dangerous state of denial about death (to varying degrees). While the first two versions are in complete denial, the third version at least admits that some evils actually kill people. But "What doesn't kill you makes you stronger" is still problematic; people who spout this platitude assume—unwisely, I think—that whatever you are going through will *not* kill you. It deeply troubles me that these so-called truisms are favorites in Christian circles. Where are the Christians who are willing to admit that some trials in life can actually kill us, or tear our faith to shreds?

Why do we keep repeating cliché-lies such as "God never gives us more than we can handle"? Suicide would not exist if this were the case. For that matter, neither would death. My best friend Suzanne died of colorectal cancer in her mid-forties. Suzanne's cancer did in fact make her many things, including extraordinarily insightful and generous, but her cancer did not make her strong or stronger. Cancer made her weak beyond measure, and then it killed her. Some things do not make us stronger; they just kill us. For what is death if not a complete and utter submission to all of the forces our body and spirit can no longer handle? Doesn't our inauthenticity do people a terrible disservice by not preparing them for the truth? Why do we try to cover up the truth, like desperate housecats clawing the litter box over and over again to bury the stink?

How can Christians, who have taken up a cross as the primary symbol of who they are and what it means to follow Jesus—deny death? Yet Christians—especially privileged Christians—in our culture do this all the time. Most of my students are twenty-one years old and have never even seen a dead body or witnessed a death. My friend who is a pastor recently officiated a funeral for a teenager who committed suicide, and members of the congregation and family specifically forbade her from mentioning the word *suicide* in the service. A big part of me can sympathize with this urge to hide a sad truth. But I worry that pretending that suicide never happens could endanger more people, especially those who might be considering suicide in their hidden hearts as a real option. Many of us Christians are masterful deniers of death and tragedy, but then we are baffled that so many people cannot take us seriously when we talk about hope and redemption. Without death, there can be no resurrection.

Outlaw Christians, however, recognize and name the painful truth that death is grisly and tragedy is real. We admit that evil crushes the life out of some folks. We confess that some people's faith does not grow stronger from an encounter with evil. Take writer Primo Levi (and countless others like him) who survived the Holocaust, but years later died by his own hand. For people like Levi, the sheer memory of a suffering so meaningless was as deadly as death itself. Outlaws listen with wide-open hearts to the stories of folks who feel compelled to take an overdose of sleeping pills because their suffering has weakened them to the point of no return.

My friend's sister, crippled her whole life by manic depression, took her own life at age forty-five in order at last to escape the prison of her own mind. Mental illnesses such as depression and posttraumatic stress disorder are overwhelming forms of torn-to-pieces-hood that cause unfathomable depths of pain, yet we are taught to stigmatize or hide such suffering rather than see it with the eyes of compassion that it deserves. How dare I, who have never had to endure either, judge the difficult choices these folks made in the face of them? Remembering that Jesus never blamed anyone for their suffering but always instead tried to heal them, we should reject the blame game.

Theologians like myself have a useful word—*contingency*—to describe the fact that human beings' lives are subject to chance, unforeseen effects, and forces beyond their control. For example, I was not born in poverty or in a developing nation, nor was I born with bipolar disorder, cancer, or any disabilities. Contingency reminds me that I cannot take credit or praise for any of these aspects of my life and most important, I cannot judge, condemn, or blame anyone whom contingency placed in hardship. This sounds easy, until you remember that we do this all the time. For how many times have you heard of a person living in poverty being blamed for their own poverty, or of an addict being blamed for their own addiction? One of our favorite cultural pastimes is redefining contingency as "choices."

We are radically contingent beings, but we forget this right up until the moment we, too, begin to suffer, because we are caught up in the lie that reassures us we are in control. *Contingency* is just a fancy word for the truth about the world in which we live, which is: *anything can happen to anyone.* Yes, contingency scares us something awful. But contingency also knits people together in the most beautiful interdependence, because if you grasp this truth about the world, you will no longer be tempted to blame other people for all of their suffering . . . and on that terrible but inevitable day when something tragic happens to you, you will hopefully have broken the habit and not blame yourself either.

But instead of teaching the truth about contingency, the faith-laws forge an invisible causal connection between suffering and God's punishment. Likewise, they feign a connection between flourishing and God's favor. I know I am guilty of buying into this. Remember how I confessed that when terrible things happen to people I love, I sometimes feel like God has broken up with me? Though cognitively I know this is a bald-faced lie, emotionally sometimes I still feel like it's true. The militant faith-laws have entrenched themselves within me like little soldiers prepared to defend with their lives the laws of the land against the dangerous enemy of more adventurous reflection about God and faith. As an outlaw Christian, I feel like within me pop-Christianity's teachings constantly battle with my real-life experiences of evil, suffering, and grief.

Consider the phrase, "There but for the grace of God go I." While I know that this cliché is meant to cultivate gratitude within us and teach us not to take credit for our near misses with misfortune, it really has a nasty side. This risky cliché masquerading as simple prayer implies that God's grace kept the "bad" things—rape, crushing poverty, mental health disorders—from happening to me, but God's grace was withheld from the people to whom these things happened. Sometimes in our culture, we judge those who suffer as somehow undeserving of God's grace (obviously forgetting that no one, ever, deserves grace and that is what makes it grace). If bad things happen to you, this line of thinking goes, it's because you somehow, someway deserved them. (Think of the popular assumption that the poor are poor because they are all too lazy to work hard enough.) If good things happen to you, it's because you have earned the reward of God's favor. I cannot fathom a more damaging theological teaching. It can persuade people who suffer injustice and sorrow to loathe not only God but also themselves. Am I just weird, or do you sometimes worry about this stuff too?

Clichés attempt a feeble reconciliation of these two truths: (1) God is good and just and all-powerful, and (2) God does not stop—or chooses not to stop—pain, death, cancer, war, earthquake, unemployment, divorce, or fill-in-the-blank with suffering from your own life. These clichés—even if partially true—wound us because they are reductionistic, oversimplified, and superficial. They pay no attention to the unique experience of me or you, the person who is suffering. Offered in the exact same milquetoast way in every situation across time, these simplistic clichés reject the sufferer as a person whose suffering is *specific* and *right now*. They legitimize suffering and make it sound easy, reasonable, and explicable, whereas most suffering feels exhausting, incomprehensible, and irrational to the person clutched in its talons. The problem with clichés is that they can make you in your deepest grief feel far, far, far away from God, as if God were a dictator in a distant land who is—inexplicably—powerless and irrelevant yet somehow totally in charge of all the goings-on inside your own house.

Maybe evil, like love, is ultimately incomprehensible. Or better, evil, like love, is only comprehensible from the inside out—meaning you can only really understand it if you wear its skin and are complicit with it. Fully understanding evil, then, is not even desirable, yet it is in every case what theodicy-clichés claim to do.

We assume that people who are suffering from an assault of evil want explanations, but usually what they really want is to feel safe in the world's arms again, in God's arms again. Claiming to a friend that "it was meant to be" for her eight-year-old to get hit by a car or for her twenty-year-old sibling to have his legs blown off in the Boston marathon bombing does not make her feel safe in the world's arms again. *What most theodicies unintentionally do is present a God who has no arms.* The clichés paint a portrait of a scary, armless mannequin-God who not only is *not* the real deal but also could never reach out to hold you.

Moreover, when we echo theodicy-clichés like this to a friend in pain, chances are a thousand to one that we subconsciously assert them for our own benefit—not our friend's. Clichés manifest our human desire to preserve order, certainty, and meaning within our own emotional and spiritual landscape. We use clichés like caulk to fill the confused holes inside of us left by a lack of explanations for suffering. We use them to disguise the doubt we are afraid to let one another see.

Wounded people feel grief because order, meaning, and their sense of the world have shipwrecked on suffering's shore. Therefore, a cliché's assertion that the world still makes sense ignores the very thing sufferers are trying to get us to recognize they grieve having lost. They do not for the moment believe the world makes sense. Parroting a pious platitude to such a person is like insisting to someone who has lost his wedding ring that the wedding ring is not really lost. When I was a kid, my mom taught me to stand up to bullies with the mantra, "Your saying so does not make it so." When we Christians just try to talk louder over people's tears with our shouts that, "Yes, the world really is ordered and going perfectly according to divine plan," people who are in the deepest places of suffering whisper in response, "Your saying so does not make it so." Can you hear them?

Let's now expose four very common yet damaging rationalizations we tell ourselves about evil.

Cliché #1: Evil is nothing except the absence of good.

Though most people don't know it, this idea comes straight from the mouth of fourth-century bishop St. Augustine of Hippo. Channeling Augustine, my student once declared, "Just like cold is nothing but the absence of heat, so evil is nothing but the absence of good." My zealous student proclaimed this truism as if he had triumphantly solved the problem of evil once and for all—robbed evil of its power like a whipped dog, tail between its legs. I could almost see him giving his classmates a theological high five. I was tempted to judge him as naive, until I remembered that I once argued the same, back when I loved the black-and-white world precisely for my ability to construct its black-and-whiteness. I, too, used to be tempted to step back and beam in satisfaction at my perfectly constructed house— but only up until the point the hurricane hit.

So as gently but as honestly as I could, I replied to my student's comment this way: "I see what you're saying, but here's my problem with it. Does cold hurt people? Have you ever known a war veteran who lost toes and fingers from frostbite? Can the cold kill you? Would it help to tell a homeless person trying to sleep in a cardboard box at 3:00 A.M. in February in Fargo, North Dakota, that cold is just the absence of heat? The problem with evil is not that we don't have a definition for it or that it's the absence of goodness; the problem is that evil—like cold—kills people." When you live in Fargo—as I do now after having grown up in the South—you learn right quick that the cold is real and a force to be reckoned with . . . always. Living here has taught me that even thinking about the world in a way that takes warmth for granted is a sign of my privilege. And *privilege* is just a fancy word meaning that some people get to live their entire lives completely untouched by the burdens and injustices that others unfairly have to grapple with 24/7.

For most people on the underside of wealth and history, the problem of evil is not a teaching moment or a matter of philosophical debate. Rather, the problem is that evil exists in our world in exorbitant heaps of annihilation and crushes millions of human lives. To list only three examples, more than 100,000 dead in the Haitian earthquake, more than 11 million dead at the hands of the Nazis, and more than 300,000 dead in Darfur. If God were really teaching us to recognize goodness through evil, then we need to question the Teacher's methods. These numbers threaten to tip the scales too far and teach those victimized a million times more (literally) about evil than about goodness.

If you talk to folks who have survived the Holocaust, for example, as I did for my first book, one of the things you learn first is that for someone who has experienced a radical evil, evil is about as far away from "nothing" as you can get. That's why this serrated cliché about evil being nothing more than the absence of good stabs some people right in the heart. Listening to them has taught me that evil's huge shadow can devour everything else meaningful in your life, the same way the earth's shadow can eclipse the entire moon.

Dorothee Soelle once said that in a world as cold as ours, we must "keep God warm."[2] The problem of evil as I see it is not that we need to keep seeking a perfect metaphysical definition of evil, but instead that we must respond to the people who are left out in the cold to suffer and die. Christians are called to keep both them and God warm.

Cliché #2: Evil is obvious. You will know evil when you see it.

Evil never parades around with a sign around his neck saying: I am evil: Follow me! The character Dr. Evil in the Austin Powers film series is hilarious rather than frightening because no villain in real life would be so transparent. Even the ultimate bad guys such as Stalin and Pol Pot and Hitler never proclaimed, "What I am doing is evil! I love being evil! Why don't you join me in being evil?" Mark Juergensmeyer's fascinating book *Terror in the Mind of God* contains countless interviews with terrorists from every religion who have slaughtered thousands of innocents. Juergensmeyer's book reveals that the most terrifying thing about terrorism is not its random craziness, but instead its rationality and convincing logic.[3] The belief that evil waltzes through the world wearing dark clothes, a nasty smirk, and a heavy accent is absurd and naïve—a Hollywood hangover from the James Bond films.

If evil were obviously evil, virtually no one would be complicit with it. No one wants to think of themselves as in the wrong or as an evil person. Thus, evil almost always *masquerades as goodness*. Evil doesn't dress in a red suit with a tail and pitchfork; evil sports an Armani suit with Bernie Madoff charm and a respectable briefcase. It is really, really important to remember this. I am convinced that the worst things many of us ever did, we did them because at the time we believed they were good (for somebody at least). Realizing this erases the black-and-white conception of the world we like to kick around like a moral soccer ball. Think of all the genocides in the world. Though monstrous and absurd in retrospect, such movements always attracted followers by making them believe they were in the right. The purpose of propaganda is to make people believe at all times in their own righteousness and the goodness and justice of all their actions. If this were not so, propaganda would not exist and evil would have no followers. Evil is a shrewd recruiter and a superlative community organizer.

Through research, psychologists have demonstrated that when we hurt another person, we often reinterpret the victim as bad rather than ourselves or our own actions. Psychologists call this phenomenon of justifying our own actions *cognitive dissonance*. Remember how the Nazis during the Holocaust despicably referred to Jews as rats, vermin, and bacteria? Similarly, in the 1994 Rwandan genocide, the Hutus, who slaughtered the Tutsis with machetes, called the Tutsi people cockroaches.

Propaganda like this works because it reduces people's cognitive dissonance. Almost no one feels guilty about killing rats, cockroaches, bacteria, or any other subhuman species who spread disease and danger; but almost everybody objects to killing a human being—a child or a mother or your neighbor's grandpa. This is why Buddhists—who believe any and all killing is wrong—have the unusual teaching that *everyone is your mother*. Adopting this view keeps everyone's humanity and dignity smack in front of your face. It is strikingly similar to the way Christians believe everyone they meet is also Christ, "For I was hungry and you gave me food . . . I was a stranger and you welcomed me, I was naked and you gave me clothing, I was sick and you took care of me, I was in prison and you visited me. . . . Truly I tell you, just as you did it to . . . the least of these . . . you did it to me" (Matthew 25:35–36, 40).

Evil relies heavily on the steady demonization of the enemy.

To fight evil, then, I think Christians must do what Martin Luther once declared—*call things by their right names.*[4] Here's another good translation of Luther's words: *Christians should call a thing what it actually is.* The world seriously lacks people who are willing to risk condemnation and unpopularity by calling things what they actually are, rather than what we are brainsoaked to believe in order to uphold our view of ourselves as righteous. The world needs more people with the courage to speak up against these lies. In a world filled with countless seductive mislabels, we desperately need to call things by their right names, which means for starters that people are always people—not collateral damage or casualties; and hunger is always hunger, not food insecurity. Euphemisms like these are masks behind which evil hides.

Did you know that Hitler was, according to his own confession, a reluctant and unwilling anti-Semite? Indeed, the title of his book—*Mein Kampf* means "My Struggle"—can really only be understood in this context. Believe it or not, Hitler claims to have struggled against anti-Semitism his whole life until some crucial experiences with certain Jews "forced" him to become an anti-Semite. And he recounts those experiences in the book, so the reader can follow his "reluctant" lead. In such ways, hate seduces us because it almost never looks like hate, but instead like a forced, unavoidable reaction to someone else's evil actions. Fortunately for us, a passage in the Bible deals directly with the human default setting of cleverly blaming other people for the violence and evil that we commit. God calls this despicable practice "the pointing of the finger," and teaches us how to avoid such sneakiness in one of my favorite scriptures, Isaiah 58.

Isaiah 58: The Pointing of the Finger

In Isaiah 58, God cautions us against the evil of "the pointing of the finger," saying, "If you remove the yoke from among you, the pointing of the finger, the speaking of evil, if you offer your food to the hungry and satisfy the needs of the afflicted, then your light shall rise in the darkness" (vv. 9–10). Here God addresses our nasty tendency to blame others for our own evil actions. In a world rife with evil, being an outlaw means to be on the lookout for this pointing of the finger.

When I was four years old, my favorite toy was a Raggedy Ann doll. Sometimes, when I could talk him into it, my older brother would play with me and the doll. Our favorite game involved one of us throwing Raggedy down our grandma's staircase and the other catching her at the bottom.

One day my brother and I got into a fight while playing this game. We stood on the landing, both clinging to the doll and pulling as hard as we could. I don't remember what we were fighting over, but I do remember vividly how in the end, I stood holding Raggedy's tiny little arm, white cotton stuffing dangling out of it. Raggedy Ann's amputation devastated me. At the sound of my wailing, my mother hightailed it to the staircase. The second she walked in, my brother, holding the disfigured Raggedy Ann in one hand, used the other to point his finger at me and shout, "She started it!" Only four years old, I learned in that moment exactly what this world teaches us to do when there is conflict: point the finger at someone else, assign guilt, deny complicity. If this story was only about my brother it would end there, but no doubt from that day forward I did the exact same thing when I faced trouble or conflict.

In the book of Isaiah, God depicts the pointing of the finger not as a form of child's play, as I have done here, but instead as an insidious adult sin par excellence, shockingly on a par with allowing the poor to starve. The pointing of the finger is, of course, the he-or-she-started-it blame game that lies at the heart of every ugly argument and grudge we carry. Have you ever noticed what happens if you ask people why they dislike a certain person? Every time, they will tell you a story, won't they, about what that other person did. "Evil is always a story," wrote the philosopher Lance Morrow, and though he doesn't mention it, we know from experience that hate is too.[5]

People in this world do horrible things to each other, and people who should love us hurt us in ways unimaginable. My heart fissures when I consider the people I know in this world who define the word *family* as: "people in this world I most struggle to forgive." One person's side of the story—the story on which their dislike, hurt, or anger is based—is often totally true. But the truth doesn't usually end there. If you went to that disliked person and said, "Hey, so and so dislikes you," he or she would likely respond, "Oh yeah? Well, I did do that and you wanna know why? You should hear what they did FIRST!" *Boom* . . . the finger points in both directions.

Lance Morrow coined the phrase "injured innocence" to describe this. Though of course some victims are entirely innocent—take, for example, any case of child, domestic, or sexual abuse—offenders usually claim a false injured innocence for themselves. This is one of the most pernicious and vile things about evil; it claims an innocence that it does not rightfully own. Think here of the abusive spouse, who right after he punches his wife in the face says, "Come on, now, why did you have to make me hit you?"

Evil slips so easily through the cracks into our homes, hearts, and communities by mimicking goodness. It cries "innocence, innocence" where there is no innocence. Christians in the twenty-first century will not ever succeed at the laborious and sticky work of discerning evil from good if we do not remember that evil is never easily recognized as evil. We need to see that evil is a master of disguise, and its favorite disguise is goodness. Evil claims, "My cause is good and just; my side is righteous, those other people *deserve* to be treated this way," and these ego-stroking claims are the main reasons why people climb on board evil's train. As Martin Luther wisely reminded us, "We were never worse, than when we appeared our best."[6]

Sadly, communities and nations point the finger the exact same way individuals do. Every violent act is justified against a political "enemy" because of what *the enemy* once did—to us. Of course, this reasoning always ignores that the other nation probably has dozens of their own stories about what your country did to them first that your history books and media never taught you; horrible, shameful things you've never heard of, let alone pondered. Just a few years ago I read the *New York Times* bestseller *Lies My Teacher Told Me* by James Loewen—and I was truly heartbroken about aspects of our nation's history I had never been taught. As C. S. Lewis once declared in an incredible essay called "The Trouble with X," we all can recite exactly how our life plans "shipwrecked" on the rocky cliffs of someone else's personhood, but we can almost never recognize, let alone confess, how someone's else plans have shipwrecked on us.[7]

The other day I tested C. S. Lewis's theory in my class with my students. All of my students could remember a moment when their life had shipwrecked on someone else. But many— okay, most—of the students were hard-pressed to come up with a time someone's plan had shipwrecked on them. They decided that in order to find out, they would need to ask the people they knew if there was a time they had hurt them and listen to their answers. The Christian ethicist Reinhold Niebuhr also urged us to practice radical listening and stop pointing the finger when he said, "No virtuous act is quite as virtuous from the standpoint of our friend or foe as it is from our standpoint. Therefore, we must be saved by the final form of love, which is forgiveness."[8]

Eight years ago, I was in Israel as a guest of the government to discuss the Israeli-Palestinian conflict. Israel at that time, in order to "stop terrorism," had recently constructed twenty-foot-high concrete separation barriers with armed checkpoints around Palestinian territories. When I met with Israelis, they said to me, "If the Palestinians stop terrorism, then we will take the walls down." When I met with Palestinians, they said, "If the Israelis will start treating us like real people rather than prisoners trapped behind walls who have to wait in check-points for five hours a day just to get to work or the hospital, then terrorism will stop." I walked out of those meetings closer to despair than I have ever been in my whole life, and it was because (1) I see absolutely no end to that Middle East conflict on those terms, and (2) what is true for the Middle East is true the world over, true for my own family and our long-standing resentments, true for myself and the wounds I just can't let go of, true for my own country and its deadly conflicts. The condition for our forgiveness and the laying down of weapons of mass destruction is that every other country has to put theirs down first. The condition for our reconciliation with other people is that they must apologize first, show sufficient repentance, and change their ways. Then and only then can we forgive.

By now you're probably sitting here thinking (and I hope you are, actually, as this is my struggle too), *isn't pointing of the finger often justified? Shouldn't Christians point to injustice and wrongdoing when they see it? Call it out on the table?* Of course this has to be the case on some level. Jesus himself overturned the tables in the temple when he could no longer bear the exploitation of the poor and the greed of the wealthy. But Isaiah 58 does not say what we expect: it doesn't only tell us to stop pointing the finger at others when we are really to blame. Now, that would make sense! No, the scary part of Isaiah 58 is God urges us to stop pointing the finger *period*, no comforting qualifiers attached. Should we stop it *even if* we are justified in our pointing—even if the other side really did start it?

God knows we have been deeply wounded in life, and often our hurt and anger are justified. So why would God ask us to do something as crazy as cease the finger-pointing, no matter what? I'm not 100 percent sure, but perhaps the act of finger-pointing as commonly practiced every day—especially in contemporary politics—makes a horrible, un-Christ-like mistake of naming an injustice while preserving our own injured innocence. In other words, when we get better at pointing a finger at another's evil, wrongdoing, injustice, or "sin," we get worse at acknowledging our own complicity in wrongdoing, evil, injustice, and sin. The pointing of the finger never reckons with the irony, for example, that though I abhor the violence you commit against me, I myself just became violent in order to stop you.

The pointing of the finger—and evil itself—lacks any sense of theological irony. I always say, "You are never more at risk of becoming the thing you hate than at the very moment when you stand up and take your most impassioned stand against it." This is why nations respond to terrorist bombs with, ironically, bombs, but do not see this as irony at all. God urges us to dispense with the pointing of the finger because God sees the problem the way God sees everything—with a lighthouse view that exposes the unseen dangers in the fog. Retribution—if left untouched and uninterrupted by Niebuhr's final form of love— never ends. It will kill us, literally. Grace and grace alone—and the human forgiveness that grows out of that divine grace—can interrupt the cycle of finger-pointing and stop it from devastating lives like a cyclone. Is it possible all at the same time to name a terrible wound or injustice, end the finger-pointing, and move toward healing?

Yes. I know because I have witnessed real stories of real people who commit astounding acts of forgiveness. Remember back in 2006 when the Amish children were shot in Nickel Mines, and within days—citing the liberating love of Jesus—the parents of the murdered children announced their forgiveness and established a college scholarship fund for the killer's kids? Outlaws are on the loose, making God's outrageous promise, "See, I am making all things new," come true (Revelations 21:5).

Doesn't every family feud begin with a pointing of the finger story? You were always nice to your aunt/sister-in-law/ cousin-twice-removed, but remember that time when she came to your house and she (fill-in-the-blank)? (My husband knows how guilty I am of this one.) My own family has its painful share of injured innocence, but also its redemptions. I didn't speak to or even know certain relatives on my dad's side until my early thirties. At that time, I wrote to my uncle and said, "I know you have a long-standing grudge against your brother. But for my part, I would like to have you in my life." I was shocked when my uncle e-mailed me back that same day. Within the year, his daughter—with whom I later traveled to Argentina—drove eleven hours to come meet me for the first time.

The global family does not differ much from my personal one. Was there ever a war that started over anything *other* than the pointing of the finger? Probably, but most wars follow this logic: "We had to do it, had to fight back. They attacked us first, and they might do it again. Or they haven't yet, but they will soon if they get the capability. We must protect our 'way of life,' our families, our values."

Isaiah 58 is a scripture I just can't shake because it makes me ask a really terrifying question: *In our own minds, are we ever the ones who started it?* If I never think I started it, neither does anyone else. This is the chicken and the egg problem of injured innocence. Maybe, just maybe, Jesus shows us the way out of this mess.

Jesus on the cross interrupted the cycle of the pointing of the finger when he said, "Father, forgive them; for they do not know what they are doing" (Luke 23:34). As Martin Luther argues over and over again in his own writing, God could point the finger at each one of us as failures and fumblers. But instead, in a feat of outlandish and preposterous grace, God chooses not to point the finger at us, and in Isaiah 58 asks us to go mercifully and do likewise to one another. By example, Jesus teaches us this lesson: *It doesn't matter who started it; what matters is who will end it.*

According to Jewish tradition, God calls every human being to participate in *tikkun olam*, a Hebrew phrase which best translates to "world-mending" or "world-repair." What a splendid calling. Who are outlaw Christians called to be in this tattered, raggedy, unraveled world enthralled with evil? We are called to be the ones who *end* it. We are called to be the ones who use our fingers not for pointing, but for mending.

If we do this, God promises at the end of Isaiah 58 that the following will happen:

> *If you remove the yoke from among you,*
> *the pointing of the finger . . .*
> *then your light shall rise in the darkness*
> *and your gloom be like the noonday.*
> *The LORD will guide you continually,*
> *and satisfy your needs in parched places . . .*
> *and you shall be like a watered garden,*
> *like a spring of water. . . .*
> *you shall be called the repairer of the breach,*
> *the restorer of streets to live in. (vv. 9–12)*

When you live in a desert of hurt, pain, and revenge, how magnificent would it be to be the person who gives other people a drink from the waters of mercy? How beautiful would that be—to repair breaches in the world—when all around you is demonizing, mud-slinging, name-calling, and fist pounding? What would it mean for God to call you, or for you to be able to call yourself, the healer of broken friendships? The mender of long-standing resentment between conservatives and progressives, Christians and Muslims, gay people and straight people?

Wouldn't we stun this polarized world if we actually lived out harmony and reconciliation? We can participate in restoring a world we couldn't wait to send our children out into, rather than locking our doors tight with a Newtown shudder of confusion, fear, and loss.

God is trying to tell us something important: the world of retribution and blame has impassable streets. If we don't become the repairers and restorers of the unlivable streets, who will? The last time I taught Isaiah 58, my students said that we should all take the Isaiah 58 challenge and challenge ourselves to go fifty-eight days without pointing the finger at anyone. Is this a challenge you would be willing to accept?

Back to Raggedy Ann. Do you think when my mom found my brother and me fighting that she cared who started it? Today I can't even remember who started it, let alone what my brother and I even fought about. But I can tell you the one thing about that story I do remember. I remember exactly *how it ended and who ended it*. My mother took the broken Raggedy Ann doll, picked up a needle and thread, and stitched the doll's tattered arm back on to its body with her own fingers. Tikkun olam.

Cliché #3: We need evil to grow closer to God and know what good is.

Many Christians, such as the philosopher John Hick, want to make a case for an instrumental view of evil, which argues that evil serves a greater moral purpose. He argues that God uses suffering and evil to make human beings more human. Writes Hick, "Men may eventually become the perfected persons whom the New Testament calls children of God, but they cannot be created ready-made as this."[9] Without evil and the suffering it inflicts, Hick argues, human beings would never have the opportunity to become like Jesus and show compassion to each other. Taking the lead from poet John Keats, who wrote the line, "Do you not see how necessary a World of Pains and troubles is to school an Intelligence and make it a Soul?"[10] Hick describes the world as a valley of soul-making. Evil for him has a positive side effect much as it does within Buddhism: compassion can't exist without it, and neither can moral or spiritual growth.

I am willing to grant that the suffering evil inflicts can teach us things—super-important things. I would be a fool not to recognize that when my mom had Alzheimer's disease, changing her Depends and making her hot breakfasts made me a more caring and patient twentysomething than I otherwise would have been. But even though that's true, it's not the point. The point is that the cost was too great—or to be more accurate, the cost was all hers and the benefit all mine.

The problem with this suffering-cliché's line of thinking is not its instrumental view of evil ("evil is a means to a better end"), but its instrumental view *of human beings*. I side with philosopher Immanuel Kant on this one—people should never be a means to something else; they should always be ends in themselves. My spiritual growth as my mother diminished didn't feel like a fair trade made by a loving God who was trying to school my soul. Instead, it felt like grotesque favoritism. It felt like the Joker in *The Dark Knight* would not stop smiling in my direction with his scarred red mouth-gash, which everybody knows is more a cause for horror than happiness. Would we praise someone who killed the person we loved merely because he boasted, "But look at all I taught you by killing her"? My thinking was always this: If God wanted to make me suffer in order to make me more compassionate, I could grow to accept that. But torturing my mother to death so I—not she—could become a better person? I'm not buying that God works this way.

In simple terms, only survivors can do theodicy. The dead can't do theodicy. Or if they do, we can't hear it. I wish they could and that I could hear them, because if redemption is real and they have achieved it, then no doubt they have everything to teach us.

Job's entire family, for example, is dead. Do we ever think about them? How did they feel about dying so that God could win some weird bet with Satan, or so that we could learn from Job's story? I once asked my students to write a letter to God in the first person from the perspective of one of Job's dead children. When they read the letters aloud, most of us were in tears. In the minds of the dead, is there a justification for their death? I hope with my whole soul that there is, but this does not justify excluding them from the conversation ipso facto, which is what an instrumental view of evil does. The dead cannot be asked for their point of view, which is all the more reason for us to consider it on their silent behalf. Elie Wiesel recoils in horror at any suggestion that God let babies be burned alive at Auschwitz in order to teach us something, let alone teach us compassion. Or as my student Peter asked just the other day, if we really believed all the dead babies are in such a "better place," why don't we just kill ourselves now and join them?

Suffering is a frail thread that, if pulled too hard, will cause the warm blanket of meaning we wrap ourselves in at night to unravel. Most people don't really even think about the word *religion* and what it means, but some scholars say the word *religion* comes from the Latin root *religare*, which means to tie back or tie up. Religion ties us to God. It tries to keep meaning from unraveling in the face of evil and suffering by tying it back together with knots of hope and acts of love. As my friend once put it, *God quilts.* As Pulitzer Prize–winning novelist Marilynne Robinson once wrote about the redemption of our lives, "What are all these fragments for, if not to be knit up finally?"[11] With theology's help, we can succeed at keeping the whole blanket from unraveling, but this painstaking work resembles sewing with the thread of a dragonfly wing.

Granting that suffering *can* teach us something is *not* the same thing as claiming that suffering exists *in order* to teach us something. If a child waits until his mother turns her back and then touches the hot stove she told him not to touch, the child will learn that stoves are hot, and touching one is a bad idea. However, this is *not* the same as saying that the mother turned on the stove, and then turned her back on purpose so the child would get scalded and thereby learn a lesson. Such a claim would be absurd . . . and abusive. What we have to recognize is that when we talk this way and use these clichés, a lot of people conclude God is abusive. This is why my student Leah, whom I mentioned in earlier chapters was raped and molested, feared God might be describable only using profanity. Too many people had tried to suggest that the bad things that happened to her happened so that she would grow or know what good was. To such folks, Leah often would turn the question back around—"But don't you still know what goodness is even though those horrible things didn't happen to you? Do only raped and tortured people know what good is? Couldn't there be a better way?" Leah has gone on in life to do amazing, life-giving things for others as a social worker. I would never deny that good things, even redemptive things, *can come from* or happen in the midst of great evils, but I will never believe that these evils exist *in order to* create a space for those good things to occur.

I make this distinction because, unlike Hick, I want to hold open the possibility that the suffering induced by an encounter with evil can teach us nothing—certainly nothing akin to compassion. First, the dead can't learn. What is their takeaway? Second, have you ever known anyone who suffered a deep injustice in life, and who now uses this as a reason to treat everyone around them with bitterness, malice, and resentment? Such people tend to drag the rest of the world down with them into their pit of misery; and they are quite successful, because they are masters of suffering, having already endured way more than their fair share. Such people are not stewards of their suffering; they are avengers of it. Sadly, I know you and I both know just such a person. Suffering did not make them stronger; it made them meaner. Suffering made them less human, perhaps even in spite of themselves, but it did not make them more. Pious clichés deny that suffering can do this to people, and that is just one more way that they fail us.

Some encounters with evil in this life are too radical and too soul-crushing to offer us any semblance of meaning for the suffering they leave in their wake. Not all, but some. Outlaw Christians have to be able to admit this, even though it hurts like blazes and makes me feel like crying even to type these words on this page. Part of this has to do with the deep listening Jesus commands us to. My cousin, whom as I said earlier was a sex crimes cop who dealt regularly with sexual assaults on children, understands this elusiveness of meaning better than most. She is the same cousin who asked, while reflecting upon the life of a young girl she met who was beaten and raped by her two foster brothers for nearly a decade and as a result of rape then gave birth to a child with a fatal birth defect, "Why is it some people are served a s*** sandwich from the day they were born?" Is there really a meaning to be found in the molestation of a tiny baby or the rape of young girls? I am going to have to say no, because over time I have learned to listen better to the people who say to me, "There is no meaning in what happened to me. Please stop trying to find one just to make yourself feel better."

When we try to peddle such wares, we traffic in obscenity. We become hope pornographers. Some suffering eludes any meaning we try to give it, at least in this lifetime; and it's high time we allow people the outlaw-freedom to confess this truth aloud—even though for now it breaks their hearts and ours to have to do so.

That being said, it's perfectly fine to assign meaning to your own suffering, because that is not the same as assigning meaning to someone else's. Please don't stop seeking meaning for your own suffering wherever and whenever you need to. But please also lovingly reflect upon what your meaning-making implies for people who don't get the same outcomes as you (people whose cancer is not cured, whose child is not saved, etc.) . . . and then ponder how you can use your own meaningful life to give theirs back some meaning.

Finally, *don't ever forget that if life bedevils you someday with a terrible suffering you cannot assign meaning to, this book sets you free to stop trying.* One of my husband's favorite childhood memories of his Italian *nonno* (grandpa) is the time they spent building jigsaw puzzles together. Eager to please his nonno, Matt often attempted to jam an incorrect puzzle piece into one of the empty spaces. Nonno always responded to this action by saying, "Don't force, Matthew, don't force." My husband, imitating his nonno's thick Italian accent, repeats this to me on days when I am trying to make something fit in my life where it does not belong. I pass this wise advice along to you. Being an outlaw Christian means you get to stop forcing yourself to believe things you do not believe and to get on with the business of living, loving, and composting your meaningless suffering. The sprouts that you grow might one day save the life of someone else who can't find meaning in everything either but still wants love and life too. *Don't force, my friend. Don't force.*

Cliché #4: Evil only describes really big, bad sins.

You may have been wondering how I could have written pages and pages about evil, and have never mentioned the one word Christians use more than any other to explain why evil happens: *sin.* Christians sometimes define sin as a failure to love rightly: we love ourselves more than other people, we love money more than God or justice, and so on. In this line of thinking, evil is a really, really big sin or a lot of sin piled up in one place or in one person. A lot of Christians whom I know have no difficulty chalking the entire problem of evil up to human sin, and then they are done with the discussion, wiping the chalk dust off their hands. They like to remind me that evil is in the world because of the fall of Adam and Eve, who committed the first sin, and that ever since then, everyone born into the entire world is a sinner. They refer to this as original sin.

On some rare days, I envy these people for their satisfaction with this simple and totalizing answer. But on most days, to me it smacks of inauthenticity. This answer fails to address my deepest concerns. In my view, the claim that the fall and original sin are the causes of evil in the world is a dissatisfying circular argument that relegates God to the role of a shoulder-shrugging spectator. To me, it's similar to saying that some babies in the world are born with leukemia, and the reason for that evil is genetics. Though this is technically true, it doesn't answer the original question of why genetics, then, is so evil that it would cause these evils, and why God would create genetics that way and then stand back and watch innocent babies die. Do you see what I mean? Original sin/the fall is not an answer or an explanation of why the world is the way it is; it's a label we plaster on our fractured world to describe what it feels like to live in it.

Sin is most assuredly one of those theology words that has become for most people, as Walker Percy once said, like a worn-smooth poker chip that has already been cashed in.[12] The word has lost meaning because of excessive overuse, abuse, and hypocrisy, so we need to rethink it.

By sin, I mean the sense we have deep down inside ourselves that very often our own most formidable enemy is ourselves. Me. Myself. Only incredibly brave people shine the required light down deep into the mineshaft of their souls to discover this, and only the doubly courageous admit to what they find there. Sin is the haunting sense we possess that a large number of the problems and pain affecting our lives and the world have their origin in ourselves, though other people, of course, run with them and make them their own too. Sin, when truly understood, means we are part owners in the world's frailty and fracturedness. We don't dwell on this on most days, though, similar to the way we don't think about being individually responsible for any portion of our country's debt to China.

The outlaw Christian does not run around assigning sin to everyone else in the world whose sins she perceives as bigger than hers—something I am grieved to admit that many Christians relish doing. Instead, the outlaw Christian regards sin as both collective and deeply personal, like this: Sin is the acknowledgment that the world is broken and that the world's brokenness is mine. I am responsible. *I am the brokenness.* Sin is the recognition that the world's brokenness is in my bone marrow. Original sin is the recognition that this is as true for everyone else as it is for me.

Reinhold Niebuhr once said that sin is the only empirically verifiable Christian doctrine. With this statement, Niebuhr meant that although many Christian ideas have to be taken on faith and cannot be proven, there is massive evidence for human brokenness. Every time I stand in line for hours at an airport and watch TSA agents pat down shoeless toddlers and white-haired grammas in wheelchairs for explosives, I know Reinhold Niebuhr was right. Imagine all the wasted hours of our life we could gain back if we never had to stand in a TSA line or have our bags checked as we enter a concert or public building. TSA exists only because sin exists. We can all agree—Christian or not—that if given the opportunity, people will kill each other pointlessly. Sin erodes our trust in one another so far down to the bone that trust becomes joke-worthy and only fear becomes trustworthy. In the twenty-first century, sin means fear is the new certainty. Would you fly on a plane where none of the passengers passed through security? See. Empirically verifiable.

When we think sin, we tend to think big, Ten Commandment stuff, etched in stone. But sin can also be the small ways most days you disappoint yourself and other people, etched in memory. Sin manifests itself as not only a fear of others (airport security) but also a fear of yourself (a firm belief in, for example, your own un-lovability). How many times have you snapped at a friend and not apologized, or yelled at your kid because you had a hideous day at work and then thought to yourself, *Why do I treat the people I love so awfully sometimes?* Sin often results in a bedeviled sensation, as described by a character in the novel *The Story of Edgar Sawtelle*, "Maybe you just don't know what it feels like to know what the wrong thing to do is, and just watch yourself do it anyway. Like you don't even control it. But I do."[13] Who among us has not had this experience?

Sin, then, is everyday disappointment, your own and everyone else's too. It's mutual neglect. It's the way you let yourself and others down, and they let you and themselves down right back. The fact that this happens constantly is why Christians call it original—not because sex is bad and dirties us all, as some of the faith-laws teach. Original means you did not set up all the conditions which you need saving from, though of course you are responsible for a whole heaping of those as well. Sin is always already there, like a birthmark or a mole you hate to look at, but were born with so it tags you as you whether you like it or not. Sin means: Anyone is Capable of Anything. Original Sin + Contingency = Anything Can Happen to Anyone.

Original sin is the troublesome suspicion you have that your parents' stories, their parents' stories, your children's stories, and the stories of everyone you have ever known or will know were already underway in all their brokenness before you showed up. Original sin is a way of acknowledging that the world was a ginormous mess before you even came into it. Original sin is the sense that even your own story was already halfway into the telling before you were ever born. So many things in play, so many characters, heartbreaks, unresolved soul work, and broken plot lines for which you are not responsible but that you must live and move within and against. In order to understand salvation and redemption in the Christian sense, you first have to see that every story is so interlaced with everyone else's that, as Frederick Buechner said, if there's no hope for just a single one of us, then there's no hope for any of us.[14]

This is why we Christians speak of redemption or salvation in the first place, as gifts we cannot give ourselves. What would it take to save you from the marrow of your own bones?

In the process of learning to accept our own redemption, to accept ourselves as accepted, many of us wrestle to forgive God too, because God created our marrow and everyone else's out of the world's brokenness.[15] Even if you believe we do get a marrow transplant from Jesus, this doesn't explain why our marrow was so diseased in the first place. God forgives us our brokenness and loves us; that is what redemption means for Christians. Every one of us, without exception, always stands desperately in need of God's forgiveness. This, however, does not change the fact that this side of Eden, many people struggle to forgive God the world's brokenness and to love God in spite of disappointment and death, which is something no one ever wants to talk about, but an outlaw Christian sees as a real truth behind what makes faith so hard.

If even Jesus genuinely felt forsaken by God, why are we offended that human beings who are not Jesus feel forsaken also and have a tough time forgiving that forsakenness? Isn't this part of the pain that the apostle Paul alluded to in 1 Corinthians when he said that now we see through a glass darkly, and not face-to-face? Why do we judge people who find they can't stay in a relationship with a God they can't forgive? Must we continue to condemn, silence, and censor those who struggle to forgive God? No doubt even my asking such a world-reversing question upsets more people than I could count.

If we don't start to change the way we understand evil, we will lose our fight against it. Evil is not sin writ large. If we define evil as only the big stuff like suicide bombs, child molestation, murder, rape, and the use of chemical weapons, then evil is not something most of us are involved in. After all, I'm not Hitler and you're not Osama bin Laden, so hey, we're off the hook from having to change. We're merely sinners; we're not evil. Jesus, however, held a radically different view. In Luke 11:13, Jesus called the disciples—and by extension, us—"evil," as if this character trait of ours was as obvious as the noses on our faces. As Jesus' words suggest, it's easier to shirk our duty to resist evil when we see evil as something "out there." When we define evil as the big, big stuff only really bad other people do, we disown it as a part of ourselves and, worse, our responsibility.

The philosopher Hannah Arendt shocked the world with her comments on evil in her book *Eichmann in Jerusalem: A Report on the Banality of Evil*. As a court reporter during the Nazi war criminal trials, Arendt learned that evil was "sheer thoughtlessness."[16] Author Shusaku Endo similarly claimed in his novel *Silence* that unintentional acts can hurt us just as bad as intentional ones: "Sin," he reflected, "is not what it is usually thought to be; it is not to steal and tell lies. Sin is for one man to walk brutally over the life of another and to be quite oblivious of the wounds he has left behind."[17] *Obliviousness, forgetfulness,* and *thoughtlessness* are not words we normally think of when we think of evil. But they fit, as we all know if we have ever been trampled upon by someone who didn't even bother to stop long enough to notice the tears or boot marks left on our faces.

Both Arendt and Endo contributed to my epiphany: evil and sin are painfully banal. The realm of both is nothing more than the disappointments of the everyday. This means I have to own evil as well. To keep things simple as well as practical and concrete, I now define evil and sin as anything we say, do, or believe (or fail to say, do, or believe) that robs us of our humanity or the earth of its dignity. Every single one of us contributes to the evil in this world, if only by not caring or turning a blind eye when we see someone else committing it. With this realization comes an awesome responsibility: *the fight against evil is mine.* And with this responsibility comes empowerment and hope: *I can do something about it because I am the brokenness.* We are not just outsiders looking in. When it comes to everyday living, we are much better off understanding all sin as evil and all human evil as sin. Otherwise, we fall into the trap of ranking everyone else's sins as more "evil" than our own.

The ranking of sins is one of our favorite pastimes. We tend to think of our own sins as forgivable, whereas other people's— the "real sins"—are beyond redemption. This is why too many Christians tend to rank individual acts like homosexual sex and murder as the worst sins, even though this is directly contrary to the Bible, which rarely mentions either. Scripture does, however, obsessively mention more than three hundred times the collective sin of keeping the poor in poverty. How theologically convenient for those of us in the majority to categorize as the "worst" sins the actions we do not consider ourselves to have committed. How self-protecting to keep things we know ourselves to be guilty of—like not working every day to eradicate poverty—absurdly low down on the list of sins, if not off the list altogether. Outlaw Christians reject this double standard by leaning on the wisdom of C. S. Lewis, whose work suggests that double standards are the result of one thing: a deficiency of loving.

When we think of sin and evil, therefore, in contrast to how we have been taught to think according to the evil-clichés, we need to think small. Thinking small reveals to us not only the terror of our own everyday thoughtlessness but also the hidden yet magnificent value of small, everyday acts of resistance and kindness. The entire last chapter of this book will be devoted to sharing some of these marvelous everyday acts of resistance. As my student Becki once eloquently wrote in her final paper, "Evil is staying at home on Election Day and watching *American Idol*." The field of the everyday and local is the only place where the battle against evil is ever won or lost. Only our own laziness can stop us, but sadly, no foe is more formidable. If you are fed up with losing out to your own apathy, then you are ready for outlaw Christianity.

God, Too, Is Over Clichés

Remember how we talked about Job's friends, and how for nearly the entire book, they utter nothing but theodicies? All of

Job's friends offer traditional answers to explain away the evil that has befallen Job, many of which blame Job for his own sorrow. Eliphaz the Temanite, for example, claims that everything happens for a reason; so if Job is suffering, it is surely God's punishment for Job's sin: "Think now, who that was innocent ever perished? Or where were the upright cut off? As I have seen, those who plow iniquity and sow trouble reap the same. By the breath of God they perish" (Job 4:7–9). But we know Eliphaz's logic cannot be right, for God has already publicly declared Job innocent and upright: "Have you considered my servant Job? There is no one like him on the earth, a blameless and upright man who fears God and turns away from evil" (Job 2:3).

Eliphaz also argues that suffering is actually a blessing because it purifies us, makes our faith stronger, makes us a better person, and brings us closer to God: "How happy is the one whom God reproves; therefore do not despise the discipline of the Almighty" (Job 5:17). Isn't it incredible that a text written 2,500 years ago could have friends within it that sound so much like our own friends? This blows me away every time I read the book of Job. For how many of us today have an Eliphaz the Temanite among our own acquaintances and coworkers?

But don't forget the book of Job's shocking twist ending. While Job is angry at God throughout the story, the friends defend God at every turn, offering every possible traditional theodicy for why God permits or decrees evil and suffering. We would expect God, who appears in the whirlwind at the end of the book, to be totally on board with the explanations for suffering that the friends offered. But no: "The LORD said to Eliphaz the Temanite: 'My wrath is kindled against you and against your two friends; for you have not spoken of me what is right, as my servant Job has'" (Job 42:7).

Of equal interest to us as outlaw Christians is how Job responds to his friends' suffering-clichés. Job is much less forgiving (or just less passive-aggressive) than we probably are when our friends recycle the same war-torn theodicies on us. Here's what Job says to his buddies when they pull the theodicy card: "My companions are treacherous like a torrent-bed. . . . In time of heat they disappear; when it is hot, they vanish from their place. . . . Such you have now become to me; you see my calamity, and are afraid" (Job 6:15–17, 21). He continues, "As for you, you whitewash with lies; all of you are worthless physicians. If you would only keep silent, that would be your wisdom! Hear now my reasoning, and listen to the pleadings of my lips. Will you speak falsely for God, and speak deceitfully for him? Will you show partiality toward him, will you plead the case for God? . . . Your maxims are proverbs of ashes, your defenses are defenses of clay" (Job 13:4–8, 12).

Job labels his friends worthless physicians because they fail to diagnose him, let alone cure him. What ails Job is that he misses God—gut-wrenchingly and devastatingly—but everything the friends say just makes God seem even further away, as well as downright cruel. Job suggests here that his friends speak this way out of fear—they can't admit they don't know the answer for why he's suffering so terribly. What I love here is that unlike myself, Job is honest and lets his friends know how their harsh words of blame really make him feel. I usually meet such words with a fake Barbie smile, and then go home feeling punched in the gut.

Job's testimony lends credibility to my theory that suffering-clichés are useful to the comforter but not the sufferer. Job too believes that we use the clichés to protect ourselves against the collapse of our sense of the world. He argues that if his friends were the ones suffering instead of him, they would never take refuge in such dishonest and oversimplified claims: "Those at ease have contempt for misfortune, but it is ready for those whose feet are unstable" (Job 12:5). Job suggests here that like armchair quarterbacks, armchair theodicists are the worst.

The more Job's friends pummel him with religious justifications for his suffering, the more Job becomes estranged from both God and them:

> I have heard many such things;
>> miserable comforters are you all.
> Have windy words no limit?
>> Or what provokes you that you keep on talking?
> I also could talk as you do,
>> if you were in my place;
> I could join words together against you,
>> and shake my head at you. . . .
> Surely now God has worn me out;
>> he has made desolate all my company. (Job 16:2–4, 7)

Many of us who have suffered deep grief in life have experienced what Job describes here: the add-on grief of becoming alienated from our friends and family by their well-intended but whitewashed proverbs of ashes.

Job's words here remind us that miserable comforters—who

99 percent of the time are sitting pretty and not suffering themselves—make themselves feel safe from contingency by always asserting that people get what they deserve. Like many of us, Job's friends want to believe that their good fortune is earned, which means that by extension, everyone else's bad fortune has to be earned as well. When we spew clichés about suffering, we act like we are defending God, but really this is a ruse. In actuality, we are defending ourselves and our own relative prosperity. Outlaw Christians are wise to this trick and can spot it in themselves as well as others. I believe the book of Job warns us not to fall into the trap of being miserable comforters, but many Christians miss this point altogether.

The next time you are suffering and feel your chest being mortared by theological clichés about "God's plan," please remember that you are not, and were never, alone. The book of Job shows us that even God rejects these painful clichés as not speaking rightly. We owe each other more than clichés masquerading as compassion. We owe each other—and God— nothing less than ourselves. In the next chapter, we will discuss how better to live a life of faith beyond clichés and to give this gift of authenticity and deep listening to one another.

Chapter Five

Scared to Tell Your Real Story?
Compost Your Pain

> *Esse est co-esse.*
> —LATIN PROVERB MEANING "TO BE IS TO BE WITH"

> *Love is the ultimate outlaw. It just won't adhere to*
> *any rules. The most any of us can do is to sign on*
> *as its accomplice. . . . There is only one question*
> *and that is: Who knows how to make love stay?*
> —TOM ROBBINS, *STILL LIFE WITH WOODPECKER*

Law #5: Never tell your real story. Vulnerability is weakness.

Outlaw Christians understand that though we may never have an *answer* for why evil happens, we are always called to have a *response* to evil. One day in class my student Coulter confessed, "Okay, I get it. Clichés are bad. But when I don't know what to say to someone who is hurting, sometimes I just stay away from them because it's so awkward." You do not want to know how many people have told me that when they were suffering the most, many of their supposed friends avoided them like the plague. But if we can't run away and we can't toss clichés, then what should we do instead? What are some meaningful, loving alternatives we can put into practice instead of avoidance or trying to say the "right" thing?

Act I: Love Listens

"If one gives answer before hearing, it is folly and shame" (Proverbs 18:13). This biblical proverb reminds us that the question, "What does love do?" has at least one clear answer. Love listens. As Paul Tillich has written, "It is [love's] first task to listen."[1] This wisdom especially applies in situations of suffering and evil when we are tempted to theodicize and wrap up evil with a pretty pink bow. Instead of always obsessing about what we should *say*, maybe instead we should obsess about how we should *listen*. If we don't know the "right" thing to say, maybe we should be honest and just say so—or say nothing. We need to listen to our loved one's pain before we leapfrog over it into exegesis and explanation.

Jesus repeats the command "Listen!" over and over again in the Bible, nearly every time he opens his mouth to speak. Note that Jesus did not say, "Listen to me." Jesus intends for us to listen, period—which most of all includes ocean-deep listening to each other. As a young Muslim student once said to me (quoting Epictetus), "God gave us two ears and only one mouth for a reason, so we would spend twice as much time listening as we do speaking." I love that. And I love also that a Muslim taught me, a Christian, such a spectacular truth. (Surely part of what it means to be an outlaw Christian is to reject the idea that our brothers and sisters of other religions have nothing to teach us. As I am sure you have noticed throughout this book, I continually break this divisive law. And if you think about it, every Christian breaks this law if they follow Jesus, because Jesus was Jewish!)

Radical listening rather than mere answering is required because, although we often forget this, evil and suffering rupture language. Think about a time when you suffered in life. When you tried to tell someone else what you were going through, did you feel there was an unbridgeable gap between your words and the sadness you were trying to express? Wasn't it lonely to not feel fully understood? Suffering shreds language the way a pit bull tears a ragdoll to pieces in its canines. No matter how much we try to share sadness, something about our deepest grief feels unshareable, especially through words. Language is an inadequate means on its own to share with one another what it means to be our human selves, which is why we communicate also through tears and laughter. Words are not enough, nor will they ever be. The apostle Paul affirms this when he says that our prayers to God are filled with "sighs too deep for words" (Romans 8:26).

Once when I was living in a country where I did not speak the language, I wrote in my journal, "Communication is never just about language but rather about whom you let your fingers touch, what you let your eyes tell, where you put your chin in relationship to the sky, when you let your tongue be still, and how well you rest your head on someone else's shoulder."

Wondering *what is the right thing to say?* is a good question, but outlaws don't just accept it at face value. We know showing love is about more than just finding the right words. Why do we believe we always have to say something? Why do we believe that saying nothing is tantamount to doing nothing? Can't we help and love others using means beyond speech?

When people we love are suffering, above all they want to be heard. I read once that we human beings have a billion and a half heartbeats to use in this life, and I propose that you use yours to hear someone else's. Along the way, remember that the suffering of the world is God's heartbeat. Christians love and are loved by a God who suffers, something I will talk a lot more about later in this chapter.

Our culture—a culture of ADHD, multitasking, tweets, interruptions, soundbites, and 24/7 news tickers—does not train us in the kind of deep spiritual listening we need to sustain one another. Consider how poorly we listen 99 percent of the time. When we are debating a hot-button issue with a friend, and he starts talking about why he disagrees with us, what happens in our minds while he is speaking? Reloading, that's what. We're so busy loading our opinion-bullets inside our mind's imaginary gun and then cocking it, we can't hear a thing the other person says.

When heated discussions break out in my Christian ethics class, I test my reload theory. I ask the strongest voice on either side to summarize the argument of the person in the room with whom they most disagree. They have to use words the other person would recognize as their own and to which he or she would respond, "Yep, that is exactly what I mean." I also call on other students in the class, who have watched the debate in silence, asking them to recap for me the argument they have disagreed with most. A funny thing happens, especially when I do this early in the term. Most students laugh. They laugh because they can't do it. Most students haven't listened well enough to be able to summarize the other person's point of view. They only know their own point of view, and what they were planning to say next. In the early days of this practice, even when a student manages to give some kind of weak recap, the person whose argument she is summarizing usually pipes up and adds some crucial point his opponent forgot.

Though my students are bad at such listening in the beginning, over time they improve dramatically. Eventually they do an excellent job presenting someone else's point of view without interjecting their own perspective into the summary. This skill is important not only in a classroom but also in everyday life, for what is a classroom if not a training ground for better living? Many of my ethics students have come to me and said they get along so much better with family, boyfriends, and girlfriends once they learned to control the reload reflex. Heaven knows my learning to control it has strengthened my own marriage. The author Joan Silber once wrote that shutting up is a good research tool.[2] For the outlaw Christian, loving well means learning when to shut up.

An important connection exists between clichés and listening. Clichés are not a form of listening; they are just another form of reloading. As the story with my students shows, we *can* listen amazingly well to one another, but we *don't*. We do not practice listening or feel we need to be taught. We misconceive listening as something that comes naturally to us, like breathing; but really, listening is more like swimming—learning not to breathe at the right time.

After the death of my mother, my friend Doug, who himself

had suffered much in life, wrote me a note. Instead of a generic sympathy card, this personal message consisted of only three simple sentences. "Jacqueline, I heard about your mother and what happened. We both know there is nothing I can say. I love you." This note meant more to me than any other. This friend didn't fill my grief glass with clichés that would gag me like a day-old cup of Metamucil. In our impulse to restore meaning to a world of death, how many of us rush to fill the blank space on the card with spam about God's so-called plan? I had lost the embrace of the person in the world who had always loved me best—my mother—and Doug realized that what I needed most of all was to be reminded that I still moved in a world where love had its arms around me.

Although Doug did not know it, at that time I had written in my journal: "I feel like God has broken up with me, left me for a younger and more beautiful person who knows how to love better than I do." My friend somehow listened through my silence, pain, and tears—all the way down to the secret sorrow I could not say and never did, which was in essence, *I feel forgotten and unloved, adrift in a world I no longer understand*. When someone you love best in the world dies, you come unmoored. But I know I am not telling most of you something you don't already know.

Reminding someone that they are loved seems obvious, but we often forget to deliver this saving good news. And even when we do remember to give voice to love in a time of loss, we may fill the space around those words with prickly platitudes or justifications for that loss that unintentionally make the person feel unloved in our very next sentence. This occurs because we have not listened deeply enough to the hurting heart murmur within our companion's chest. For outlaw Christians, the cross means not that God micromanages the world and is all-powerful, but instead that God—for outlaw reasons of Love's own that we cannot fully understand—has chosen to suffer alongside those who suffer rather than remain on a throne in a divine castle we have built in our minds. Immanuel, one of the names in the Bible for Jesus, means "God is with us."

But suffering feels like rejection. Like being forgotten. Like being a five-year-old who peels off the pin-the-tail-on-the-donkey blindfold and realizes all the other kids at her party have left. Folks who grieve and suffer death feel rejected by God, and this is why even Jesus asked, *Why, O God, have you forsaken me?*

Perhaps when someone we love is suffering, one helpful thing we could do is remind them that the world they live in still has love addressed to her or him. I once wrote to my friend how appreciative I was for all of the interfaith work he does for our community, in spite of his own struggles with cancer. At the end of the note I said, "Consider this e-mail a love letter from the world." We need to hand deliver love letters from the world to each other. We also should remind people who suffer that even though it may not look like it, God still loves them, because the God of the cross knows what suffering tastes like. (Acknowledging that God is no stranger to feelings of rejection and sorrow is *not* the same thing as saying that someone's suffering is part of God's plan.)

I cannot explain why God neglects us or at least why it feels like God does. Maybe God is like those parents who cannot explain why they hurt the very child whom they love more than life itself. All I know is that usually those very same parents who hurt their kids claim to love them and not to have meant them harm. I believe that in most cases they really do love them, in spite of all that they do wrong. Even though one day I hope to stand corrected, for now I have to confess it feels like the Almighty does a poor job showing equally abundant love to all God's children.

Once after my sister and I had a huge fight over something stupid, my brother-in-law came into the bedroom where I was sulking and announced, "I don't know what's going on with you two, but I do know your sister loves you. Now come on out here, I've ordered Domino's." He went into my sister's room and said the same thing. These words—and not the smell of sausage pizza—brought me and my sister out of our respective rooms. *I love you* is not a cure, but it is a continuance.

In the same way, suffering makes us worry God has rejected us, and the biggest challenge we face is showing each other that God really *does* love us, despite all evidence to the contrary. When we struggle to overcome our addictions, await oncology test results, sign divorce papers, or bury the remains of our miscarried child, we sigh into our pillow, "God, I feel so forgotten by you." At those times, we want and need to hear back from God and one another: *You are loved.* We cannot say it enough. I love you. God loves you. Loved. Are. You. It's practically impossible to believe this on our own. Sorrow and shame can drown out God's voice, if and when God is saying anything.

This is why we need community—to remind one another God really does love us. Christians call this the church. Every church should have over its door the wonderful bumper sticker I once saw (and immediately bought and placed on my office door): GOD BLESS THE WHOLE WORLD: NO EXCEPTIONS. Nothing sucks more than to realize that for many people, church is the place where they've learned who they should reject, and feel righteous doing so. As Anne Lamott has said, "You can safely assume you've created God in your own image when it turns out that God hates all the same people you do."[3] If the church does not proclaim God's outrageous and wild love, or if it excludes a single soul from the scope of this radical love wake-up call, then the church has failed not only itself but all of us. The church's first calling is to announce the good news— the news that you are loved in spite of everything, in spite of the crap you and everyone else have done or left undone. The church fails to deliver this good news every day, and it rips my heart into jigsaw pieces. But frustration is no excuse for allowing such absurd failure to continue.

So let me tell it straight. Thankfully, the world does not have to be ordered, perfect, evil-free, or even coherent in order for you to love and be loved. No amount of crazy can stop you from loving and being loved. This is the real meaning of Romans 8:36–39, which says, "As it is written, 'For your sake we are being killed all day long; we are accounted as sheep to be slaughtered.' . . . For I am convinced that neither death, nor life, nor angels, nor rulers, nor things present, nor things to come, nor powers, nor height, nor depth, nor anything else in all creation, will be able to separate us from the love of God in Christ Jesus."

The problem is not that we are not loved. The real problem is that none of us believe it. Paul Tillich wonderfully defines faith as the courage to accept that you are accepted. My version is that *faith is the courage to love the fact that you are loved*. The secret to faith is trusting that you are actually loved. I mean really believing it the same way you believe the sun is hot and the American flag is red, white, and blue. But almost none of us believe deep down in the belly of our souls that we are love-able . . . and I can prove it to you.

If I were to tell you that the human body is made up of DNA, that three years ago I visited Copenhagen, Denmark, and that an albino squirrel lives in my yard (all three of which are true, by the way), would you believe me? You believed me, didn't you, in spite of the fact that I only told you once and that you have no evidence whatsoever of any of these claims. But if your child, mom, dad, brother, sister, grandma, best friend, boyfriend, girlfriend, or spouse told you only *once*—one single time in your entire life—that they loved you, would you believe them? What about once a year? Once a month? Even if they never did anything to disprove that love, would you believe they still loved you if they didn't repeat it—ideally every day? If I could get away with it, I would ask my husband every five minutes if he loves me, because the truth is I love to hear him say it. Every time he does, I feel, as Elizabeth Berg once wrote, like I am "sitting in the lap of God."[4]

Unlike other truths that we do not need to hear repeated, most of us need to be reminded every day that the fact of our being loved remains true; and the reason for this is that virtually no one believes they are loved, at least not enough. The cross is proof that God understands this about you, and would die alongside you as a person just like you to show you how real that love is. Yes, God's love disappoints us in the same way that human love disappoints us—namely, over and over again. But this does not mean the love is a lie. God may not be anything we expect, think, or even on some days want, but I do believe with all my heart that *you are loved by a God who is Love itself.* We need to remind each other of this on the dark days when we can't believe it on our own, because those days are as real as any other.

The way outlaw Christians remind ourselves God loves us is by deep listening to Jesus' entire life story. We listen for what that story really tells us about God rather than what we presume it should tell us about God. Jesus' story reminds us that God someway, somehow, took up the nail-biting, hair-raising, preposterous project we human persons undertake every day—which is to live, die, be loved, and be largely misunderstood. Let's be honest. If I were God, I would be tempted to sit on a throne stitched of cottony clouds, put on my noise-canceling headphones to drown out the sounds of gunshots and Wall Street worship, and get some much-needed rest from constant disappointment. Surely God has witnessed the ungodly mess we are making of things down here. Only love would drive the Divine to become one of us, because this morass of being human is as hard as it gets.

If everyone you loved was lost in a foreign country, at war in a jungle full of hidden minefields, would you join them—become one of them—in order to get them out? Or would you, like Claire Danes's character on *Homeland*, use all your skills and gadgets—like a GPS, cellphone, and helicopter—to rescue them from afar while you remained safe in the control room? Your choice of how to save these people would undoubtedly depend on how much you loved them. If your love for them was stronger than anything else in your life, you would rather die in the war alongside them than risk surviving and living without them. The cross tells us that God made the former outlandish choice.

But come on, are you that surprised? Think of the craziest thing you have ever done in life and then ask yourself, "Why did I do it?" I'd bet my life your answer is love. When friends ask my husband what is the craziest thing he has ever done, he often answers, "Once I took an all-night Greyhound twelve-hour bus ride from Manhattan to Charlottesville, Virginia, and then back again the very same day. All night I sat in front of a stench-filled toilet next to a drunk man who made a pass at me and my unprotected left thigh every time I started to fall asleep. And I did it all for a two-hour picnic in the rain with Jacqueline." When these same friends then ask Matt why he did it, he always answers, "Well, duh. Because I love her."

Love is the only possible explanation for the incarnation, for God taking on our ridiculous flesh that scratches and scars, freckles and farts, yawns and yearns, hungers and hurts, wrinkles and wonders. If you could pose the question *why* to God over a cup of coffee—why God lived as a person on this earth and continues to live inside all of us—I like to believe that like my husband's answer, God's answer too would include both *duh* and *love*. More than we know, we are made in God's image.

Maybe we have things backward when we say faith is about us seeking to understand God. Maybe God's faith in us is the real faith seeking understanding. Dorothee Soelle once wrote that while most people worry that they will stop believing in God, her real concern was that God will stop believing in us. Maybe God wants to understand us as much as we want to understand God. Maybe the street is not one way. Perhaps God knew that without becoming one of us, God could never understand us. The whole thing reminds me of the line from the fantastic novel *Extremely Loud and Incredibly Close*, "I hope that one day you will have the experience of doing something you do not understand for someone you love."[5] I don't know if

God understood what was involved in the reckless task of being a human being and walking among us. All I know is that once God took that one on the chin, I understood God's love for me in a way I never would have believed without such astonishing, fleshy evidence.

By radical listening to Jesus' life as well as his death on the cross, we find that God understands the peculiar torment of being human. A God who had never suffered could not be a God of love, because all love carries suffering on its sails. If I thought God did not understand what it means to walk around in a world where one out of four women is raped, where once my student's father took me out for coffee to thank me for teaching his daughter and then tried to rape me in his car, I would consider God hopelessly out of touch. I would not pray to a clueless God who had never known love or love's loss any more than I would ask advice from an armadillo.

The God Christians profess to love and turn to when they most need healing is a God who has experienced being half out of Love's head with longing, just like us. When the leper came to Jesus begging to be healed in Mark 1:40–41, the Scriptures say that Jesus was "moved with pity" and healed the man. The weird word in the original Greek that Mark uses to describe Jesus in this verse is *splagchnizomai*. The term is way more graphic than the toned-down translation of "moved with pity" lets on. The word literally means "have the bowels/spleen/intestines yearn." In other words, Jesus yearned all the way down into his bowels to heal the hurting man in front of him. Have you ever looked at someone who was suffering and yearned all the way down into your own guts for his or her healing and wholeness? I know I have, and never more than when my students and I went to

South Africa and held AIDS orphans in our arms, wiping the snot and the flies from their beautiful faces.

We know Jesus gets what it means to be out of one's head with love and longing when we read about the night before he died. In the Garden of Gethsemane, Jesus' sweat-blood mixed with tears because he couldn't stop thinking about his own arrest and death. He begged God—calling him *Abba*, meaning daddy—to find a better way. "Abba, Father," he cried out. "For you all things are possible; remove this cup from me" (Mark 14:36). Jesus begged his friends to stay awake, but they all fell asleep on him: "He came and found them sleeping; and he said to Peter, 'Simon, are you asleep?'" (Mark 14:37).

Who among us has not felt the way Jesus must have felt that night? Who among us has not let the screen door slam behind a friend or partner, even though every cell of our being is screaming, *Please don't go, I'll never make it through the night alone. Stay.* Sweating blood is a powerful, poetic description of how it feels to plead for love to stay but not be heard . . . and also how it feels to be too scared to plead even if we wanted to—for fear we might be heard but then rejected.

When we suffer, we can't escape the feeling that God has forgotten us (which is terrible enough, for is there anything worse than being forgotten by someone who claims to love you?). Even worse, we may feel God has left us and is tormenting us like a lover who kisses someone else and forces us to watch. But nobody wants to talk about Jesus' cry of dereliction—the line when Jesus asks why God has abandoned him—because Jesus' despair seems so strange and blasphemous. Outlaw Christians who are serious about listening to Jesus' story—especially the not-so-pretty theology of the cross—discover that it does not teach us about God's all-powerfulness. Instead, it reveals God's willingness to be human, get hurt, and risk rejection in order to better understand us.

A God who understands that the worst thing about suffering for anyone who loves God is the dreadful fear that even the Divine has up and walked out on them, well, *that is a God who gets it*. For me, Jesus' forlorn "why have you left me" question is the moment when God experienced at last what hurts most about being human. When people ask me how I can go on loving God in spite of everything, I tell them this moment is the main reason why. If God had no clue just how much it can suck to be a human being, then I couldn't love God, because God would be the only person in the room who didn't know.

Being understood changes things. The cross sends this message in a bottle: *God understands you*. When life is crap and you feel abandoned by everyone you know, God understands you (the cross). When your friends fall asleep on you, betray you, and act as if they don't even know you, God knows what this feels like (Peter). When your friend dies the second you leave town and you did not get to say good-bye, and all you can do is sob even if you do believe he will live again, God has felt the same way (Lazarus). God knows how ugly-awesome being human can feel, all right. If you ask people what they most fear, so many answer dying or being alone. What I see in the cross is that God has done both—died and felt horribly alone—and thus experienced our worst fears.

In a world roiling with rot and rancor, here's my best answer for what God is up to: suffering and drawing near to us in our own suffering. The cross does not signal to us that our suffering will soon stop or even become meaningful, but instead offers hope that it might someday come to be redeemed in spite of its possible meaninglessness. I believe the only meaning—if we can even call it that—found in deep suffering may well be that we are not alone in it. I believe God is present whenever and wherever we suffer, God's face sitting right there in the pile of manure life has dropped in your lap. I believe that God's presence can comfort. As Jesus promised, "I will not leave you orphaned; I am coming to you" (John 14:18). The Bible repeats this promise of comfort, as if God knows we can never hear this enough times to really believe it. "As a mother comforts her child, so I will comfort you" (Isaiah 66:13). "Then the Lord God will wipe away the tears from all faces, and the disgrace of his people he will take away from all the earth" (Isaiah 25:8). "God will wipe away every tear from their eyes" (Revelation 7:17). "Blessed are those who mourn, for they will be comforted" (Matthew 5:4).

I know this promise is not a pipe dream because wondrous people in my life have comforted me and *made* the promise more than mere smoke ring. As my brilliant student Rachel once said in class, "Why should theodicies only be words? I think we need to *be* our own theodicies. We need to be theodicies to each other." I now have this written on a Post-it note above my desk: *Be the Theodicy the World Is Longing For.* While I can respect the longing and the care behind theodicies, I am always disappointed by the colorless world where they end up. For me, the jury is still out as to why horrible stuff happens. I know this makes me an annoying person to be around, but as my friend likes to tweet: #sorrynotsorry.

More than answers, I want to provide the world compassionate action—as modeled to us Jesus-style. Jesus never explained why evil exists, but he constantly resisted evil through a hundred daily acts of self-giving agape. Likewise, Jesus never found a cure for leprosy, but he did heal lepers. He didn't speak theodicy; he incarnated it. My spiritual director once told me that when she became depressed and overwhelmed with the question of how a good God could let children die, she started volunteering twice a week at our local hospital's pediatric oncology ward. Can you think of a better theodicy?

Suffering is dizzying. When someone you love is suffering deeply, you usually cannot make the world stop spinning out of control for her, nor is that even what she expects from you. Instead, she wants you to understand that she cannot stand up without leaning up against you. Rather than endless philosophizing or wordy defenses of God, we need to offer up our arms.

People all too often suffer and die without having been shown this support—which is a massive, tectonic failure on our parts. Yes, some rare people can discover and glimpse God on their own, in the same way that some people are born with better-than-perfect vision—20/15 and even 20/10—but most people are not this way. To them, God is an escapee, a refugee, a nomad without a forwarding address. God is so stinking hard to find much of the time. No one will be honest about this except outlaws. Martin Luther—who was quite literally designated an outlaw by his government—bravely called God *deus absconditus*, meaning "the God who hides or is hidden." Maybe that's the purpose of life—to help each other find God's hiding place, to call Love out of the closet.

If I do not show you God's face and you do not show it to me, odds are good that neither of us will ever lay eyes on it. I say this because people in my life have shown me how to win at hide-and-seek with God, and without them, I would have called a permanent time-out long ago. Now it is my responsibility to share the tricks of the trade.

Outlaw Christians understand that God can be both ridiculously hard to find but also strangely present where we least expect it. We don't need to force ourselves or other people to choose between the two. Outlaw Christians live a life liberated by the both/and in a world enslaved by the either/or. In the Bible, God is found in the unlikeliest of places, including in a first-century-Palestine version of the electric chair; a tree that's on fire; the saliva on a blind man's eye; the wilderness; the tax man's dining room; a hooker's irises; a wrestler's arms; a famine; some frogs' legs as they jump out of the Nile; the laugh of a hundred-year-old old barren woman; and a horse barn full of manure and donkeys and poverty. Perhaps most preposterously, Jesus can be found inside us. As I once heard the theologian Stanley Hauerwas say, we are Jesus' hometown. Who is God, then, if not someone who is so hard to find, (s)he might just show up anywhere?

Act II: The Arts of Accompaniment and Presence

Another way to be there for the ones we love when they suffer is accompaniment. By accompaniment I mean walking alongside others, meeting them where they are, joining our arms in theirs, and sharing in their joys and griefs. For those of you who are musicians, you know that the accompanist plays music alongside the soloist, making the soloist's music richer than it would be on its own. Love can *always* accompany, though this role can be very, very painful for the outlaw who audaciously chooses it. Accompaniment taxes your time, patience, and the comfortable state of mind you enjoy when you avoid staring death, distress, and affliction in the face. But any love that does otherwise does not deserve to be called by that name. Love that accompanies is a miracle, and it is the only authentic love there is.

My husband and I, like you, have known people throughout the years who were not willing to accompany us off-road. We call such friends our Good Time Friends. Like rental car companies whose rider clause says they will not insure drivers who go on unpaved rough terrain, so too our Good Time Friends will only ride along with us on the smooth roads. Apparently, they fear the dents and scratches our sadness-gravel might cause them and their happiness paint job. Their friendship comes with no insurance.

In contrast, our best friends are our All the Time Friends. It's depressing as heck to admit, but there's nothing like real suffering to reveal which friends are which. These friends, in contrast to the Good Time Friends, do not suddenly stop answering their cells when the road we're driving down has signs that start to read "Really Bad Crud This Way." Instead of jumping out of the moving car James Bond–style, they not only stay put but also offer to drive awhile. They have shown me glimpses of God's face when I had just come to believe that suffering had evicted God from the place where the Divine used to live—which was once within me. From these marvelous friends, I have learned more than I could have from a thousand theology books.

Above all, they taught me this: The worst part about suffering is its loneliness; but mercifully, there is a cure. Loneliness's cure is togetherness, or at least a shared acknowledgment of our loneliness. In my experience, sharing with a friend the truth about your marrow-deep loneliness can take the edge off lone-liness's chill like a shared fleece blanket. Elie Wiesel defines friendship like this: "What is a friend? Someone who for the first time makes you aware of your loneliness and his, and helps you to escape so you in turn can help him."[6]

In the lovely Buddhist parable "Gotami and the Mustard Seed," the young mother, Gotami, loses her only child—a baby boy—to a tragic illness. Devastated and adrift in the deepest realms of grief, Gotami goes to the Teacher (the Buddha) and asks, "What can I do to bring my son back? He was everything to me!" The Teacher tells Gotami that in order to bring her son back to life, all she has to do is find a house in the village where no one has ever died and ask them to give her a single mus-tard seed.

So Gotami goes door-to-door to every house in the vil-lage, clutching her dead baby in her arms. At each and every house, the people inside compassionately explain to Gotami that at one point in time, a loved one who lived in their house died, so they do not possess the seed she needs to resurrect her son. At the very last house in the village, Gotami experiences her epiphany: no such house or mustard seed exists. Everyone Gotami has met is no different from herself—they too have lost someone they loved to death's talons. But Gotami had forgotten their heartache, or perhaps never taken the time to notice it. Gotami, along with the rest of her community, then gives her son a proper funeral and starts to heal.[7]

My own personal interpretation of the parable is that nobody's life is untouched by grief or death, and realizing this can strangely help take the sting out of death's slap in the face. This Buddhist parable has made my Christian faith stronger than ever, because I think a theology of the cross bears a related message. For Christians, the cross means that God too is no stranger to grief or death, and grasping this truth means healing can begin. Think about support groups. Why do they work? When people share stories of walking through similar pain, they find comfort in knowing that others understand what they are going through. Sharing scars often soothes like a mysterious balm. We cannot stop death's forward march. So we must defeat death the only way we can—through authentic sharing with one another the grief left in its wake. Wherever such authentic sharing takes place, resurrection happens.

The Christian poet Wendell Berry tells us to "practice resurrection."[8] One way we can practice everyday resurrection is to stop delegitimizing people's grief by avoiding the subject or the grieving person. Instead, we can invite them to share their secret pain in all its rawness.

In the upper Midwest where I live, stoicism—the endurance of hardship without complaint or emotion—governs life with an iron fist. But every day I see how badly people crave authenticity, and so I have tried to become a cultural outlaw who *never makes anyone feel ashamed for their sorrow.* We can't bring anyone back from the dead, but we can help one another retrieve our own grief from the island of misfit feelings where it has been banished. We can take a vow of vulnerability—the honest sharing of feelings, emotions, and unhealed memories with each other. Only when hearts take off their coats can they connect.

Social psychologists have come up with the term *disenfranchised grief* to describe grief that society has deemed illegitimate. Disenfranchised grief is the grief you are told you do not have the right to feel, so you had best get over it quickly and privately.

In cases of divorce, miscarriage, infertility, absent parents, and even retirement, people don't feel allowed to grieve. I, in fact, would go further than social psychologists and claim that though some forms of grief are far more disenfranchised than others, our culture and its ferocious faith-laws disenfranchise virtually all grief to some degree.

If my sixteen years of teaching students who constantly honor me with their sadness, scars, and secrets has taught me anything, it has taught me this: like Gotami, everyone carries around a corpse of some kind. What deadweight do you hold inside the coffin of your heart that you have been taught not to let anyone see? We must become the kind of person whom other people meet and think, *Yes, they can be trusted. They will not shame me for my secret. My sadness will not scare them.*

Gotami's parable also teaches us another important lesson: grief is an audacious liar. Everyone caught in grief's seductive embrace says to herself or himself, *I am the only one who has ever felt this horrible. I am the only one whom love has caused to suffer like this.* We should recognize grief as a wily adulterous lover who—while seducing us with swells of emotion—makes each of us genuinely believe we are the only one to ever feel his embrace. In reality, however, he has slept with every single person in the entire town . . . or one day will.

In fact, "Grief Casanova" uses the same exact sleazy pick-up lines on each one of us: *You, you are the only one I have ever made feel this way. Shhh. Keep these feelings a secret, because no one else will understand.* Outlaw Christians, however, understand what grief is up to and shout in the streets, "Grief, you are a liar and a thief. I will no longer be played." If you take one thing away from this book, please let it be that there are people out there who understand your sadness from the inside out. They have grief-wisdom to offer you if only you will take all those heavy winter coats off your heart.

One of those people is God. The message of the cross is twofold: *God stays* and *God has a story of grief just like you do.* God realized that in order for us to know we are accompanied even in death—the time every human being feels most forsaken by God—God would have to die and feel forsaken too. God, quite literally, like Gotami in the parable, carries a dead child, and that child is Jesus, and all of us too.

God—not the domesticated god of our imaginations, but the actual outrageous God of the cross—*is a God in grief.* When Jesus saw that his friend Lazarus was dead, the Scriptures say that he wept. Jesus cried even though he knew he would resurrect Lazarus five minutes later (!). Notice Jesus did not fill the air with clichés about why Mary and Martha and everyone should stop being sad because "it was part of God's plan" and "God had taken Lazarus home."

Instead, Jesus grieved his heart out and hoped like mad at the same time, which is the perfect authentic life-model for the outlaw Christian. Jesus' tears reveal that even though Christians believe in redemption and resurrection, we can and should mourn death. Jesus' cries show us that it is okay to cry and wail our hearts out whenever and wherever the world tramples on hope's face with its steel-toed boots. What could God be doing through Jesus' tears besides showing us that all of our tears are legitimate, and never more so than when someone has died?

In this way, even God is an outlaw. We imagine God to be someone who transcends grief, but this is certainly not the God revealed in Jesus. This sounds scary at first, but only until you realize this means grief, doubt, and despair must be added to Paul's epic list in Romans 8:38–40 of things that we fear separate us from God but ultimately do not: "For I am convinced that neither death, nor life, nor angels, nor rulers, nor things present, nor things to come, nor powers, nor height, nor depth, nor anything else in all creation, will be able to separate us from the love of God in Christ Jesus." In spite of the fact that this is true, we will still often *feel* as if our grief separates us from God.

Outlaw Christians understand that this happens because we are taught to think of God as supreme and powerful instead of purposefully weak and vulnerable, which the God of the cross actually is. The God revealed on the cross is a confusing one— more the God-No-One-Expected than the God-We-Imagined. Everything in the Old Testament points to the messiah as being a massively powerful and popular political and military leader, but Jesus is neither. I'll never forget the day I was babysitting for my wonderful, orthodox Jewish friends and their son, Noah. Noah, who had just learned I was not Jewish like himself, exclaimed, "But you don't really believe that God can die, do you, Jacqueline? God can't die! God is God!" The child had a point. This God of the cross is more like us than any philosophy or common sense would dream up.

As wacky as it sounds, the God of the cross is weak, alone, afraid, misunderstood, and dying. And yet when someone says the word *God*, even Christians' minds don't run to any of these characteristics. Martin Luther recognized this problem and remarked that most Christians have bought into a "theology of glory" and not a "theology of the cross."[9] We forget Good Friday's tragedy for the sake of Easter bows and bells, which is like telling the "Hansel and Gretel" story to kids but omitting the part about a witch trying to kill them, which renders the whole story, breadcrumbs and all, nonsense. When you realize that we have forgotten all about the weak, lonely, dying, and afraid parts of God's story, it becomes less surprising that in our own stories, we also forget that God accompanies us during the times when we feel the exact same way.

My mentor Tony Abbott once told me a story about his granddaughter who was furious with God about the world's evil and suffering. At age fifteen, she announced, "I am ready to give up on God, Grandpa." Tony replied, "That's okay, sweetheart. Just don't give up on Jesus."

We give up on Jesus when we hide the true depths of our anguish from one another. If you have not asked the key players in your life about their own personal grief and suffering, please make sure you do. I never asked my mom for hers and I regret it, for now there are parts of her I will never know. The truth is, we do not really know anything about each other until we've shared the sacred stories behind our deepest scars.

Have you ever considered the telling fact that the Latin word *stigmata* that Christians have used for centuries to describe Jesus' scars is just the plural of the English word stigma, meaning a mark of shame, disgrace, or humiliation? Here, our very language exposes the tragic teaching that all scars—even Jesus'—are stigmas. But outlaw Christians remember that in the scriptures Jesus refuses to see his scars as a source of humiliation or shame, or even as a thing to keep hidden. Instead, Jesus readily and boldly shows his scars to his friends. As I see it, Jesus flat-out rejects the idea that we should be ashamed and secretive about the unjust and terrible things other people have done to us. As we already mentioned in chapter 3, not only is Thomas unafraid to ask Jesus about his scars, but Jesus is also unafraid to show them to him. Both are heroic actions.

Why then are we so terrified of showing our scars or asking anyone about theirs? Are we missing the point of the story, which might just be that scar-sharing brings resurrection? Thomas is like that character in the novel *Little Bee* who says in one of my favorite quotes of all time: "A scar is never ugly. That is what the scar makers want us to think. But you and I, we must make an agreement to defy them. We must see all scars as beauty. Okay? This will be our secret. Because take it from me, a scar does not form on the dying. A scar means, I survived."[10] While many Christians remember Thomas as the loser who doubted Jesus' post-resurrection appearance, outlaw Christians remember Thomas instead as the bold friend who, because he refused to believe scars were stigmas, cared enough to ask Jesus about his scars that he survived. Inspired by Thomas, we go and do likewise with our friends.

We do not know the hidden pain people are carrying around inside of their chests like a secret tiger unless we take the time to break taboos, sit with, be with, share, ask, and listen. We must not fear vulnerability—neither our own nor someone else's—the way we have all been taught to fear it like our own nakedness. I sometimes have a nightmare in which I am walking down my high school hall, breezing past the lockers buck-naked. In our culture, fear of vulnerability borders on pathology. Outlaw Christians intentionally break the law that insists *vulnerability is weakness*. Both Jesus' life and death point to an opposite truth: *vulnerability is strength*.

If we are not wailing and tearing our clothes to reveal the nakedness underneath, how do we expect people to know that grief is swallowing us whole? Grief is just as invisible in our time and place as it was in Gotami's ancient village. Where within our culture are the resources that teach us how to give voice or representation to our grief? We have funerals, sure, but after the funeral? Nothing. But no one's grief ends with the funeral. A funeral instead marks grief's birthday. A funeral can be a cakewalk compared to the months of emotional-wasteland to follow.

In the eighteenth century in Tahiti, in contrast, women in mourning who had lost a loved one used a shark's tooth to cut a small but deep scratch in their foreheads. That cut would leave a permanent scar of grief on the woman's face for all to see. Similarly, in Victorian-era Europe, widows and mourners wore all-white or all-black mourning clothes for as long as two years to signify to everyone around them, even strangers, that they were the emotionally walking wounded. Some mourners wore a simple black armband for months to let people know they were still grieving. On the hit show *Downton Abbey*, one of the wives whose husband died in the war walked around for several episodes with a black band on her arm. I know these traditions sound strange or even morbid, but my point is this: Isn't it more honest to show our scars than to pretend we don't have any?

Personally, I wish we could bring back the armband tradition, or one like it. I would walk more softly around certain people when they needed me to, and they would return me the favor. What does it say about us that we no longer have any acceptable cultural means of showing other people that we are grieving?

I longed for a black armband the day after my best friend Suzanne died and I went to work, business as usual. I had no real choice. My employer—like most Western employers—did not offer any grief days like vacation days or sick days. It's as if we do not expect grief to happen to us in the same way we expect to catch a cold several times a year. Because of this denial, grief always takes us off guard, surprising us with a sucker punch to the gut.

After the funeral, we expect everyone to be right back at work within a day or two, being productive once again. "Moving on," we like to call it, as if the permanent loss of a human being is no different than a car passing us on the freeway. "Get over it," we like to say, as if death were a stomach flu and forty-eight hours from now we will be downing a cheeseburger, completely forgetting our Technicolor yawn. Statistics show that 16 to 20 percent of Americans—more than 35 million people—suffer from depression. But talking about depression is taboo too, because much depression is caused by grief.

The truth is, however, that we cannot "get over" some deepest forms of grief, though we can become stewards of it. The truest thing anyone ever said to me about the death of my mother was, "Every day you have to learn how to live without her." Every day. I wanted someone to tell me that all the hurt would end someday but now I know: time does *not* heal all wounds. (Go figure, another cliché that lies.) As Jesus verified, deep wounds leave scars. Time just gives us the opportunity to become better and more compassionate stewards of those wounds. Or time can just help us learn how to live again in spite of the fact that we are *not* healed and might never fully be.

Frederick Buechner said it best when he said we are called to be "good steward[s] of [our] pain."[11] Some people are stewards of their pain, while other people are salespeople of theirs.

The salespeople say, "I can't believe this s*** happened to me!" (bitterness), but the stewards take their outrage to the next level, "Now that this awful thing has happened to me, what can I make of it?" (resistance). The most important question of your life and personhood may well be: *Which one am I, and which do I want to become?* The only way to turn still-oozing wounds into scars is to put our own woundedness to work, using it to help other people muddle through theirs.

Buechner also wrote in one of his novels, "I'll tell you about s***.... If you don't pile it up too thick in any one place, it makes the seeds grow. . . . God so loved the world he sent his only begotten son down into the s*** with the rest of us so something green could happen, something small and green and hopeful."[12] I love this idea, but I have my own take on it. In my backyard, my husband and I have a compost pile where we pile up a ton of waste and rot. In time, as I sift the soil, I am always astonished at how dark and rich and wriggling with life it becomes. Stewards of pain know how to use even the stinkiest of garbage to make something green sprout and grow, even if it is not in their own gardens. Stewards of pain, I like to say, compost their sufferings.

As followers of Jesus, we are called to be composters of the world's stinkiest, still-steaming manure pile. As the poet Rumi beautifully advises, "The ground's generosity takes in our compost and grows beauty. Try to be more like the ground."[13] Theologian Henri Nouwen summons us to be "wounded healers."[14] Wounded healers never give up trying to compost what the rest of the world has labeled as garbage and shame and ugliness. Wounded healers don't kid themselves—they know they are as mucked up as anyone else. They reject the either/or and choose to live in the both/and, saying, "I am screwed up, *and* I can use my own particular screwed-upness to comfort other people." They see the garbage of this world as something perhaps not meaningful, but nonetheless useful. They refuse to give into garbage's stink by helplessly throwing it into a landfill and poisoning the earth even more. Instead, they recycle.

One of my favorite professors at Yale was the Reverend Dr. Marilyn McCord Adams, who taught a course on evil and was a consummate composter of the rot life handed her by the truckful. Dr. Adams openly shares that she was sexually molested and physically abused by her own family, and she taught us that "theology is something you do with your whole self, but you can't afford to wait to do it until your self is whole for this reason: many of us called to be theologians become whole by doing theology!"[15] Perhaps we can only become whole by accompanying other folks to healing in the midst of our brokenness, rather than waiting until we are whole ourselves to get in step beside them. As my best friend Suzanne once said in a sermon, "We have to free ourselves from the illusion that we can only help others from a place of strength."

With such understanding comes an awesome responsibility, for I now recognize that I *never* have excuses for not helping someone. Even if I feel brokenness and despair, or worry that I haven't worked through all my own mess, I can still share and listen to someone else. Authenticity heals. As Catholic activist Dorothy Day once wrote, "The only answer in this life, to the loneliness we are all bound to feel, is community."[16]

I love being part of a community of people who are hard at work composting their own crap but are still willing to lift their heavy shovels to help me compost mine. It's how I, as an outlaw Christian, would define the church. But a lot of folks would turn up their noses at this dirty definition.

As for you, what is some crap from your own life you have composted or want to compost? Write it out here to remind yourself that you can:

_____

_____

_____

I'll never forget the day soon before she died when Suzanne, a proud African American woman, outlaw Christian, lay pastor, and huge political activist, threw a massive Passover party that doubled as an election party for Barack Obama. Suzanne knew that if he got elected, she probably wouldn't live to see it (she was right); so in her hope, she threw a party in advance. Seated in a plastic lawn chair with plate of lamb in hand, a chemo-ravaged Suzanne spoke to the crowd about life's gifts and the ways life's evils had passed us over. The irony of this mini-sermon seemed lost on her—the one person whom death was *not* passing over—but left not a single dry eye in the backyard barbecue.

Later, too exhausted to continue enjoying the party, Suzanne went to bed. I found her up there, crying, and assumed it was because she hated having to leave the fun. But when I asked Suzanne what was wrong, she sobbed and mumbled, "God is so good" over and over again. She went on to tell me that someone with political connections at the party planned to offer her eighteen-year-old son—who that year was voting in his very first election—a job at the state house. (He wound up working there for years and has become such a renowned community organizer that recently he was selected to meet President Obama.) Though Suzanne never lived to see any of that, I was struck by how that night she somehow foresaw it all.

At the time, Suzanne's words astonished me, mostly because I feared deep down that if I had been her, I would have been cursing everything in sight, *not* serving up the fatted lamb with a side-dish list of blessings. I was also amazed at how cancer couldn't stop her from throwing a party and from using this celebration to help her compost her pain into promise for her son. As if that weren't enough, Suzanne's dream had been to rent a limo (she had never ridden in one) and drive around Columbus on Election Day, picking up people from the poorest parts of town and driving them to the polls to vote in one of the most historic elections of our country. Cancer robbed Suzanne of this chance, but Suzanne's husband and kids spent all of Election Day driving inner city residents to the polls in stretch limos fit for rock stars.

Another thing I learn from Suzanne's story is that redemption is not the same thing as reversal. Though beautiful, redemptive things happened to others because of Suzanne's incredible generosity, Suzanne's own cancer was never cured. The cross does not promise that God will deliver us from ugly, painful, and unjust situations. I wish to God that it were so. It's a mystery to me why sometimes God seems to have a hand in the miraculous—like the time I survived accidently driving down the wrong side of the road at dawn—but at other times it obscenely feels like God has not only failed to rescue but abandoned. Where, for example, is the miracle for the thirty-five thousand kids a day who die from starvation and simple infections? The outlaw Christian is unafraid to acknowledge the fact that God delivers some and not others; delivers sometimes, but not always. We have no clue why this is, and we do not lie about it—neither about our cluelessness nor the sad truth of undeliverance.

No matter what, though, God can and does accompany us as we become stewards of our scars. I would never want to take away anyone's life-story of healing. However, a massive amount of the time God does not cure the cancer, take the gun from the shooter's hand, get us our job back, enact justice, or remove bacteria from water so people can safely drink it. Those things are up to us to do for one another whenever and wherever we can. Why can't we be honest about this, as painful as it is to admit? By holding on to the belief that God is all-powerful, we let ourselves off of the hook for not doing the things God wants and needs us to be doing.

To admit this *does not mean* the death of hope. By no means. To admit God does not do these things *for* us gives us more responsibility and more empowerment, not less. God's choice of powerlessness is our empowerment, because whatever God doesn't do, we have to. No more sitting around waiting on God. We have to enact justice and limit suffering because God is obviously not going to do these things *unless through us*. My national church's tagline is "God's work, our hands." Yet I have to tell you; nearly every time I show a group of folks Dorothee Soelle's poem "When He Came," some people in the room get outraged by a line in the poem that suggests God needs us. A God who *needs* us offends many, many Christians. Yet didn't Jesus have disciples—disciples who healed the blind and the lame and fed the hungry just like he did? Didn't Peter resurrect Tabitha from the dead? Jesus knew that we would object to

God's need for us, which is why he said, "Blessed is anyone who takes no offense at me" (Matthew 11:6).

Dorothee Soelle explains that God is not an "interventionist" but an "intentionist" whose will we can know: life is for all.[17] Jesus himself says, "I came that they may have life, and have it abundantly" (John 10:10). God's intentions for us are clear: we need to give each other our humanity back. In an age where cable news reports death 24/7, we need to make our own newsreel of life-giving acts of accompaniment, compassion, service, and resistance. We, not God alone, are the interventionists who must do what God intends. God tells us where we need to intervene, which is everywhere the "least of these" are languishing: "Truly I tell you, just as you did it to one of the least of these who are members of my family, you did it to me" (Matthew 25:40).

When Suzanne was dying of colon cancer, I could not cure her cancer or explain it, but I did do other things that she asked me to do. I passed the Smartwater. I put her favorite movie, *The Awful Truth*, in the DVD player fifty times. I laughed my head off when she tried on the wedding dress she had not been able to fit into for twenty years and joked, "Wow! It fits! This cancer diet is really something!" And when she whispered, "Don't leave," I stayed. I found hope in the Jewish saying that "each visitor is said to take one-sixtieth of the illness away from the ailing person."[18]

Though we think we want someone to fix our problems, in the end maybe all we really want is someone who promises to stay and keep coming back to be with us no matter how bad it gets. God makes that promise to us on the cross, but God keeps that promise with our help.

Speaking of promises, I once heard the theologian and

teacher Terry Fretheim say that anyone who makes promises can never be all-powerful, because to make a promise is to be purposefully self-limiting and to bind yourself to limited courses of action. If I make you a promise, then there are choices that I have eliminated as possibilities for myself. I take this to mean that our God is a God of promises, and not of power—at least not as power is normally understood. Certain promises can always be kept even when the world believes we have lost all our power, and the prime example of this is the promise *I will always love you.*

Examples of Accompaniment in Our Own Lives, the Bible, and Art

Personal Example

I want to share with you a story from my own life that best taught me what accompaniment and the vocation of presence looks like in practice. When my mom was dying and I was suffering from crippling depression, my friend who was worried about me came to visit. This friend, named Matt, listened to me talk and cry all night about how much I loved my mother.

The whole time I cried, Matt had one hand in mine and his other hand on my arm. At one point—I'll never forget this—he leaned into my shoulder and cried with me. A strange comfort spread to every place his body touched mine. He did not find a cure for Alzheimer's, tell me my mom's death was meant to be, make my mom remember my name, or take my grief away. He did not even say a word, except to whisper in my ear, "I know how much you miss her." Matt did, however, do three important things that night. First, he did not leave or fall asleep. He did not leave me comfortless, and in this way reminded me of

Jesus' promise that God will never do that either (John 14:18). Second, he held my hand and passed me Kleenex—and in that way practiced the vocation of presence. Third, he grieved alongside me and acknowledged that in my mother's illness, the world had genuinely lost something. In so doing, he showed me what Romans 12:15 looks like in real life, "Rejoice with those who rejoice, weep with those who weep."

Oftentimes, accompaniment saves lives. Six years later, I married this loving friend—a testimony to how grace reconstructs ruins.

"Allow your community to hold you," says the Buddhist monk Thich Nhat Hanh in one of my favorite quotes of all time.[19] As a member of your community, God wants this for you, and from you too. I know that some days you simply cannot hold on to God any longer. I know this because I feel this way myself a lot of the time. The rope is too frayed, too long, too slippery with sea-slime, and your arms and legs are too tired from dog-paddling. But the good news is this: You do not have to hold on. You only have to *let yourself be held on to*. This is what accompaniment means.

The sum conclusion of all this is that powerlessness is an illusion—a proficient liar just like grief. Taken together, both the cross and life of Jesus teach us we are to heal, mend, feed, provide, fix, allay, teach, listen, learn—and even when all or none of these things can be achieved, always, always we can accompany and comfort with presence.

Accompaniment in Art: Lars and the Real Girl

In the popular 2008 film *Lars and the Real Girl*, Lars's girlfriend Bianca gets very ill and dies. During Bianca's illness, the women of Lars's church come uninvited to his house and bring food, books, and knitting. The women sit on the couch in silence, never saying any clichés such as, "Bianca will be fine, we just know it" or "God is getting ready to take her home." Lars, confused, eventually asks the women why they are there. The women look up at Lars as if he has missed the most obvious fact in the world. They explain, "That's what people do when tragedy strikes. They come over and sit." They proceed to sit all night long, even after Lars goes to bed.[20]

Ever since the day we watched this film in one of my classes, my students and I adopted the word *sit-with*. I have overheard my students saying to one another in times of grief, "Do you want me to sit with you?" I have witnessed one female student accompany another male student to our health center because his depression had reached new lows. Two students told me recently about the time they stayed up all night just sitting with a friend who was waiting on news about her mother's surgery. I myself once received a text message from a friend when I was going through a tough time that said, "Would it help if I sat?"

But at this point perhaps you are wondering, *Doesn't the God of the Bible do more than just sit around and accompany? Doesn't God also offer real healing and real change?* Yes, but the truth is, even God's healing is local. I can offer you a story that speaks to this, but not an explanation. Though the church father Thomas Aquinas once famously penned that the Christian faith is about seeking understanding, my faith does not seek understanding—though it would be a great comfort—because I know full understanding is impossible. I would describe my own faith as faith-seeking-love-and-living-love-in-spite-of-not-understanding. The best part about learning to love God without understanding is that it's great practice for learning to love human beings, whom most of the time we have to love the same way.

The following story brought me a couple centimeters closer to learning to say to God, "God, I love you, even if I do not understand you."

It was the middle of winter in the Midwest of my soul, and nothing green or alive had survived, or so it seemed. Even my prayers were frostbit. Frostbitten prayers. I had become like the character Baby Suggs in Toni Morrison's novel *Beloved*; I craved color. My cousin invited me to Argentina, and I stepped off the plane into a January summer. Everywhere I looked, my eyes found the colors for which they longed.

During a hike in the Andes, I nearly stepped on a tiny flower. The flower stuck up proudly out of the ground like one of those flags mountain climbers thrust into the earth to say, "I was here, remember this." A swath of snow, white as the Ohio sky I had just left behind, surrounded the flower's purple pinwheel-petals. But when I bent down and looked closer, I saw something else. For a few centimeters all around the flower, the snow had melted. A perfect donut of brown, rocky earth encircled the flower's thin, green shoot of a stem, like a coin of infinite value, like the earth winking color. *Flowers breathe*, I realized. I did not know this. The flower's breath was slim and fragile, yet powerful enough to melt winter so thoroughly that none of the plant's outstretched purple arms touched any of the snow-walls that probably that very dawn had pressed in on them like a frozen prison.

I found myself thinking that my calling—my vocation to love others, resist evil, and act compassionately—is like this.

God's love and healing is like this too, which often disappoints us. Though we wish God's love were a huge hurricane crushing any force in its way, the cross reminds us that God's love is frail and local like a flower's breath. Nonetheless, if you are the person whose arms no longer touch ice every morning, you understand better than anyone that nothing could be more infinite and life changing.

The paradox of healing one another through accompaniment is the same as God's: our actions are frail and local, yet they make an infinite difference. I can say in all honesty, I would not be the person I am today without the people who've let their love accompany me into the dankest corners of my own mountains. Heck, I might not even be alive, and I know I'm not the only one. But stubbornly, our society still refuses to create a religious or cultural space for sharing our grief or our laments. The new slang word *overshare* can be cultural code for *we do not want to hear about other people's pain, don't even think about going there.* The subliminal message of this word is that grief is taboo and better left unsaid.

To sit, therefore, just sit with someone else, like the women in the movie, when tragedy has moved in, is a beautiful and redemptive form of accompaniment, but we don't usually recognize the power in these small acts. This power looks too much like weakness for us to stop and notice the small, melted circle of once-ice that surrounds its breath. However, maybe it's only privileged and relatively empowered people like me who can't grasp the subtle but profound impact accompaniment can have. Empowered folks expect to be able to enact significant change in the world without needing help from others. Our privilege lets us go for big chunks of time buying into the fairy tale that we don't need other people and that accompaniment can't make a difference.

Suffering deconstructs this myth of independence and reveals it for the illusion it always was. Indeed, the cross suggests that even God is interdependent with us human beings, albeit by a radical choice made for love's sake. We learn from God's example that accompaniment may well be the most empowering action we can take.

Accompaniment in the Book of Job

Though the book of Job provides us with armchair theodicies and suffering-clichés aplenty, the very same book also provides an astonishing example of accompaniment at its best. Given how Job's friends in the story screw up horribly, you might wonder who in the heck actually gets it right. Well, the totally ironic answer is: Job's friends. His friends get it wrong *and* get it right, as if to show that there is hope for every one of us to get this right in the end.

If the alienating behavior and the accompanying behavior toward Job had come from *different* friends, the story would offer us no hope. Such a story would suggest that some people know what to do and some people do not, which would let us get away with our usual cop-out thought, *I'm not the kind of person who knows what to do in situations like this.* The real story proclaims the fantastic opposite. Even those of us who screw up massively and sometimes hurt the very people we love also possess all the resources necessary to offer genuine comfort and consolation.

In the very beginning of the story, Job's friends haven't resorted to mumbling clichés yet. What do they do?

Now when Job's three friends heard of all these troubles that had come upon him, each of them set out from his home— Eliphaz the Temanite, Bildad the Shuhite, and Zophar the Naamathite. They met together to go and console and comfort him. When they saw him from a distance, they did not recognize him, and they raised their voices and wept aloud; they tore their robes and threw dust in the air upon their heads. They sat with him on the ground seven days and seven nights, and no one spoke a word to him, for they saw that his suffering was very great. (Job 2:11–13)

What is most effective about Job's friends' response is that they (1) shut up and do not offer up words to explain away Job's pain; (2) refuse to leave Job; and (3) cry with him. The similarities with what Matt did for me on that dark night of my soul are uncanny. Yet for years, I read the book of Job and always missed this. Job's friends stayed with him for seven days and nights. Can you imagine sitting on the ground with a friend for that long? Such solidarity! Job's friends demonstrate the two most important aspects of the sit-with: silence and staying. Here the friends demonstrate that the best way to mourn with those who mourn is through accompaniment that embraces and listens, not through clichés that estrange and isolate. Only later, once Job's friends resort to wordy rationalizations and spin-doctoring, do things start to go wrong.

In Judaism, the practice of sitting-with is a marvelous custom known as sitting *shiva*, for which Christianity regrettably has no real equivalent. During shiva, mourners sit for seven days and nights, completely ceasing their normal lives of work and leisure. The community cooks for the mourners and brings them meals, so they can devote themselves full-time to grieving. The mourners embody their mourning by sitting on the ground or on chairs close to the ground, to symbolize that their grief has brought them low. When friends come to visit the mourners, they too sit low. The visitors do not speak to the mourners but wait instead for them to initiate any conversation. The only appropriate thing to say to mourners is the following sentence, which exists in the tradition in a couple different versions, including, "The Omnipresent will comfort you (pl.) among the mourners of Zion and Jerusalem" and "May you be comforted by *Hashem*." By referring to God as the Omnipresent rather than the Omnipotent, these expressions emphasize God's presence and comfort instead of God's power.

As a symbol of the griever's broken heart, Orthodox Jews who sit shiva wear a shirt or vest with a torn spot over their heart. Conservative and reform Jews wear a torn black ribbon pinned to their clothes. The torn *keriah* garment is never worn again or mended, as a reminder that the dead person will always be missed—a permanent tear in the garment of the mourner's life. In today's practice of sitting shiva, only certain parts of the Bible may be read—notably, Job and Lamentations are among the few acceptable texts.[21] Outlaw Christians learn from the stunningly rich Jewish spiritual practice of shiva that it is possible from within faith to honor grief on its own terms.

A New Understanding of Authentic Power

I once got into a huge theological debate with one of my graduate school professors. I said in class that though suffering had no real answer and evil had no real reason, one thing I knew for sure as a Christian was that whenever we suffer, God suffers alongside us, with us, and through us. My professor found this terrifying and insulting. He challenged me in front of the whole class, "I don't find that comforting at all. What can possibly be comforting about a suffering God?"

My professor believed that a suffering God would be weak and powerless, able to do nothing to help us. I couldn't disagree more, and I told my professor so. Just because God isn't all-powerful doesn't mean God is doing nothing, sitting around on the clouds playing Xbox or embroidering tea towels. Similarly, just because God knows what suffering tastes like doesn't mean God is powerless. As my story with Matt shows, in one moment we can be both powerless to change some things, but powerful enough to change others. Matt couldn't cure Alzheimer's, but he could help cure the loneliness my grief had inflicted upon me. God can do the same. My professor assumed that only omnipotence could get things done and that suffering paralyzed us completely.

My professor's worrisome line of thinking implies that when we human persons suffer, we can't do anything to help one another either. My professor not only underestimated God's possibilities for action, but also ours. We need a word in our language for the power to comfort (comfort-potence?), but notice there isn't one, which reveals that we, like my angry professor, do not grasp comfort's peculiar power.

The cross suggests God exchanged divine omnipotence for radical empathy, felt from the inside out. Without going through it, how could God know what it feels like to be a human being and to suffer and die? I do not want to ever let go of my understanding of God as loving and just. I have let go, however, of my understanding of God as all-powerful, but only in so far as that term is traditionally conceived. Most Christians consider omnipotence to be like a superpower—the raw and formidable ability to do whatever one wants, to whomever one wants, with a mere flick of the wrist. But this understanding does not come from looking at the nail-driven hands of the God on the cross. As an outlaw Christian, I want to throw out this naïve conception of omnipotence, because it's holding us back from living lives in service to one another. When people renounce power and violence, they acquire a mysterious power that we do not understand, yet somehow admire; we see it embodied in people such as Gandhi, Nelson Mandela, Mother Teresa, and Martin Luther King Jr.

Jesus and these individuals teach us that power is something radically new and different from what we have always believed power to be. As human beings influenced by patriarchy, we define *power* as being over and against others. We are taught—by people in power!—to believe that power is the ability and authority to force others to obey our commands or pay the price. But real power, as God tried to demonstrate on the cross, is beside and with, *not* over and against. *Authentic power shares power with others.*

Here's a real-life analogy. I am a teacher who has all of my students sit in a circle, no matter the class size. The message of such a classroom design is that we all share the authority. I do not lecture. When necessary, I give mini-lectures, but for the most part, if you sat in on my class, you would hear student voices more than my own. A friend of mine who is not a teacher once sat in on my class and joked, "But, geez, you are just sitting there, hardly doing anything and letting the students do all the work! How easy is that!" But as any good teacher recognizes, learning when to shut up so that students can find their own voice is an art that takes years to master. It took me nearly a decade. The worst mistake I ever made as a new teacher was doing all the talking, and not nearly enough of the listening. Just ask my poor students.

Dorothee Soelle wrote that the only real power is that which empowers others. In her words, "Power is empowerment."[22] Authentic power is not an either/or, but a both/and, both yours and mine. We know this deep down, because it's why we prefer democracy to dictatorships, but somehow we still forget. To those who crave traditional power, authentic power looks like weakness, because it renounces simple dominance and substitutes shared empowerment in its place. This is why Jesus said, "My grace is sufficient for you, for power is made perfect in weakness." It is also why the apostle Paul wrote, "God's weakness is stronger than human strength" (2 Corinthians 12:9; 1 Corinthians 1:25).

The cross reminds us furthermore that traditional unshared power is a weakness in its own right, because anyone with such power has to spend 99 percent of their time defending and maintaining it, crucifying those who challenge it, and constructing lies in order to justify to themselves and others why they have so much while others have none. People in "absolute" (unshared) power know how tenuous and flimsy that kind of power actually is; if this were not so, censorship, prisons, lies, AK-47s, concentration camps, militaries, propaganda, and nuclear weapons would not exist.

Consider Jesus and how our interpretation of Jesus depends on where we stand. Leaders used to absolute power saw the power Jesus shared with the masses as a loss-moment. Both the religious and secular Roman authorities wanted Jesus dead; his popularity and his message threatened to redistribute the authority they hoped to hoard all to themselves. On the other hand, the disempowered understood the cross rightly as a gain-moment, because now the power was shared with them. We tend to forget that Jesus came not just to bring good news, but specifically *good news to the poor.* Jesus' command to share is a delight to those who have nothing, while the same command feels like a burden to those who have everything and want to keep it that way. "Jesus, looking at him, loved him and said, 'You lack one thing; go, sell what you own, and give the money to the poor, and . . . then come, follow me.' When [the man] heard this, he was shocked and went away grieving, for he had many possessions" (Mark 10:21–22). This battle rages on today in our society (think: taxes, health care reform, and the way Americans are taught to believe socialism is one of the greatest evils on earth).

So what does this discussion of power mean for our everyday lives? First, it means that the paradox of power is that you are never more powerful than when you share yours. Nonetheless, you may feel less powerful, for it goes against all you have been taught by the laws of the land. Likewise, the paradox of freedom is that you are never more free than when you are fighting for someone else's freedom, but this fight may well result in what feels like the loss or suspension of your own freedom.

Consider as powerful examples, Nelson Mandela and Vaclav Havel. These two men spent a combined total of more than thirty-five years in prison as political rebels against oppressive regimes before they both became presidents of nations—South Africa and Czechoslovakia, respectively. Would you say they are powerful, free men? Yes, but would you have said it while they were behind bars? Wasn't it still true even then, because their free choices to try to make others free landed them there? Deeply powerful and profoundly free, both men knew they could really be neither until everyone else was both.

Second, our new understanding of authentic power means we need to be on the lookout for myths about powerlessness. The unwritten law—that you are powerless if you share your power with others—is seductive, but outlaws reject this insolent lie. We'll talk more about this in the last chapter where we look at some of the most radically powerful people in history whose names you have probably never been taught. But for now, simply remember that the person(s) in power over you wants nothing more than for you to believe in the myth of your own powerlessness. When you feel this way, you have internalized what someone else believes about you, which is how oppression always works. Oppressors and bullies want you to believe that you are a second-rate loser, when in actuality you are an outlandishly loved child of God. Once you realize who you really are, oppressors beware. "Whoever wants to be first must be last of all and servant of all" (Mark 9:35).

Friends I have met the world over have taught me that your so-called powerlessness can never rob you of your sacred right to tell your story. When Nelson Mandela was in prison, he shared stories with other prisoners by writing on pieces of toilet paper.

Because it's wrong to ask people to do something scary you yourself would not be willing to do, I end this chapter by sharing one of my own scar-stories. What follows are pages torn straight out of my own journal. This story involves the person I love most in this world, but when I asked him if it was okay to tell you about it, he said yes. He knows what it means to compost pain.

FEBRUARY 24, 2013

*In the midst of winter, I found there was, within
me, an invincible summer.*

—ALBERT CAMUS

Faith is the transformation of affliction.

—THICH NHAT HANH

I just looked out the window after reading that line above from Thich Nhat Hanh's book *Power* and started crying. As I put the book down in my lap and looked at the white stillness outside, this thought overwhelmed me, "Anything can be transformed. Any grief. Anything." I cried because most days I do not believe this, even though I desperately want to believe nothing is more true. Yet in that moment, I cried because I knew it was absolutely true in a world where love still exists.

My whole life is a story of my awestruck admiration of people who survived horror and nonetheless transmitted nothing but love to the people around them—Elie Wiesel, Tony Abbott, Desmond Tutu, my own mother. I always knew—and even have often said—that these people possessed the secret of living, even though I was never quite sure how they came by it. Yet what I did not realize is how much I would one day need their example. I certainly never realized that one day, unless I became like them, the suffering of the world would climb in my windows and strangle me to death.

Now, today, I feel like the character Owen Meany in John Irving's novel *A Prayer for Owen Meany*. Owen spends his whole life practicing one shot in basketball, which seems absurd at the time. But Owen feels he should keep doing THE SHOT, as he calls it. And in the end, he realizes why he had to practice THE SHOT all those times. It enables him during a terrorist attack to take a grenade and throw it out of a high bathroom window, saving a huge group of people. I have been practicing my own version of THE SHOT for my whole life, though I never realized it until today.

I have always been troubled by evil, plagued with it and the suffering it ushers in. Everything I teach involves evil, forgiveness, nonviolence, mercy, and grace—my whole life is committed to trying to understand and live this strange tango between compassion and suffering. Thich Nhat Hanh defines faith as the transformation of suffering. As a Christian, this makes me think to myself, *of course that is what faith is.* But I am embarrassed to say I never thought of it this way. It took a Buddhist to unlock for me what the cross is really about. Faith is trust that *yes*, all *dukkha* (the Buddhist word for suffering) will find a way to transformation, or at least it can find its way there. All things are possible.

Everything I claimed to trust, believe, and teach was and is put to the test that dark night in bed when Matt shared his horrible secret of evil, of the unbearable pain of what had happened to him.

Normally I would want to write next something dramatic like this: that was the night our whole life changed. In one way that is true, and in another way it isn't. Now I want to write what feels closer to the truth: that was the night I realized that horror must not be allowed to change you or who you are. And: that was the night I realized that rape in all its ugliness has always been our problem as long as it happened to one innocent human person in this world, but I never realized this until it happened to someone I loved—my spouse— and in that way had happened to me. Rape was always something out there—looming large, and appalling, making itself known as statistics like one in four (women) and one in six (men). These numbers are astronomical. This means that when I look at a class of my students, five people in the room at a minimum have been raped or molested. I never once considered this, in spite of having heard those statistics many times. I feel terrible that I never did.

I always believed this act would scar a life beyond recognition, like I feared it did my friend Mary Beth in high school, whom I now realize put that deadbolt on the door of her bedroom because her adopted brother was raping her. If this act scarred someone's life and they could not recover, I would be unable to judge them for it. Had it happened to me as a child, I think I'd be tormented eternally. I have always thought that, and considered myself secretly "lucky" to have not undergone such violence and even having been spared it during that one close call in my own life. So what is most surprising in the situation we now are living through is the utter naiveté of all my assumptions.

In the days since the horrible thing happened, I have watched Matt walk around baking homemade bread, hosting wine-tasting parties at our house, writing a screenplay, and making Bret and Dylan crack up with his jokes. When I watch him, I feel astonished at people's sheer ability to survive—to flat-out refuse to let the feces the world force-feeds them stop them from living. To not stop them from making a beef stroganoff, to not stop them from attending a friend's funeral and sobbing that that friend could no longer share this life with the rest of us (also things Matt did recently). I have never been more surprised by my own reaction to anything or by the reaction of the person I most love. For here I sit, and I can write these two absurd sentences in the same breath:

(1) Six months ago, my husband was raped, assaulted, and beaten by three men in Louisiana who punched him in the head over and over while they called him Yankee faggot, robbed him, and abandoned him at the side of the road in a swamp.

(2) I actually believed today for a moment that all suffering can be transformed—meaning this one included—if washed in love daily.

This is of course a long, hard road. . . . But Matt and I are like Gotami in the mustard seed parable. We know there is no house in the village that has escaped unscathed and this is oddly and impossibly comforting. Grief cannot tell us the lie of aloneness and make us believe it. She cannot say, "No one knows what you're going through. No one else knows how much this hurts and eats your dignity alive with jaws of shame." *We know this is a lie.* Knowing this has perhaps saved us or at least saved something of who we once were and still want to be.

Even Matt said this when he came home from his support group at the Rape and Abuse Crisis Center last Monday. He said he felt like every time he told the truth aloud to someone who did not make him feel ashamed, the person listening carried away a milligram of his hurt for him. Everything in my life has prepared me for this shot—John Irving, even the writing of my book *Outlaw Christian*, which I had started years before this happened. Now of all my emotions, the one I am feeling most is disgust at evil and shame at culture, and not anger at God at all. Shame—and the way we all buy in to it by teaching others that certain things must be kept hush-hush—allows evil to keep on and on in its filthy winning. I am disgusted with evil for never feeling dirty itself for the ugly things it does, but instead for making us feel dirty for the terrible things it does to us.

I feel like a girl who lived on the equator her whole life and yet these odd, older, wiser strangers from the Arctic came to her house every day and dropped off cross-country skis, snowshoes, goggles, snow globes, eighteen Alaskan words for *snow*, thermostats, dogsleds, down parkas, thermal heat glove inserts, scarves, wool hats, and incredible stories of blizzards survived and surmounted. I feel like the best thing—the best grace in my whole life—is the astonishing fact that as a child of the equator, I actually listened to these arctic strangers and did not disbelieve in a winter I had never seen, but instead accepted their gifts.

I feel God sent me and Matt all these snow-knowers for the day when the winter hit us in our 44th year, so we would at least have some sense we do not go out into the blizzard alone. This is even more true for Matt than for me. I think of the movie Matt made exactly ten years ago, *Speak*, which is about date rape. I think about everyone who unfortunately understands that film all too well—snow-knowers every last one of them. I think of how even before anything like that had happened to Matt, he always told people that the film he was most proud of having helped make was *Speak*. I am so grateful that we took all of these snow-knowers' arctic-gear offerings and kept them in the basement rather than throw them away, because we can and must use each of them now that we ourselves have moved north.

I am writing all this down as proof that I once believed it, because I know on hard days I will not and will need reminding. Sharing, instead of hiding all of our shame, sadness, and suffering, is the secret to joy. The secret to joy is shedding our secrets. Listen to the snow-knowers, for they will always tell you the truth.

Chapter Six

Longing for Hope?
Seven Ways to Find It

There is no me without you.

—HAREGEWOIN TEFFARA

*Pay attention. It's all about paying attention.
Attention is vitality.*

—SUSAN SONTAG

*The very least you can do in your life is figure out
what you hope for. And the most you can do is live
inside that hope. Not admire it from a distance but
live right in it, under its roof.*

—BARBARA KINGSOLVER

Law #6: Always believe hope comes easy as pie for those who truly love God.

Let there be no doubt about it, despair is my nemesis. (Given
that you have made it this far in the book, I can almost hear

you laughing right now and saying, "As if I hadn't noticed!") But seriously, I once discovered the haunting German word *Weltschmerz* in a novel. I found out that Weltschmerz means world-weariness. Ever since that moment, I use the word to capture how I feel on my bad days. Some days after reading the newspaper, I feel weary to the bone—the way my great-grandma, rocking on her front porch, said to me just days before she died, "I am so tired, Jacqueline, I just want to go home." World-weariness.

During my many years spent caregiving for my mom, I battled depression, and I have accepted that this is one battle I will not get to stop fighting any time soon. At my lowest point, I took antidepressants for months, and hid this fact from nearly everyone I knew. I was ashamed and did not yet understand that depression is an actual illness like a bacterial infection, meaning that if it's bad enough, you need medicine to fix it or it might well kill you. The problem of evil and suffering are a soul-eating bacteria for me. In order to reclaim my soul, I have spent hours with a grief counselor, and even more hours talking to close friends about my grief over my mother's death, Suzanne's death, the sick babies I've held in South Africa, and in general, the world's grotesque and soul-scarring injustice. I am a strong believer in what Elie Wiesel once said in an interview, "I believe in therapy, particularly between friends."[1]

I confess my despair to you as a preface to this chapter on hope and joy so that if you are a person for whom hope sometimes looms like a mountain with an unreachable summit, when I start to talk about hope, you will hear me out. Especially I am here to tell you that although in life we usually do not get to choose which battles we will fight, we always get to choose whether we will fight them or not. What our world needs right now, more than anything, is more hope foot soldiers.

The saddest part about despair is that just like grief, despair is a social and spiritual taboo. Christians learn that despair is the greatest of sins, and many characterize it as the cryptic unforgiveable "eternal sin" Jesus speaks of in the Bible (Mark 3:29). So for most of my life, until I decided to become an outlaw, I kept my own despair a secret. But the truth is that feelings of despair are not sinful, they're just honest. Jesus felt them too. The other truth is that despair is like grief in Gotami's parable: it is everywhere, but nobody wants to talk about it. To live outside the law and overcome despair, honesty is required.

What happens when we sweep our true secret stories of grief and loss under the rug and don't share them? All the incredible true stories of hope get swept under there too, and mate with the dust bunnies of complacency, disappointment, and apathy. As they say in Al-Anon, you are only as sick as your secrets. Keeping our hope-stories secret is definitely making us sicker by the second. Amazing people have gone before us in the struggle for hope and joy and community, and they have wrestled with hopelessness and won. But because we don't want to face the filth that made their struggles necessary, we lose their victorious stories of survival too.

Outlaw Christians like to wear these hope-stories as protection against despair the way cops don bulletproof vests. Human history can be read as a book of evil, but those of us brave enough to dust off the jacket and dig in will discover a hidden transcript of resistance and hope so compelling and creative, we will never see the world the same way again. We must tell and retell our own stories of hope, as well as other people's. In this chapter, I want to tell stories that give us back our humanity—tales that get lost when we let history be written by the so-called victors.

Everybody wants to have the last word because they know, down to their bones, that to have the last word is a triumph. In this book hope comes last, because I believe hope wins.

There's a faith-law that suggests hope comes easy as pie, that it comes natural to Christians who love God. But the truth is that if we really want grace, joy, hope, and resistance in this life, we will have to struggle like heck to cultivate them. They easily get choked out by the weeds of evil, suffering, and loneliness. But I know you've seen those crazy green shoots growing up even through concrete. The truth is, we can grow them on any street.

Hope = Good News

Remember when we talked about theology, about placing our own life-stories next to God's? Christians wrestle every day to reconcile the world's gruesome news with God's good news, to live within this tough tension. Both kinds of news pulse with significance, but we have collectively screwed up by allowing the bad news to jade us and eclipse the good.

When I give public lectures and teach classes, people lament to me that they cannot stand to watch or read the news anymore. It's not that people don't care. It's that they are overwhelmed because almost all of the news stories are about horror rather than hope. We are a people parched for a drop of good news. As we already mentioned, the biblical word *gospel*—*euaggelion*—literally means "good news." Our word *evangelism* comes exactly from *euaggelion*. Evangelism, then, taken literally, simply means the sharing of good news.

It's amazing how clearly the first-century Jesus speaks to our twenty-first century longing for good news. In the Bible, Jesus proclaims his mission exactly in these terms more than fifty times, "[Jesus] said to them, 'I must proclaim the good news of the kingdom of God . . . for I was sent for this purpose'" (Luke 4:43).

Jesus, as one who walked among us, understood how much we long for a break from the litany of atrocity. Jesus brings good news of in-your-face mercy, world-reversing justice, wild abundance, outrageous generosity, defiant hospitality, radical humanization, breathtaking compassion, nonviolent solidarity, and revolutionary patience. From him comes the following wondrous news: *If I share my bread loaves and fish, there really is enough to go around. God's love is so crazy-expansive it reads like a guest list for a wacky dinner party that seats millionaires next to the homeless and crack addicts beside CEOs. Those who believe themselves despised and lowest of the low are in fact the beloved. Small acts such as washing someone else's dirty feet are the hinge upon which the entire future hangs.*

How telling it is that both the religious and the secular authorities wanted to kill Jesus for his stupendous news. They understood that ordinary folks could achieve revolutionary self-empowerment if they dared believe him. Jesus says that our mission, in turn, is to go out and tell everybody we know the good news we have heard. "And [Jesus] said to them, 'Go into all the world and proclaim the good news to the whole creation'" (Mark 16:15).

What this means for us at the practical level is that anywhere good news happens, the gospel—or at least a glimpse of the gospel's message of the holiness of the everyday—happens. I mean it. Not only pious or obviously religious stuff but *all* good news, like yesterday as you sat on the porch a blue dragonfly landed on your toe for three minutes. And last Thursday when you saw a young man at Target stop to help a white-haired stranger reach a two-liter bottle of Cherry Coke on the top shelf. The gospel is the good news anywhere and everywhere we find it; and it's our job to tell it, share it, and shout it from the rooftops. If we want to be alive rather than be what some friends I met in Belize call the "dead-alive," we'd better get started. "Whatever is true, whatever is honorable, whatever is just, whatever is pure, whatever is pleasing, whatever is commendable, if there is any excellence and if there is anything worthy of praise, think about these things" (Philippians 4:8).

Outlaw Christians believe the good news that can restore our souls is everywhere, but we are taught a lot of lies that keep us from spotting it. We have to break down the doors of deceit that keep us from dwelling under hope's roof.

Lie #1: You can't beat the man.

If you ever even for a minute believed that you can't fight city hall or beat the man, put this book down right now and go buy a copy of Paul Loeb's *The Impossible Will Take a Little While: A Citizen's Guide to Hope in a Time of Fear.* Everybody needs a go-to book with true stories of why we should still have hope and faith in the world, one another, and God. This fantastic, horizon-altering book is mine. Nearly everyone to whom I have recommended it so far has reported back to me that it has become their go-to as well. (I promise I don't know the author or get a commission . . . but I should.) The book is a compilation of short, real-life tales of people who, as the saying goes, make a way out of no way, outrunning despair and injustice with wings on their heels. Contributors range from famous folks such as South African president Nelson Mandela and American bestselling author Bill McKibben, to more ordinary folks like Danusha Goska, an adjunct professor who has lived most of her life in poverty. If we regularly shared with one another the kind of stories in this book, the swamp of despair in which many of us wallow would become as dry as a California cistern.

And yet, why have most of us never heard 99 percent of these stories? Why does "news" mainly mean awful news? Maybe it's because bad news sells, and like addicts we keep coming back for more. We all still gawk at the umpteenth car accident at the side of the road. And maybe it's also because some powers-that-be realized that if you can create a culture of fear, fearful people are way easier to control and subdue than the courageous.

Fear, not despair, is hope's opposite. Fear paralyzes us into apathy, while desperation drives people to great feats of creativity and resistance. If more of us average, everyday citizens told stories that created a culture of hope, together we would be unstoppable. Don't ever forget this. Much of what we do not know and are not taught is precisely because of how powerful we would become if we only knew.

The following four marvelous stories—the first two of which come from Loeb's book—will make you want to raise your fists over your head Olympic gold–medalist style and shout, "Yeah! Take that!"

The Cha-Cha-Cha Uprising

First, meet Julia Chikamonenga and the Cha Cha Cha uprisers. Black Rhodesians like Julia and her friends had suffered for years under violent, racist oppression and discriminatory apartheid-style laws enforced upon them by British colonial rule. During the 1960s, they decided they had had enough. At that time, Ms. Chikamonenga and the people of Northern Rhodesia (now Zambia) followed Gandhi's lead and organized themselves into a nonviolent uprising called the Cha Cha Cha. The Brits grew frustrated with the people's resistance and decided to send in a new administrator to stop it. Instead of accepting this new leadership as yet another fait accompli defeat at the hands of a wealthier, more powerful enemy, Julia came up with a plan of her own. She gathered together the biggest, most beautiful female friends she could find and organized an extraordinary "welcome" committee for the new administrator. Vern Huffman, who reported this story, writes, "When the new administrator stepped from his plane, he looked across a sea of huge Zambian women, all naked, singing songs of greeting. When he got his mouth closed, he stepped back onto the airplane and ordered the pilot to return him to London. Within weeks, Zambia was an independent nation."[2]

The Poet Robert Desnos

Second, meet Robert Desnos. Desnos, a relatively unknown poet who wrote frequently about the transformative power of imagination, was arrested by the Gestapo during World War II for being part of the French resistance. A prisoner in a concentration camp, Desnos one day found himself in the back of a flatbed truck bound for the gas chambers. Everyone in the truck was dead silent and filled with despair.

Out of nowhere, Desnos leapt up from his seat. He grabbed the hands of the men around him and, with joy on his face, started reading their palms. Though the men were all headed for the crematorium, Desnos proclaimed out loud that their lines promised long life, happiness, and many children. No one could believe their eyes—neither the prisoners nor the guards. Writes Susan Griffin, "How can one explain it? . . . They [the guards] are in any case so disoriented by this sudden change of mood among those they are about to kill that they are unable to go through with the executions. So all the men, along with Desnos, are packed back onto the truck and taken back to the barracks. Desnos has saved his own life and the lives of others by using his imagination."[3]

The Mothers of the Plaza de Mayo

Third, don't ever forget the Mothers of the Plaza de Mayo. In Argentina in 1976, a brutal military junta took over the government. The new government declared a "war on subversives" and secretly began to kill, imprison, torture, and rape those citizens who even remotely disagreed with the regime. An estimated thirty thousand people became "disappeareds," virtually all of whom were murdered. Mothers, at the time desperate to find their sons, daughters, and husbands, traveled every day to prisons and concentration camps to inquire after them, but the government never released any information. Eventually the women—almost all of them housewives who had never been active in politics—began recognizing each other at the gates at the prisons. In April of 1977, one of the *madres*, Azucena

Villaflor de Vicenti, declared that the women should all start meeting together in front of the Casa Rosa, the Argentinian version of the White House, in the bustling main square known as the Plaza de Mayo.[4]

Azucena had the idea that if they each wore one of their children's white cloth diapers as a headscarf, then the outlaw mothers would recognize each other. They would also wear the scarf as a visible symbol of protest—a white swath of proof of their child's stolen life and innocence. In time, all the madres wore white headscarves on which was handsewn the name of their missing child. Once a week and often for twenty-four hours straight, the mothers marched silently in front of the president's house. Though some of the women were beaten, arrested, or became disappeareds themselves, most of them survived. The mothers explained, "They [the military] didn't destroy us immediately because they thought we couldn't do anything and when they wanted to, it was too late. We were already organized. They thought these old women will be scared off by the arrests. . . . On the contrary, we used to shout at them, 'Aren't you ashamed?'"[5]

The government, which controlled the media through intense propaganda, did a masterful job hiding its human rights abuses from the outside world. They banned any publication critical of the regime. So whenever someone from another country came to Buenos Aires, the women tried to meet with them to tell their stories and share the truth about their murderous, repressive government. When, for example, a group of doctors from all over the world were in Buenos Aires attending a global conference on cancer, the madres slipped them notes explaining their plight. The women started writing their stories and pleas for help on peso bills and giving them to international visitors to the nation's capital, ironically using the very thing the dictatorship worshiped—cash—as a tool of resistance against them. Some of the women even met with the pope, who sadly did nothing to help them.[6] But the mothers did not give up, give into despair, or fold their hands in their laps and say, "You can't beat the man."

The turning point came in 1978, when the World Cup came to Argentina. A plethora of journalists came to Argentina to cover sports, but instead they discovered the Mothers of the Plaza de Mayo. Eventually private donors, Amnesty International, the Red Cross, and the United Nations became involved, and the mothers became too well known to be made to disappear anymore.

Because the government could no longer violate human rights with impunity, the nasty dictatorship toppled after a few more years of struggle. To this day, people worldwide credit the Mothers of the Plaza de Mayo for ending the reign of terror. They were even nominated for the Nobel Peace Prize. Now, would you ever have believed that unarmed old ladies who wore not guns but diapers as headscarves could topple one of the most violent regimes in history? Yeah, me neither.

But we have to ask ourselves, "Why not?" When did we stop believing in the truth? Why do we believe that evil is more real than hope, when both are verifiable? How did we come to stop believing in the possibility of successful resistance to injustice? The lesson I get from the madres is that when hope becomes an impossible possibility, community makes hope possible. In other words, anything is possible, but only together. In the words of one madre who lost all of her biological family to the dictatorship, "My family now are the Madres de la Plaza de Mayo. . . . Recently we were saying what could be better than to be together like this . . . because we each have the same pain. . . . When one weakens or gets disheartened there's always someone standing by her side to give her strength . . . to continue the struggle."[7]

Ever since I first read about these fabulous women twenty years ago, I was dying to meet them in person. When I visited Buenos Aires in 2010, I got my wish to meet with these magnificent mothers, who are now grandmothers (*abuelas*). Incredibly, these seventy-some-year-old powerhouses still march every Thursday at 3:30 P.M. in the Plaza de Mayo, as they have for nearly four decades. They have since taken up other human rights causes, because as one grandmother confided to me, they refuse to give up *la lucha* (the struggle). I heard the words *la lucha* more times that morning than any other word, aside from *justicia* (justice). The day I was there it was ninety-nine degrees outside and these seventy-year-old *abuelitas* (little grandmothers) were in the plaza for hours, marching, chanting, and giving speeches about human rights and land reform only a few yards away from the president's door. They wore their white headscarves with the blue writing, and one of them gave me a pin with their web address on it, madres.org, which made me grin like there was no tomorrow.

The famous madres invited us bystanders to walk with them in their circle around the plaza's center statue, but most people held back. I chose to walk with the petite gray-haired women in the white headscarves and the men in yellow hard hats—immigrant workmen—and protested for worker's rights. We walked counterclockwise around the circle, which felt significant. Two of the grandmothers I was walking behind held hands as they held the top edge of a blue banner. Though the cops glared on, the madres seemed relaxed and filled with joy, like people who had outgrown fear and planted laughter in its place.

Interestingly, only the day before, my local Argentine friends expressed horror when I told them I planned to go meet and march with the Mothers of the Plaza de Mayo. Their mouths gaped with concern and incredulousness, and they said, "I really don't think you should do that. You might get arrested." This exchange revealed to me that even today, the grandmothers still face opposition from "the man" and are therefore every bit as courageous as ever.

As I traveled across Argentina to cities more than a thousand kilometers away from Buenos Aires's Plaza de Mayo—Mendoza, Bariloche, Neuquen—I noticed the white headscarves painted everywhere, on buildings, streets, and monuments as a symbol of outlaw resistance. I stood in a square in Bariloche, where hundreds of youth were listening to a live band, and I looked down and saw graffitied on the black asphalt: white headscarves, complete with the names and disappearance dates of victims of state terror. In the same square, I spotted a white headscarf, spray-painted on a brass horse-and-rider statue in the center of the plaza along with the Latin words—*Memoria Justicia*. Remember Justice. Less than a foot away, on the horse's hindquarters, I noticed a graffitied swastika. I snapped a picture of both graffiti tags in the same frame—an image that captures in a way words cannot the world's tug-of-war between forces of evil and resistance. Though the pulling continues and many of us have the rope burns to show for it, it's important to ask, who is winning? The Nazis are no longer in power anywhere, but if you go to Buenos Aires on any Thursday afternoon, you will find the grandmas alive and well, laughing and holding hands.

The Chilean Women

Fourth and finally, remember the *arpilleristas* of Chile. On September 11, 1973, the dictator Augusto Pinochet seized power from Salvador Allende in a military coup. Like his dictatorial neighbors across the border in Argentina, Pinochet abruptly killed, imprisoned, or kidnapped thousands of "disappeareds." The only successful political resistance movement against Pinochet turned out to be a group of destitute mothers who lived in shantytowns in Santiago. Inspired by the Mothers of the Plaza de Mayo, they started a unique resistance movement all their own.

Throughout the 1970s and 1980s, unemployed Chilean women in Chile who were desperately poor under Pinochet's brutal regime formed quilt-making groups at local churches to export their handicrafts and raise money. The government, presuming the women to be poor and therefore powerless, failed at first to notice that the squares of the *arpilleras* (quilts) revealed gruesome stories about present-day abductions and tortures of the seamstresses' loved ones. Through colorful, deceptively simple storybook-like images, these quilts told the outside world of the unknown suffering of the Chilean people under the brutality of that regime. Today, the arpilleras are one of the most precious historical and spiritual documents of the era, on traveling exhibit throughout the world.

When the government finally noticed and condemned the arpilleristas as subversive and unpatriotic, these outlaw

Christian women continued with the help of the Catholic Church to smuggle the quilts out of the country through foreign visitors. When the women suffered beatings, imprisonment, and detentions for their work, they did not give up. Instead, their numbers grew.

The word *arpillera* in Spanish means burlap. The quilts were indeed nothing more than leftover scraps of material sewn on the backs of grain or feed sacks. When resources ran scarce—which was always—the women refused to give in to defeat or despair. When the electricity was shut off because bills could not be paid, the women would "borrow" electricity by connecting wires to city electric poles. Much of the fabric used on the figures in the arpilleras came from old clothes the disappeared loved one used to wear. The women sewed used matchsticks into the scenes to represent policemen's clubs. And when they ran out of yarn for hair for the arpillera dolls, they cut hair off their own heads and used it. As poet Marjorie Agosin reports in her fascinating book *Scraps of Life*, "In more ways than one, each quilt was truly a piece of the woman who had created it."[8] With every stitch, the arpilleristas mended their world and resisted oppression and evil. Adds Agosin, "What courage, what strong weapons are hidden in [their] fingers."[9]

The women reported becoming tremendously empowered through telling and sharing their stories together. "I have become so keenly fond of my arpilleras because they give me food, but also because they also help me kill my sorrows. . . . I see God as one who gave his life for a better world. He is present in each one of us. We have experienced the Way of the Cross because of our missing relatives and the people who listen to our story, like you, for instance, in this moment, help us to bear this calvary."[10]

The women, much like the madres of Argentina, testified repeatedly to the curious strength of community. Notably, they felt comforted when people simply accompanied them and took the time to listen to their stories. One arpillerista remarked that the women became each other's family; the quilt workshops made them feel "accompanied in their sadness" and gave them back "a sense of dignity."[11] The arpillerista women learned the highest form of resistance; they became stewards of their pain. They composed their grief into art.

This seemingly small act of resistance—storytelling pain through quilting—led to incrementally larger and more public acts of resistance and tikkun olam (world-mending). The outlaw arpilleristas from each workshop across Chile formed an Association of Families of the Detained-Disappeared. Once, these association women chained themselves to the Congress building with large photos of the disappeareds hanging around their necks. Another time, in 1978 when a mass grave was discovered in a mine outside Santiago, the association formed a human chain of more than 1,500 people holding hands from Santiago to the mass grave site in order to draw people's attention to the hidden atrocity. But perhaps most poignant of all, many of the women took to dancing in the streets in an act of resistance and protest that came to be known as *la cueca sola*.

La cueca, meaning "handkerchief dance," is the national dance of Chile. Pinochet took this beautiful dance and made it a symbol of terror by having performers dance la cueca in military marches. But the Chilean women protestors decided to reclaim la cueca. They took to the streets with large black-and-white photographs of their disappeared spouses held in their hands like priceless paintings they were about to hang on a wall. Wearing black evening gowns to signify mourning, these women stood in silence in front of government offices and police stations. And there, right underneath the office windows of the people who had raped, tortured, unjustly imprisoned, and even executed their loved ones, the women danced la cueca, all alone (sola), with nothing but a photograph.

You can imagine how these women's wordless performance of lament haunted the conscience of the people and the military as they walked by on the street. I am still haunted by it, and I have only seen it on YouTube. The government did not arrest the women for dancing la cueca sola. It was, after all, the national dance that symbolized patriotism. Moreover, if the regime had arrested them, it would have been an admission that such (supposedly) weak and powerless women posed a real threat. La cueca sola was the perfect act of nonviolent resistance, because the authorities' pride prevented them from ever taking action to stop it.

If you have an hour and want to be inspired, rent the documentary *La Cueca Sola*, a film by Canadian filmmaker Marilu Mallet. If you have only five minutes, check out the handheld video version of the women dancing la cueca sola on the street on YouTube.[12] While you're there, watch the video of the singer/songwriter Sting, who wrote a song about the Chilean women called "They Dance Alone" (1988), in which he openly criticized Pinochet for the unspeakable anguish he had brought to his people.

Due in large part to the international attention that the dancing women and the arpilleristas brought to Pinochet's policies, Pinochet fell from power. Do we still think we can't beat the system?

Lie #2: The world is going to hell in a handbasket and no one cares.

The next time someone says to you that "the world is going to hell in a handbasket," or that "young people today don't care about anything except video games, crystal meth, and being in street gangs," I want you to remember a group of eighteen-to twenty-two-year-olds whom I know well.

All semester long in the spring of 2008, the students in my social justice and service-learning class served with me at various places in our community including a local Lutheran Social Services food pantry, a homeless shelter, and Community Refugee and Immigration Services ESL classrooms. When two of the students who volunteered at the food pantry heard that the facility was going to be closed for four days over Easter weekend for staff vacation, they approached the director and asked if they might open the pantry on their own. The director said that it would require at least ten volunteers to run the pantry by themselves, so the students approached the rest of the class. Within minutes, we had twelve volunteers.

Because the university where I taught was Lutheran, we had nearly a week off for Easter. During this substantial break, most of our students went to see their families, boyfriends, or girlfriends, or just took it easy after stressful midterm exams. Instead, my students got up at 7:30 A.M. on a snowy, dark Ohio morning and singlehandedly opened and ran the food pantry for the next eight hours without so much as a lunch break. None of the fifty-six families they served that day would have gotten any free bread, apples, baby formula, or frozen chicken thighs had it not been for these young people. They could have done a thousand other things with their Saturday, but they chose to serve.

The students also gave the hundred kids who came into the pantry bags of Easter treats and crayons, which a local church had donated. Easter bags that I couldn't help thinking would have been distributed *after* Easter had it not been for them. While my students' actions did not reverse the injustice of poverty, they certainly revealed that to practice resurrection thaws lives in that same way we talked about a flower's breath melting snow.

Later that year, at our city's celebration of World Refugee Day, my class won Outstanding Volunteers of the Year. For me, not to have hope would be to betray my own students who show me every day that hope is possible . . . and that hope happens best when we get up off our duffs and cook some up for someone else.

Lie #3: Nothing ever changes, and people can't change either.

If you believe that people never change and nothing ever changes, I recommend you go out and read *Mighty Be Our Powers: How Sisterhood, Prayer, and Sex Changed a Nation at War* or watch the documentary *Pray the Devil Back to Hell.* Both the film and book are about Leymah Gbowee, a Liberian woman who was sick to death not only of her own husband's domestic abuse but also of terrorist warlords, endless civil war, and her government's corrupt president. Leymah believed that if she and her Christian sisters could unite with their Muslim sisters in an organized campaign of nonviolent protest, together they could stand up for justice and end the war. And the women did just that. They overthrew the regime using all kinds of wild methods of nonviolent resistance, including going on a nationwide sex strike.

Ms. Gbowee won the Nobel Peace Prize in 2011. My students and I invited her to our college, and she came in November 2014. She was three-standing-ovations phenomenal. Leymah shared with us that every inspiring act of hope starts with one small crazy idea. She argued that if you have an idea for changing lives or communities, and people look at you and say, "You're crazy!" then that's exactly how you know you are on the right track. And she would know, because that's what everyone told her.

Another fabulous read is Nelson Mandela's biography. Though inequality and injustice still exists in post-apartheid South Africa, it is also true that apartheid—a government-endorsed racist system of discrimination and oppression against black South Africans—was brought down by people like Mandela. Mandela spent twenty-seven years in jail as a political prisoner, only later to become president of the country and a winner of the Nobel Peace Prize. Whenever I get sucked into believing that nothing has ever really changed, I consider how much it would hurt people like Leymah Gbowee or Nelson Mandela or Martin Luther King to hear me mutter such preposterousness. Believing such lies show that I know nothing about being in prison or living under war and then becoming liberated, because if I did, I would understand the word *change* in a whole new light.

These are examples of larger-than-life famous people, but I have others. Whenever someone says, "You can't change the way you were raised" (which is often code for "hate will never end"), I remember my mother, Charlotte Bussie. Charlotte grew up and got married in a small, rural midwestern town that was inhabited back then by some of the most openly racist people I have ever known. I am ashamed to admit to you that some of these folks are or were members of my own family, so I know my mother lived with and went to school with people who regularly told racist jokes and used the *n* word.

I grew up in a similar kind of town in the cotton-and-peach-growing deep South. Our house was just outside Atlanta, Georgia, and nearby was a grocery store called the A&P. When I was little, my mom would drag me there to shop. One day at the A&P there was an enormous line—only one checkout register was open. My mom and I went to the back of the line and parked the shopping cart, and I climbed in to sit among the Pop-Tarts and frozen peas.

Out of nowhere, a smartly dressed lady with an overflowing cart came up and cut in in front of everyone, including my mom and me. As a savvy five-year-old, I knew a thing or two about lines and how they worked, and I knew this lady had broken every rule. The weird part was, everyone else in the line just let her go ahead of them, though she had not said "sorry" to anyone nor explained why she wanted to go first. Even the cashier didn't get mad at the woman. Worse yet, the lady looked back at my mother and snorted. She made some kind of condescending remark to my mother—to this day I can't remember exactly what she said; she must have used a grown-up word I did not understand—but I remember getting that yucky feeling kids get in their gut when they know that adults are about to do something like fight or yell or hit. I pulled on my mom's shirt and asked her in as quiet a voice as I could, "Mommy, why did that lady get to cut in line?" My mom, in a not-so-quiet voice, with a drawn and fierce look on her now-red face, said, "I'll tell you when we get out to the car."

As we waited our turn, I stared out from my shopping cart perch and observed that all of the people in front of us in line had brown skin, but the lady who had cut in line had pale white skin, like us. I wasn't sure if this had anything to do with it, but I wondered. When we finally got out to the car, my mother put all the groceries in the trunk, squatted down to my eye level, grabbed me by both shoulders, and told me why the lady had cut in line: "Some people believe they are better than other people just because of their skin color, but they are *wrong*. Do you hear me? *WRONG*. God loves everyone the same." Then she slammed the trunk, shot a dirty look back at A&P, climbed into our green Chevy, and drove us home.

To this day, whenever anyone grants nasty behavior a get-out-of-jail-free pass by saying something like, "You can't help the way you were raised," or "You can't teach an old dog new tricks," I can hear my mom saying in that skeptic voice she reserved for sulky comments or similar predictions of doom, "Hmm. Well, now, we'll see about *that*, won't we?"

Lie #4: I can't make a difference. The problems are too big, and the world is too much of a mess.

The next time you see a homeless person on the street, see graphic images of an earthquake on the Internet, or read harrowing statistics about poverty and cancer, and find yourself thinking, *No one person can make a difference in all of this,* remember Jesus' commandment to set the good news of the day right alongside the crap. The bad news is: you probably can't make a difference on your own. The good news is: you're not expected to because *we* are expected to. It's *together*, in community, that we're asked to make a difference, not alone. Remember the madres of Argentina and the Chilean women, who said over and over again they would've given up if they'd had to face what they did without each other?

My ego loves to try to persuade me that I should be able to make a difference on my own, because then I can take pride in my own strength. The ego is a liar. Behind every ground-shaking change that happens in this world is an enormous community of like-minded individuals who suffered and sweat and eventually succeeded, even if these people didn't get to see the success for themselves. Consider, for example, the U.S. civil rights movement, the women's suffrage movement, India's struggle for independence from England, and South Africa's overthrow of the racist apartheid government. Sure, these movements had leaders, Mandelas and Kings and Gandhis and Cady Stantons, but none of them could have succeeded without the millions of others who joined the struggle. In the future, when you despair that no one can make a difference, reflect on this remark from Nelson Mandela: "It's always impossible until it's done." Then try to remember the following people.

First, Irene Siegel. As I'm sure you are aware, the Israeli-Palestinian conflict rages on and on, as does the hate and resentment on both sides. But what you probably do not know about are the people on both sides of the conflict who refuse to be defined by the hate they are taught. Irene Siegel is one such person, and so is her Palestinian hostess Magdalene. Irene, a Jewish woman and peace activist, for several years took part in a human shield campaign in Palestinian territories. The idea behind the movement was to have Jews live with Palestinians in their homes, in hopes of deterring the shelling and destruction of Palestinian homes by the IDF, the Israeli army. Irene and her friends risked their lives by putting their bodies in harm's way. Yes, that's right, there are people in this world who are willing to be human shields in order to save someone else—someone they have been taught to hate, no less.[13]

Second, Haregewoin Teferra. Haregewoin's story is told in the incredible book *There Is No Me Without You: One Woman's Odyssey to Rescue Her Country's Children*, which I highly recommend you go out and read if you need an inoculation of hope against despair. I won't spoil the whole story for you, but I'll give you a foretaste. In Ethiopia, where antiretrovirals are either unavailable or too costly for most people, AIDS is a pandemic that kills millions and leaves even more millions orphaned. When Haregewoin's own beloved daughter died of AIDS, her grief overwhelmed her. Friends tried to tell her that the death of her daughter and husband were "God's will," but Haregewoin saw their deaths as injustice and waste.[14] She decided to renounce the world—as is possible within the Ethiopian church—and live out the rest of her days in silence in a hermit hut in a cemetery. She thought, "Everything, everywhere is ruined for me. . . . I am *mena* (useless, without value)."[15] But when she approached a local Catholic priest, he had another idea for her. What if she took in a child recently orphaned by AIDS who had no place to go?

Haregewoin said yes, and before long, she had more

than forty orphans living with her. They slept on top of one another (and her) inside her two-room "house," which consisted of a rusty boxcar and a windowless old cargo container. What is incredibly refreshing and real about this story is that Haregewoin, foster mother to hundreds of children over time, was not a saint. She was every ounce a person like you and me. She got frustrated with the kids, forgot names, lost her temper, fell asleep sitting up, felt like throwing up at the sight of another diaper filled with diarrhea, and wondered what in God's good name she had done with her life in her old age. At one point, she even got arrested for making some really bad decisions.

Haregewoin's biographer, Melissa Fay Greene, lived with her for months and eventually adopted one of the orphans herself. She writes of Haregewoin, "My hero is no saint. . . . You don't have to be a saint to rescue other people from suffering and death. You can just be an everyday, decent enough sort of regular person, nothing extraordinary, and yet turn lives around."[16] Greene, reminding us here of Nouwen's concept of the wounded healer, urges us to accept that our heroes don't have to be saints. We can be heroic without being perfect. In fact, no other kind of authentic hero exists in this broken world of ours. This realization is scary, but also radically hopeful, because it means none of us have an excuse not to be a hero to someone.

What's also wonderful about Haregewoin's story is that once again, she could not have done it without her community. Her community neighbors thought she had gone off the deep end, but they still left money on her coffee table whenever they dropped by, without which she and the kids would often not eat. Through it all, Haregewoin never stopped grieving for her dead daughter but recognized that taking in all these children was a way of resisting grief's tyranny over her life. With every snotty nose she wiped and every good-night kiss she gave, she let fly a punch that landed squarely on AIDS jaw. Sometimes AIDS hit back, such as the time Haregewoin woke up to a dead child in her crib, but more often than not, Haregewoin won the fight, because the girls in her house didn't have to live as prostitutes, and none of the kids had to eat garbage anymore.

If Haregewoin's story inspires you to keep on keepin' on in the face of impossible odds, then go out and rent *Angels in the Dust*, a phenomenal documentary about a South African white woman named Marion Cloete. Marion, along with her husband, abandoned her suburban life of wealth and white privilege to build a makeshift compound in the slums, where she lives with and raises 550 AIDS orphans. You will never be the same once you have watched this astonishing film.

Yes, millions of children orphaned by AIDS still die tragically alone on the streets of South Africa and Ethiopia, and a cynic could argue that the work of these women is only an infinitesimal drop in an ocean of suffering. But if you asked any of the orphans who found their way into these homes—many of whom now call either Marion or Haregewoin mama—if one person can make a difference, what do you think they would say?

Lie #5: The people with the guns and gold make the rules.

When I was growing up, my dad often infuriated me by repeating, "The real golden rule is that the people with the gold make the rules." Of course, this is sometimes true, but it is not the rule. The next time you find yourself bemoaning the fact that only violence in our world accomplishes anything and only people with guns and wealth and power prosper, I want you to recollect not only every story I've told so far—not one of which involves guns or violence—but also two more amazing ones.

First, South Africa. For decades under the apartheid government, black South Africans were second-class citizens who suffered many forms of violence and discrimination, including being forcibly removed from their homes and relocated to slums. Black South Africans lacked the money and power that white South African colonists possessed. Eventually, the people on the underside joined together and decided they had had enough. The people demanded regime change, and they got it in 1994 when Mandela became president—but without the bloodshed everyone expected. Instead of guns, the people ultimately toppled the government through truth telling.

South Africa established a Truth and Reconciliation Commission (TRC) to hear every gross human rights violation perpetrated under the apartheid regime, with the agreement that instead of punishment, the state would grant most perpetrators amnesty in exchange for the truth. The TRC, headed by Archbishop Desmond Tutu, took as its motto the South African concept of *ubuntu* (remember its meaning: "I am a person through other persons"). The televised hearings lasted three and a half years, which meant that everyone in the country got to hear the victims' pain as well as the perpetrators' confessions of their crimes. While globally everyone expected these public confessions to provoke a terrible violent backlash against the perpetrators, most of whom still walk the streets, to this day not a single confessor has been killed in revenge. Of course, things are far from perfect in today's South Africa, and the question of how to undo decades of economic injustice and systemic poverty still looms large. All the same, would you ever have imagined in your wildest dreams that *truth* was what ultimately ended apartheid, rather than war and bullets?

When I went to South Africa with my students and spent the day with one of the TRC commissioners, Glenda, she said something to us that I have never forgotten. Glenda explained that part of the reason the human rights hearings were so difficult was that each victim was allowed to tell their story in their own language; and in South Africa, there are dozens of dialects. Allowing everyone to speak in their native tongues required constant translation and thousands of additional hours of trial time. When one of my students asked Glenda why this decision was made, since most South Africans also speak the common language of English, Glenda answered, "We believe that everyone has the right to speak in the language in which they dream." It was one of the most beautiful sentences I have ever heard, and I believe it defines hope. *Hope is our right to speak in the language we dream.*

Second, I want you to recall the outlaws Jurek Roslan and Wladyslaw Misiuna, two Polish Christian teenagers who lived during World War II. Though neither boy knew the other, they have similar stories of courage. (You can read their incredible stories and hundreds more like them in the book *Conscience and Courage: Rescuers of Jews During the Holocaust.*) During the Holocaust, when Jurek was a twelve-year-old boy living in Poland, his family took in several Jewish orphan boys. One little boy, Sholom, was only nine years old and had lived for months on rooftops, forced to lie prostrate all day long for fear of being seen. Unfortunately, all of this hiding took a toll on the little boy's health. After Sholom had lived with Jurek's family for several months hiding in a hollowed-out couch, he became seriously ill. They tried everything in their medicine cabinet to help him, but to no avail. Jurek and his family realized that the boy would die without medical attention.

At the time, of course, the law forbade doctors from seeing Jewish patients. Jurek's family had no like-minded doctor friends who might illicitly see the boy. And naturally, if Jurek's family took Sholom to the doctor, the doctor would figure out from an examination that he was Jewish (at that time in Europe only Jews were circumcised, and this led to countless arrests). Then the boy would be dragged to a concentration camp and executed, along with Jurek's family for their treasonous rescue attempt.

Wladyslaw's story resembles Jurek's. During the war, the Germans forced Wladyslaw to work at a concentration camp as the supervisor of thirty young Jewish women. He was horrified at the conditions in which the women lived, and almost immediately, at the risk of his own life, he began smuggling food to them in his coat pockets. One day one of the Jewish women he supervised, Devora Salzberg, fell dreadfully sick. No one could figure out what was wrong with Devora. She had open lesions on her arms and could not work. Everyone could tell that if she did not get treatment, she would surely die. Wladyslaw knew that if he told the guards at the camp that she was sick, they would execute her. And as we said, no doctor would care for a Jewish patient. His options were dismal: do nothing, and the girl dies; take the girl to get help, and the girl dies.

What would you do if you were in an impossible situation like Jurek or Wladyslaw? I don't know about you, but when I first read about both of these dilemmas, there appeared to be no way out. But I discovered that I reached this doomsday conclusion only because I was not creative enough to imagine a form of resistance. Also I was too selfish to spot the obvious solution both teenagers put into action.

What Wladyslaw did was this: He cut himself on purpose and rubbed his own wound up against Devora's bloody lesions. His plan worked. He infected himself with her terrible mystery illness and then went to the village doctor. The doctor prescribed a medicine. Wladyslaw took only half of the medicine and shared the other half with Devora. The medicine cured them both, and they both survived the war.[17]

As for Jurek, he came down with scarlet fever himself from the hours he spent caring for Sholom. Jurek was hospitalized, while Sholom continued to die at home. All on his own, Jurek, horribly sick, decided he would take only half his medication. This of course meant that Jurek ran the risk of not having enough medicine to cure himself, but he did not let this fear stop him. When she came to the hospital, Jurek's mother was shocked to find that Jurek was stashing half of his pills underneath his pillow, along with instructions he had written down describing exactly what care the nurses and doctors had given him so she could do the same for Sholom at home. When questioned about their family's heroic rescuing behavior, Jurek's dad commented that his grandmother had always taught them, "We are all God's children."[18]

As I hope you are beginning to see from the good news I have already told you, part of our problem with resisting evil is that we assume we have to stoop to the same level as the evil-doers and use the same means they do in order to defeat them. As I mentioned earlier, we are never more at risk of becoming the thing we hate than at the very moment we stand up to defend ourselves against it. Another way to state this paradox is that at the very moment when we stand up to defend what we most love with all we have, we are more at risk than we are at any other time of compromising the very thing that we love and are standing up for.

Nowhere is this more obvious than in the struggle against violence, where everybody seems to buy into the myth that only violence can defeat violence. Why don't we recognize that if that were true, we certainly would have defeated it centuries ago? If you read literature about World War I, you learn that everyone called it "the war to end all wars." If only that were true. In the fight against violence and weapons, our own hasty resort to violence has crushed our creativity. As every single one of the stories I have told thus far shows, violence numbs us to more creative nonviolent possibilities of resistance. Moreover, unlike nonviolent tactics, it robs us of our integrity and our humanity. For Christians, the person we become by our actions is as important as the actions themselves. As Jim Wallis suggests in *God's Politics*, we need to become the people we have been waiting for.[19]

The Jewish thinker Martin Buber once wrote, "Success is not a name of God."[20] Such a powerful insight is important for outlaw Christians. What about the Bible and especially the cross would indicate God's name is success? The names of God in the Bible include Love, Life, Truth, Light, and Comforter. But success? Well, that doesn't appear anywhere. We forget that Martin

Luther King Jr. lived only long enough to see a bullet meet his chest—not to see full integration, a street named after him in every major city, or Obama's presidency. Obviously King, who received death threats every day, thought it was worth doing what he was doing even if he never would get to see his dream fulfilled.

Our spiritual heroes like King set us free to do things because they are right—not because they ensure success or change in our lifetime. How limiting it is for us only to do the things that we can guarantee will succeed. Often our actions do end in success or victory, but that cannot be the main reason why we do them—we do them because our humanity demands it of us. Episcopalian bishop Shelby Spong calls this way of living *solar ethics*: just as the sun shines because it is the sun's purpose, we do what it is right because doing right is our human purpose, made as we are in the image of God. Way cool.

Sharks have to swim. If they stop, they die of anoxia. This is exactly how I feel about hope. It doesn't always makes a difference in the world around me, but without it, I would surely die.

According to Dorothee Soelle, hopelessness is the luxury of the privileged. For me and my students, this was one of those sentences we read on a page and then had to step back and say, *Ouch. Guilty as charged.* What Soelle means is that despair is universal, but only the relatively rich have the luxury of succumbing to its paralysis. (There are exceptions to this, such as those who suffer from mental illnesses that inflict despair. Soelle here is not talking about them; she is criticizing only healthy and privileged folks who can choose hopelessness.)

Let's face it. When I fall into despair, as sometimes happens, and I can't get out of bed to face the day, the worst that happens is that I don't go to work and my students get a day off from class. But if I am a single mother of three living in Nigeria, if I don't get out of bed and walk the requisite eight miles to fetch clean water for my kids, my children will die of thirst and my hopelessness will have killed them. A lot of people in the world don't have time for despair, and if I have that much time on my hands, I need to get off my butt and fight the very thing that makes me despair so hard.

We think we have so much to teach the poor—namely, how to get rich—when, in fact, the poor have everything to teach us, which is why Jesus spent all of his time with them. My education among those who live in poverty has taught me that they understand their interdependence—the truth that there is no me without you—better than anyone I know. As Pastor Roberto in the San Jose, Costa Rican slums once said to me, people of means have so many things they can rely on and put their faith in—education, money, power—but the poor can only have faith in two things: God and other people (and that includes you and me). I have thought about what Pastor Roberto said ever since. All anyone ever has in the end is God and each other, but wealth and privilege bury this truth about our humanity under community-crushing illusions of individual strength, independence, and a gross misunderstanding of authentic power—which, if real, is always shared.

Whenever we travel abroad and spend a considerable amount of time living in marginalized communities, my students do not romanticize the living situations of those who live in poverty. But they do come home mourning the fact that our own culture glorifies individualism to the extent that we possess no real sense of community. When my students and I got home from South Africa, we had to devote hours to talking about our depression and severe loneliness. How many people do you know in our culture who are lonely? Almost everyone I know is lonely in some acute, fundamental way they cannot even name. Though we have much material wealth, when it comes to living in authentic community, we are the poorest people I know.

In South Africa, when we arrived home every day after working at the crèche with the orphans, a huge gathering of children would jump into our arms the second we hit the street. Most of them spoke Xhosa, so we couldn't even talk to them, but everyone understands smiles and hugs. I couldn't help noting that when I walk home from work in the United States and my feet hit the street where I have lived for eight years, no one even notices, let alone rushes out to greet me, and the entire winter can pass without me seeing my own neighbors even once except through the window of their car.

In contrast, one afternoon in South Africa I was giving my host mother a bottle of wine as a gift when I realized to my embarrassment that she probably did not own a corkscrew. She did not, but before I could even say pinot noir, her son had run across the road to the one person on the street who had one, and he was back in the living room with the corkscrew in hand—neighbors in tow hoping for a taste. In Khayelitsha, no one person had everything, so the need to borrow drove everyone daily into one another's arms and houses. Middle-class North Americans, on the other hand, have confused their lack of *material* need with a lack of *spiritual* need for one another. Finding their true home in community, my friends in Khayelitsha shed the myth of independence we still wrap ourselves in like Betsy Ross's flag. The people we met in South Africa understood that of all the places where hope can be found, the most likely place is each other.

Dorothee Soelle, who traveled and lived extensively in Latin America, concluded that she must hold on to hope for one simple reason. The people she met in life who in theory shouldn't have any hope at all—such as the women who sift through trash in Brazil for a living—still managed to have it; so she, a privileged European who had every good reason *to* have it, had absolutely no excuse not to. Do you know anyone similar to the women Dorothee met, whom life has mortared with an unfair share of suffering, but they still have hope? I imagine that you do, and that they have taught you heaps. When my mother was dying of Alzheimer's, she never gave up her hopes for me. Even though she had no idea what year it was or who the president was, when I told her I got a full scholarship to Yale for my master's degree, she sobbed like it was the happiest day of her life.

When I was in college, I remember looking at the face of my mentor and professor Tony during a Christmas concert and thinking as clear as a bell, *That man has the secret to living.* In time I would learn that Tony's daughter, his only daughter, had died on Easter of a sudden and terrible illness when she was only four years old. And yet Tony was—and still is—one of the kindest, most generous and loving people I have ever known. He will sit with you and talk to you like you are the most important person on earth. We owe it to Tony, my mom, and all the other life-teachers like them to have hope, if only for the simple reason that they were brave enough to sow hope in a place where they could have sown bitterness—namely, in us. The secret to hope is becoming a steward—a public gardener—of your own pain and bitterness. I was right that people like Tony and Mom possessed the secret.

Practical Ways to Cultivate Hope and Joy in Our Lives

Keep It Real

Soren Kierkegaard, the Christian philosopher, once defined hope as the passionate pursuit of the possible.[21] Hope is not just believing, it's doing. A few years ago I was on a public panel with pastor and activist Jim Wallis, author of *God's Politics: Why the Right Gets It Wrong and the Left Doesn't Get It.* Jim's definition of hope is "believing in spite of the evidence, then watching the evidence change."[22] During our panel discussion, I took him on a bit and said, "I don't believe we just watch the evidence change, I believe we have to try to be the ones who change the evidence." Given Wallis's own activism, no doubt he believes this too (he didn't disagree with me), but it's important to call a thing what it actually is. My hope believes it is possible for all of us to become *human* human beings, and especially if I find myself in a place where no one is acting like one, I had better become one *tout de suite*. To hope is to reclaim our humanity.

That being said, I appreciate Wallis's reminder that hope always involves waiting, even when we are busy doing. In Spanish, to hope and to wait are the exact same verb, even though in English the two verbs share no common root. Language shapes the way we see the world, and in this case, only Spanish honestly prepares us for what hope in the trenches really looks like. Whenever I say the sentence "I hope" in Spanish—*espero*—I am also saying the sentence "I wait"—*espero*. I love this because if you are going to live a life of hope in this wrecked world, you had better get ready to do a whole heckuva lot of waiting. "But if we hope for what we do not see, we wait for it with patience" (Romans 8:25).

Most of the time, however, Christians don't talk about hope this way, and this is where we fail most deeply to be authentic. The way we talk about hope most times makes me gag, the way those awful x-ray bitewings do at the dentist. The way we talk about hope is usually Pollyannaish, quietistic, and sugar-nasty, and doesn't acknowledge either the deep horrors within which some people find themselves or the role we people of faith must play in making the world a place where hope sounds less ridiculous.

Outlaw Christians, on the other hand, explore new ways to talk about hope. We can't leave the starving, the sick, the bereft, the bereaved, the dead, the poor, the marginalized, the abused, and the oppressed standing in the street, saying, "You're kidding me. Is that all you got? Words? Can you show me that you love me? That I am loved? That what you say is true?" Hope in our day has to be about showing other people God's face so well that they begin to second-guess themselves when they've decided that God doesn't care and has abandoned them.

Hope for outlaw Christians is a lifestyle of embracing and giving life in a world of death-dealing. As Isaiah spells it out, "Do good; seek justice, rescue the oppressed, defend the orphan, plead for the widow" (1:17). When we tell a homeless veteran that God loves him, but then we deny him proper health care, do you think he believes us? When we thank God for our dinner of steak and potatoes, but our neighbors go to bed hungry, do we expect them to thank God for their growling stomachs? When

223

we claim "God is just" to a former bank employee who lost her job and pension because of the sub-prime mortgage lending scandal right after her CEO got a $3 million bonus, do you think she will believe us? "Happy are those who observe justice, who do righteousness at all times" (Psalm 106:3). Christians always ask people to place their hope in God's goodness, life, and love, but outlaw Christians realize God calls us to give them reasons for doing so.

In my experience, if we do not speak authentically as people of faith about despair and calamity, no one will listen to us when we try to speak authentically about hope. On this point we come full circle with the previous chapters. When we keep our grief, shame, and feelings of despair in the closet as the faith-laws demand, then we closet our hope as well—which means that when we finally take it out, it reeks of decay and mothballs. By hiding our grief, despair, and loneliness from others, we call our own credibility into question and have nobody to blame but ourselves when our words of redemption fall on deaf ears.

We are like the child in the folktale who falsely cried wolf so many times that no one listened when he cried wolf for real, but our situation is the reverse. We are overrun with wolves every day, but we never cry wolf. Nevertheless, we expect people to jump up and down for joy and sing alleluia when we announce the wolf is gone and hope has slayed him. That, my friends, makes no sense, but it's how a lot of Christians sound when they open their mouths to talk about redemption and hope in the twenty-first century, which is a world filled with wolves on every side if there ever was one.

We outlaw Christians need to talk about wolves when we talk about hope, instead of pretending that they don't exist.

When we say God is just, we also need to confess that a U.S. CEO's salary is 373 times the salary of his own average worker[23] and 264 times as much as public school teachers; 1.2 billion people in the world are without access to clean drinking water; 2.6 billion are without access to sanitation; the world's richest five hundred individuals have a combined income of more than that of the poorest 416 million, and one-fifth of humanity spends $4 a day on a cappuccino while another one-fifth lives on less than $1 a day.[24] And if we say "God is love," or "God is in control," we need also to confess that 10.7 million children a year across the globe do not live to see their fifth birthday, more than 1 billion people live in abject poverty, and more than 1.5 million people in Haiti were left homeless by the 2010 earthquake. Outlaw Christians lament aloud that the world's heartache is exponential.

These facts depress us, I know. But the key to an authentic life and faith is not to hide from personal or global hope-corroding facts but instead to lament them, protest them, despise the crud out of them, talk to each other and God about them, and resist them daily in a hundred small ways through our vocation and our actions.

Hope is hard. Hope becomes a lie whenever we ignore the realities that make hope such a dire necessity. One of the best math teachers I ever had in high school would fail us on our calculus homework if we just wrote the answer down on the page. "You must show your work!" she always insisted, wiping chalk dust off her skirt. She was right, of course. Authentic hope shows the work.

Dostoevsky once wrote that "love in action is a harsh and dreadful thing compared with love in dreams,"[25] and I want to say the same of hope. Hope is a heartbreaking, never-ending struggle, but none is more important. Real hope sweats. Real hope gnashes its teeth. Real hope has dirty fingernails and muddy boots.

When we talk about God's love and our reasons for hope, we tend to come off sounding like God's jesters. Instead of jesters, we need to become God's finest public-relations agents. Our actions should prove to people that God's promises aren't just packs of lies we tell to maintain the status quo of our own power. Evil already has fantastic PR agents—the media, our despair, and our belief in being powerless against it. Outlaw Christians are God's new PR agents, and we are calling for change.

Become a Hope Sleuth

Outlaw Christians recognize that if we want to have hope in life, we have to become hope sleuths. Because of the prevalence of bad news in the world, we should become hard-boiled hope-detectives who follow hope around every day in our tricked-out panel van complete with surveillance equipment, forensics lab, and flashlights. We are looking for clues of everywhere hope was last seen.

Like all good detectives, we need to interview witnesses. We need to start listening to those who are hot on hope's trail, especially to those who on the surface of things appear to have little reason for hope at all. We need to ask people we know who have gone through deep grief and suffering, "Why hope? How did you not give in to despair?"

My students can always count on me, no matter where we go in the world, to ask people about the hope they have. When we were in Costa Rica, I asked Juanita how she kept up hope. Juanita was a young widow who had lost her husband to cancerous toxic chemicals that multinational corporations had put on banana plants on the plantation where he worked. Juanita told us that to keep the families away from the killer banana fields (where DDT is still used), Juanita and her other female friends—nearly all of them un-coincidentally widowed in their late twenties as well—formed a coop. The men of the community at first scoffed at the idea. But the women forged ahead with eco-tourism right there out of their own wooden houses on raised stilts, taking in guests like us and teaching them how to make chocolate and medicinal tea from plants growing in the rainforest. The women cook their guests rice and beans, make and sell simple jewelry, and share all the money they make with everyone in the village. And it works. No one from their town works on the banana plantations anymore. Juanita has hope because she, in community with her friends, stood up to injustice and composted the terrible loss of her own husband.

Similarly, I asked my dear friend Christine in New Haven, Connecticut, how she sustains hope. Christine has two kids in public school, a biracial marriage that both sides of her family scorn, a health care job with decent pay but obscene hours, and a manic-depressive underemployed husband. "I have hope because I don't have time not to, really," she answered. "You just get up, pack the lunch, put the kids on the school bus, go to work. You do what you gotta do."

In South Africa, I asked Glenda who worked on the Truth and Reconciliation Commission how she maintained hope during her three-and-a-half-year term, which involved listening for sixteen hours a day to the tearful firsthand testimonies of nearly seven thousand apartheid victims. She began her answer by saying that the chair of the TRC, Archbishop Desmond Tutu, insisted that everyone in the group practice self-care. One time he said to her when she was utterly exhausted, "As archbishop, I order you to stay home today!"

Glenda said she tried talk-therapy for a while to help her hold on to hope, but in the end massage therapy gave her the hope for which she yearned. Jokingly she told me with a laugh, "With massage therapy, at least I got a break from the question, 'So, how are you feeling?'" Serious once again, she looked out the window and said softly, "Touch at that time was beautiful and gentle for me."

She continued, "It's not really possible to work with someone like Desmond Tutu and not have hope. What can you do?" As for Desmond Tutu himself, he wrote in his book *No Future Without Forgiveness* that during the hearings, he harbored hope by insisting upon taking Communion—the sacrament of receiving grace—every morning before work. A sip of wine and a bite of bread. Whatever it takes.

Of course when I got to meet Elie Wiesel in person, I jumped on the chance to ask him what gave him joy and hope. Wiesel, whose entire family was killed by Germans in Auschwitz, smiled and said, "My students. I wouldn't want to live in a world without them. Every year I make it a point to take in students from Germany and become their mentor." If that is not living right inside your own hope, right under its roof, I don't know what is. And once, in the early stages of her Alzheimer's disease, I asked my mother what gave her hope and kept her keeping on. She looked straight into my eyes, chuckled as if I were missing the most obvious fact in the universe, and gave a one word answer: "*You*."

Reader, if I were able to speak to everyone in the world who knows each one of you, I guarantee that someone in this world would credit you with the hope that they have. If for no other reason, on your darkest days, remember that this is a magnificent reason to never give up. Other people are counting on your hope to give birth to theirs.

I am struck by how practical and simple all of these people's answers are about what sustains their hope—music, students, massage, cooking rice and beans, packing a child a lunch, sharing port and bread, teaching students, resting at home for a day, and you. If hope is to be found anywhere, outlaw Christians have figured out it is in places like these where we are going to find it. Hope is extravagant, yes, but it is found in the minutiae of the everyday. Whatever that thing is for you—only you know what it is—you've got to find it and hang on for dear life.

We often look up into the sky longing for hope, laying on our backs on futons or beach blankets, our minds filled with visions of transcendence and an afterlife. But we forget to look down at our own dirty fingernails or at a bologna sandwich in a kid's lunchbox. Rest assured, we can seek hope in the immanent without denying its origin in the transcendent, in God. The message of the cross is that hope is incarnate—meaning right here and now, inside us and among us.

Pay Attention

Paying attention to the world around you is another wonderful way to cultivate hope. In other words, think small and look hard. To paraphrase the brilliant poet Mary Oliver, prayer is paying attention. Similarly, Dorothee Soelle said we need to live eyes-wide-open, and I think this applies well to hope. Paying attention and staying awake are forms of prayer outlaw Christians cherish. How often does Jesus get upset with his friends, the disciples, for falling asleep just when he needed them most? Wrote Paul in 1 Thessalonians, "Let us not fall asleep as others do, but let us keep awake" (5:6). When it comes to hope, we need to stay awake. Fortunately, I know a couple of good strategies.

Seek Art

Turn to art. I read recently a scientific study that exposed depressed people regularly to beautiful art, which transformed their mood. The best artists take it upon themselves to be our senses when ours are tired out, and in so doing they reawaken us to appreciation and wonder. When our nose smells nothing but rotting garbage, the artist shows us the beauty of a plastic bag parasailing in the breeze—as in that famous scene in the film *American Beauty*, which if you are like me made you think, *Wow, I never thought of a plastic bag as beautiful before now.* Remember when you were a kid and you learned what to do for crossing the road? Stop. Look. Listen. We need to do the same thing to find where hope is hiding out: slow down, take notice, behold beauty. We've got to put our noses on hope's trail like a drug-sniffing K-9 at a border crossing. Nobody does this better than artists, except maybe you at the moments in your life when you have been in love.

Some spectacular works of art help us rediscover how to live eyes-wide-open, the way we once did as kids. One favorite I highly recommend is the German film *Wings of Desire*, which is a film about angels who long to be human, and which, trust me, will infuse you with wonder and marvel at your own humanity. Another great option: one of my all-time favorite poems,

Stephen Dunn's "Loves." It's an absolutely gorgeous ten-page list of tiny things that Dunn loves about life—everything from iguanas to mushrooms sautéed in garlic and wine to the fact that "a marriage must shed its first skin in order to survive."[26] Read this poem aloud to yourself, or better, read it aloud to a friend. Then try your hand at writing your own personal version of "Loves." The exercise will reorient you. I just said a silent prayer that you will find and read Dunn's poem by the end of this week.

Keep a Hope Journal: To List Is to Listen

Another fine strategy for learning to pay attention is to begin the spiritual practice of writing down things you notice, especially the things that give you hope. Frederick Buechner called this listening to your life, and I want to say we should not only listen, but also write down what we hear. I have taken up this practice and keep what I call a hope journal. Before falling asleep each night, I try to write down one moment of redemption, hope, or grace for the day. Nothing big, just a sentence or a phrase.

For example, one day when I was caregiving for my mom and had had a rough morning, the only moment I could think of to jot down was the fact that when I washed my Tupperware dish out after lunch, I squeezed the bottle of Dawn dish soap and a hundred tiny color bubbles came out like confetti and decorated the silver sink. On a random Monday, I wrote that I found comfort in the way my husband, Matt, puffed out his cheek when he shaved his face. Another day I was walking home from a long, overly political day at the office when three women drove by in a white Pontiac. The women shouted out the open window, "We love you, Dr. Bussie!" and as I peered in the car at their faces, I realized that I hadn't had a single one of them in class for more than two years. I treasure this journal. Over time, I started living differently because of it, watching out of the corner of my eye for the moment in the day that would make it to the page.

In lieu of a journal, Gail Sher recommends writing a haiku once a day for three months in order to rediscover appreciation and presence in the world around you.[27] Another author, Georgia Heard, says that we should fall in love three times a day and write down the three things we fell in love with in a notebook.[28] All of these strategies help us live a life of presence, which we sorely need within our culture of text messages, tweets, and iPhones. In order to cultivate appreciation, we have to find creative ways to rediscover, as the Buddhist saying goes, that "heaven is the now." However you choose to do it, outlaw Christians know that committing our hopes to paper is a life-enriching way to live into 1 Peter 3:15: "Always be ready to make your defense to anyone who demands from you an accounting for the hope that is in you."

When my now-husband, Matt, and I were sixteen years old, we struggled with how rough life was for a lot of people we knew. One day we were both pretty bummed out by the whole process of becoming an adult, so we grabbed a sheet of paper and divided the page down the middle into two columns. On the top of one side, we wrote, *Things That Rule*. On the top of the other, *Things That Suck*. We then started filling in each column. We decided to make our lists separately, then compare notes. Under *Things That Rule*, Matt wrote items I can still remember—things such as Double Stuf Oreos (with whole milk, not skim). People who smile a reasonable amount of the time. Jacqueline Bussie. Seeing U2 live and in concert at Madison Square Garden. Zero candy bars. Under *Things That Rule*, I put things such as fresh picked peaches from a Georgia orchard, whippoorwills, seesaws, Matt, yearbooks, and letters from my best friend Jennifer detailing every moment of her summer vacation down to what soda she drank on the plane (usually ginger ale). Under *Things That Suck*, I had scribbled: people whose crankiness robs you of joy, war, sex as a game or tool, people who are cheap, when people die too soon for you to really have gotten to know them, being called a geek, Uncle Richard's divorce, etc. We kept going and going; our lists were huge.

We were both surprised by how much fun it was and how we got to know each other better. And even though we had started off with the intention of just getting down on paper all the things that sucked, our *Things That Rule* list was even longer than the *Things That Suck* list (true for both of us). These lists reoriented us, reshaped the world as more of a both/and place, rather than either a totally bleak or totally sunny place—both of which are a lie if told as the whole truth. Matt and I still make these lists from time to time, especially when things get bad and our eyes need to readjust to the spring light after a too-long winter. I strongly recommend you try this at home. Nowadays you can buy books like *Listography: Your Life in Lists*, which are great, but Matt and I had already figured out in the '80s that all you need is paper and a pen. To list is to listen.

On a whim one day, I tried asking my students to make these lists in class. It went so wonderfully I have done it every semester. At first, my students lovingly mock their professor's hopelessly outdated 1980's slang words *suck* and *rule*. But they take out their pens and draw the line down the center of the page anyway, because I've asked them to and it's way better than talking about the reading they forgot to do.

They start to write. Slowly at first, digging around in their memories. Then faster. The exercise possesses them. No one sneaks a glance at their phone's text messages hoping I won't notice. I love to watch their faces as their thoughts ricochet from dreadful to delightful and back again. I always have to call time. Without fail, they want to read their lists aloud and they beg me to read mine, so we do. When they read, everyone's ears in the room stand at attention as if they are listening to a poet laureate. Usually their list-sonnets are the most splendid song I have heard in months, and I want to add their lists of *Things That Rule* to my current list of *Things That Rule*.

I then tell them that becoming a hope-detective is like becoming a poet, because noticing is what poets do best, as my mentor Tony Abbott describes in his unpublished poem "Effluctress":

> *Today my daughter made up a word . . .*
> *"Effluctress," she says, are things*
> *That can only be seen by 4-year-olds*
> —*Scott Owens*
> *Four-year-olds, darling, yes I agree,*
> *completely—it's only the only*
> *I have a problem with. Poets,*
> *sweetheart, and lovers, lovers*
> *especially, can see all sorts of things.*
> *So give us a break, my dear,*
> *because we love what you can see*

and you'd love what we can see,
too. The other day I was walking
home from church, and all of a
sudden, I said out loud: "Even
the streets are holy." That's right,
out loud, and I looked down
and there in the cracks between
the sections of the sidewalk
I could see I was right. God was
there, in the pieces of the sidewalk . . .
I know I'm not four anymore
but I sure want to be effluctress
and I just wanted to know—well
how am I doing?[29]

When it comes to holding on to hope, we all need to become effluctress. This is not as hard as it sounds if you are willing to let yourself fall in love with the world once again and with the people in it, even if only for a few seconds a day. We need to become, as Henry James famously wrote, "people on whom nothing is lost."[30]

Tell Your Stories of Enchantment

I have an acquaintance in Detroit who has the strangest job in the world. She is a professional (paid!) water-sniffer. She literally has a sense of smell like a superhero. She can smell people she knows walking down the hall long before they are even in sight. And for her job, she can smell water from any county and be able to tell you down to the molecule (no, I'm not kidding) what minerals and chemicals are in it. Her analyses' accuracy have been repeatedly verified by expensive scientific experiments, so now that she has a solid national reputation for detecting microbes, bacteria, toxins, and the like, cities just pay her to sniff their water and tell them what's in it to see if they need further treatments.

Last summer I taught a mini-seminar on enchantment, and I thought of my friend the water-sniffer. Most of our readings argued that we live in a disenchanted world, but one day I argued to the class that maybe we are the ones who are disenchanted. The truth is we have to sniff out the trace elements of the world's enchantment like my friend the water-sniffer, because usually these mystical moments are only a millionth of what is going on down here in the muck and the mire. They are happening, but not enough of us are talking about them, even though to do so might well save our life. I want to share with you a few of my enchantment stories.

During the fall of my first sabbatical, my husband and I rented a house on Lake Michigan. In October, I became friends with one of the neighbors, who taught me that the brass sculptures on the lawn of our house were of calla lilies. They were his favorite flower as a child. I had stared at the copper-colored version of these flowers for months, basically never seeing them at all, never caring or questioning what kind of flowers they were. Calla lilies. Now I knew.

The next month, December, we went to Santa Fe to house-sit for a friend. Santa Fe was the home of Georgia O'Keeffe, a fact I had not known but learned when Matt and I visited her museum in downtown Santa Fe off San Francisco Avenue. As we walked into the first room of the museum, I gasped. The walls bloomed calla lilies. I stared at the calla lilies, seeing them for the first time as calla lilies and not just some strange flowers that looked too much like reproductive organs for me to be comfortable in the same room with them.

Paying newfound attention to the art as a tribute to my friend, I learned things I would not otherwise have learned from O'Keeffe. I paid a new kind of attention. I wrote this in my journal:

> I used to think O'Keeffe must have been crazy or morbid or tripping on LSD to paint all those flowers floating around in the sky next to skulls. When I was in college, I used to hate those O'Keeffe posters hallucinating all over my dormmates' walls. It is obvious now that the self I was then did not understand that beauty is an agonist. I did not want to believe at that time that the glaze covering the whole world's artistry was ambiguity. But now I know that O'Keeffe was exactly right but I resisted learning from her. Flowers are lies unless they are depicted alongside bone. And the reverse is also true: hollow-eyed antelope skulls are a lie unless painted alongside a hollyhock, to which their carcass gave birth.

If it hadn't been for the calla lilies, I never would've learned anything from O'Keeffe, because I would not have stopped to listen or look.

After this trip to Santa Fe—the city of holy faith—Matt and I went to Los Angeles—the city of angels—in February for his job interview. We stayed in a friend's apartment right off Sunset Boulevard, amidst the urban sprawl. We arrived at night. The next morning I went out for a walk. I stopped short at the foot of the stairs. My scalp tingled. Three perfect white calla lilies—the exact color of O'Keeffe's—in full bloom sprayed up from the ground like a static fountain, no more than three inches from the stair entrance. I looked up and down the street. They were the only flowers in sight anywhere. Calla lilies pursued me across the United States that year, which is even more astonishing when you consider that the months they found me were between October and February—when most flowers were no more than a thought-seed hibernating in the cold ground.

Another story from around the same time. I had recently written a short piece entitled *Helium*, comparing the graduation of my students to the letting go of helium balloons, when a former student whom I was thinking about when I wrote the essay came to visit us in Michigan. As we walked on the shore, he retrieved from the waves a deflated yellow birthday balloon with a white ribbon still attached. He hung it on a fence nearby, because he didn't want any wildlife in the water to get tangled up in the string, and because he wanted it to remind me of him after he left. The balloon hung there until the day I moved away, and I took a picture of it for posterity.

One week later, I was in Montreal for a conference. I wanted to take a picture of my friend Cheryl in front of the creperie restaurant where we had just had lunch. I raised my camera to my eye, and the second I snapped the photo, a woman carrying a yellow helium balloon on a white ribbon walked right in front of Cheryl and into my camera lens. The picture only captured the balloon and the stranger's retreating back. I have not seen a yellow balloon since.

One last story. When I was in college, I worked one summer at the Autism Society of North Carolina as a camp counselor for autistic kids. It was a hard job, but one I loved. One day an especially difficult teen camper attacked me and pulled out a massive clump of my hair. The next day my friends Angela, Emily, and I all decided we needed to take our day off away from camp to regain a little sanity. We climbed into Angela's car, put our picnic basket in the backseat, and she said, "Girl, let's get lost," and took off at high speed. We drove around all afternoon. None of us were from the area and the camp was in the total boonies, so we did indeed get lost. Angela stopped the car, took a map out of the glove box, and wondered aloud, "Hmm, where are we on here?" To find out, we all looked up at the green street signs right in front of our car. We were at the intersection of Emily Road and Martin Avenue. All three of us stared at the signs for a minute, and then died laughing. The full name of my friend Emily who was in the car with us was *Emily Martin*.

You could, of course, say all of these stories were mere coincidences, rather than signs that the world contains trace elements of the enchanted. You could say they're cheesy and hey, you might be right. I teach teenagers who can sniff out cheese from a mile away, so they have taught me to keep my cheese-o-meter accurately calibrated at all times.

But all I can tell you is this: every time I saw the calla lilies, I laughed just a little bit way down in my chest. The sight of the calla lilies' white coronets trumpeted a strange sense of home in each non-home place where I was, and helped me remember the much-missed friend who had taught me about the lilies. The same goes for the yellow balloon and green street signs. Amid a terrible year when I felt like God had broken up with me, each calla lily I saw suddenly made me feel as if God had sent me a little text message casually saying, *Hey. Thinking of you.* Not, *Jacqueline, I made this happen*, exactly—just a small and sincere,

Hey, you. Maybe the world makes more sense than you realize.

By acknowledging the possibility of an enchanted world, I found glimmers of hope floating like lily pads in the stagnant pond of my own hopelessness. To pretend that these events did not make me feel this way would be a lie. But I'd also be lying if I told you that experiencing these enchantments made me as certain of God's hand in my life as I am certain that I 100 percent hate lima beans. The outcome for me of acknowledging enchantment is not certainty, but instead a shapely trust. As breakable and beautiful as a ballerina's ankle.

I once saw online the artwork of a guy named Willard Wigan. Wigan, a dyslexic who can barely read and write, creates in the eyes of needles or on the heads of pins colorful, intricately detailed micro-sculptures, most of which are barely visible to the naked eye.[31] He has created 160 such pieces, most of them 4/1000 of an inch, including one of Alice in Wonderland. Alice, in the micro-sculpture, is 1/3 the size of the period at the end of this sentence. Wigan also recently sculpted the Obama family holding hands in a needle's eye, and used an eyelash to put the president in place. As a paintbrush, he often uses a hair from a dead fly. To keep his hands steady, Wigan must sculpt between his own heartbeats. When seen under a microscope, Wigan's art is wondrous and replete with impossible detail.

When I started taking note in my life of enchanted moments like yellow balloons and calla lilies, all I can tell you is I felt exactly like I did when I first looked at Wigan's sculpture of the Statue of Liberty, made from a speck of gold and perched atop the head of a pin. Enchanted. Outlaw Christians want to *become* water-sniffers and visionaries like Wigan, people who can see liberty on the head of a pin and smell hope where other people smell nothing.

Seek Joy

When people ask me what joy is, I always start by saying joy and suffering are twin sisters. I am not the first to notice joy's strange kindred with sadness, which is why when we speak of both we say our heart aches. Joy is when love, appreciation, and beauty outwit pain and despair, yes, but the weird thing about joy is that it always seems aware—just below the surface—of what it is outwitting. Joy is aware of its own finitude, like my grandma who once said, "I know I will die, and soon"—then smiled and took a bite of a chicken leg.

Joy's beauty is in its awareness of its own fleetingness—like the life of a monarch butterfly, who lives only twelve weeks but manages to fly from Canada to Mazatlán in that time. Joy is keenly aware of its eventual fade out into absence. On a movie set, the director shouts, "Last looks!" after the final rehearsal. This marks the moment when they are about to do a take and commit the details of the scene to film forever. When we experience joy, something in our heart cries out at that very moment, "Last looks!" Joy is never far from suffering's frame.

Joy is when your morning coffee smells like fragrant possibility released from its husk. Joy is the feeling that the present moment is a tree you want to climb. Joy means loving others for the love they can give you rather than the love you want. Joy is gratitude so overflowing, it comes out the corners of your eyes.

Whenever someone asks me if there is a difference between happiness and joy, I say yes. When I was young, I will admit that I was often happy. Deep down I believed I deserved all the good things I had, though I never would have admitted this. I had bought wholesale into the lie regarding haves and have-nots, smugly including myself in the former. At that time in my life, I lived eyes-wide-shut when it came to other people's deep suffering. I dutifully believed success was a name of God. When I began to live eyes-wide-open, all of that changed. Members of my own family rejected me. People got mad and called me a socialist and other names I won't mention. It took me a long time to realize outlaws make other people really uncomfortable.

Authenticity about pain does not make you popular, but it does keep you honest, and therefore makes you dangerous. My new life was harder than the old one, because honesty hurts. I remember one day thinking, *Oh my gosh, what happened to the happy person I used to be? Why am I always getting myself in trouble?*

The truth is, however, what replaced my so-called happiness was not unhappiness, but joy. Happiness can carry with it a sense of smugness or deservedness, which is why happiness is often the luxury of the privileged. Happiness comes from living in security, from believing all is right, reasonable, and ordered within the world. Joy, on the other hand, bears no such illusions. Joy comes from living in the truth, and from setting yourself free from the lies you tell yourself about yourself, God, and creation. Happiness is almost always *because-of*, while joy, like grief, is almost always *in-spite-of*. What this all means in practical terms is this: while happiness can be taken from you by misfortune and suffering, joy can *never* ever be taken from you, because joy by its very nature resists suffering and dances on its grave. That is why I like to tell everyone I love, to quote Shakespeare, "I wish you all the joy that you can wish."[32]

As much as outlaws commit to composting sorrow, they commit to cultivating joy. When I read Alice Walker's novel *Possessing the Secret of Joy*, I read every page with baited breath, eager for the author to unveil what was indeed the secret to possessing joy. Her answer, once I read it, was what other smart people like her had already taught me: resistance. Resistance is the "secret of joy."[33] Resistance is also the secret of hope, because every single story of hope I have told so far—the madres, the arpilleristas, Haregewoin, my mother, the black South Africans, and all the rest—entails resistance. Resistance is the path of the outlaw Christian, whether in resistance to oppression, habit, injustice, silence, lukewarmness, loss, death, despair, killer faith-laws, or haters.

We are created for joy. I believe this. But I also know that joy, like hope, needs to be cultivated and received, which is a struggle through and through in a world filled with so much sadness. Every strategy I have listed already for cultivating hope would work for joy, too, but here are a few more.

Practice Authenticity

A first major way to cultivate joy is through *authenticity*, something I have already alluded to a hundred times in this book. The reason why we think nobody really knows us is because we have not let anyone actually know us. And if we don't feel known, how can we feel loved? When we let ourselves be vulnerable, shed secrets, and show each other the deepest sides to ourselves that we never let anyone see—the pain, the grief, the ugly, the fear—we will find that many people love us anyway, either because of ourselves or in spite of ourselves. The beautiful upshot of authenticity, then, is the knowledge that the love you receive from others is at last love for the real you, and not the mask-wearing you. This kind of love does not feel like the other, which leaves us paranoid and fearful of being found out as a fraud. Once you experience love born in authenticity, you will never want to go back.

As I said at the beginning of this book, in the house where I grew up, unspoken pain dominated and damaged our lives. My own personal resistance to dysfunction has involved becoming a person who refuses to allow silence to reign as queen any longer. From silence to stewardship there is but a step: *voice*. Take the risk of authenticity and tell someone you trust your true story; it's how you resist a world where most people live a lie. You will find joy there, I promise.

Don't Forget Humor

Second, don't forget that most humor is an irreplaceable means of finding joy amid the absurdity of life. One of my favorite stories of resistance humor comes from my friend Shawn. One spring Shawn did not get accepted into a single graduate program in creative writing. As an act of resistance, he decorated his wall with dozens of rejection letters rather than hide them, which he said would have made him feel ashamed. Defiantly, he decided to compose a letter of rejection back to each of the schools that had rejected him. The letter began:

Dear Sir/Madam:

I regret to inform you that because of the overwhelming number of rejection letters I have received this year, I am unable to accept yours at this time . . .

The letter made me laugh so hard and so long my cheeks hurt. Shawn, who took great joy in making people laugh, posted this letter on his fridge and would read it to friends every time they came over and asked how the application process was going.

Oftentimes, when I feel like God has walked out on me and prayer won't come to my tired tongue, my husband asks me to repeat aloud after him an outlaw prayer inspired by Shawn that we once wrote:

Dear God, this world often sucks. (This world often sucks.)
   I know that you know this. (I know that you know this.)
   We feel like you abandon us sometimes. (We feel like you abandon us sometimes.)
   We just want to let you know. (We just want to let you know.)
   We regret to inform you, but we reject your rejection of us at this time. (We regret to inform you, but we reject your rejection of us at this time.)
   Sorry, but no thank you. (Sorry, but no thank you.)
   We are sticking with you anyway. (We are sticking with you anyway.)
Amen.

Faith, for me, is not only accepting acceptance, but rejecting rejection.

Move Your Body

Third, cultivate joy by having your body express it even when your heart feels anything but. Dance is the best example of this I can think of, and sex and playing sports are other good ones. (Turning cartwheels is also one of my personal favorites, especially when you need to see things upside down for a bit.)

One summer night after we got home from visiting Suzanne in hospice, my thoughts chased the night like fireflies. At about 4:15 A.M., I couldn't take the insomnia lying down anymore. I grabbed my iPod, went out to my back porch, and danced my heart out in my underwear under a blue Ohio moon. I could not stop. I didn't care if anyone saw me looking like a half-naked crazy person, because it was what my soul so desperately needed. I danced not because I felt joy but because I felt joyless. It was strange how my heart, though, followed my body to a place of joy-as-resistance. I danced my furious dance for Suzanne but also against what was happening to her and millions of other people in the world right at that very moment.

I did feel like in some strange way that my dance was kicking death's derriere. Only as I sat here typing this did I realize the music I listened to over and over again as I danced on death's neck was from Coldplay's album *Viva la Vida*, which translated means "Live the Life." Later I also remembered that within the Jewish tradition of Hasidism, the people sometimes dance on graves to summon God's presence into the moment of grief. Rather than accept the felt experience of God's absence, the Hasidim insist God show up—and they will resort to dancing at the most unlikely moments if that's what it takes to get God's attention. All I know is, I will feel a certain satisfaction if people who love me dance on my grave one day.

Months later, I told my husband the secret of my midnight dance. A couple of times since then, when things have gotten bad, my husband with a sparkle in his hazel eyes has turned off the lights, turned up the stereo full-blast, and proposed, "Dance party?"

Practice Your Vocation

A fourth and final way to best resist evil, grief, and suffering and to cultivate joy is through the practice of our vocations. The word *vocation* means calling, and Lutherans like myself grow up believing everyone has one. Luther in the sixteenth century stretched the term out, applying it not just to priests but to everyone—from moms to shoemakers to streetcleaners. In the twentieth century, Frederick Buechner wrote the much-beloved definition, that your vocation is "the place God calls you, the place where your deep gladness and the world's deep hunger meet."[34]

I like both of these definitions, but I believe we don't have one vocation but many. We have multiple vocations in a lifetime or even every day, the way we are a student, daughter, accountant, neighbor, and best friend. Each role summons us in its own special way to become more human human beings. I would therefore define *vocation* as anything you commit to in life that presents you with the chance to give someone's humanity back to them. This could be anything. The someone could even be yourself. Understanding yourself to have a vocation means looking forward into each day's endless array of possibilities and thinking, *I wonder what will be the moment today when I and only I will have the chance to give someone's humanity back to her?* Your vocations are how you wrestle in the world every day to bring us one percent closer to The-World-We-Want-to-Live-In.

My vocation of being a teacher has brought me more moments of joy than I could ever describe to you using mere Microsoft Word. I am thinking of when one of my recent graduates Jordan told me about her work doing HIV testing on skid row and counseling fourteen-year-olds scared out of their minds, and I was so proud to know her that my hands shook as I held the phone. I'm thrilled when my liberation theology class was supposed to have ended at 3:15 P.M. and it's now 3:35 P.M., and nobody, and I do mean *nobody*, has made a break for the door because time doesn't matter compared to what Megan is saying now about Fazeel, the Somali refugee whom she is teaching English as part of our class' weekly community service and who, though dead-broke, baked her food as a thank-you. I am thinking of the day my student Elise from chapter 2 read her lament on the lawn and when she started to cry and I feared she could not go on, her classmate Eddie reached out and held her hand until she was able to speak again. My students are people I genuinely love, and if my vocation did not let me be around such awe-inspiring people all day, much of my joy would vanish from my life.

The other day a student interviewed me for a class assignment. The last question she asked me was, "What is one thing you would want everyone to know that you have not yet said?" I want to leave you with the same answer I gave her, because it sums up best all I want to say as an outlaw Christian about vocation, grace, hope, and joy.

Every day during the warmer months of the year, I walk to work. My walk is a couple of miles, and it is beautiful. The Red River divides the city where I live—Fargo, North Dakota—from the city where I work—Moorhead, Minnesota. A pedestrian bridge that I have to cross hangs over the Red River. Every time I cross this bridge, I feel as though nature itself helps transition me from work to home or home to work and back again. Whenever my feet hit the bridge's wood slats, no matter which direction I am headed, my heart sings. Heading west in the morning, I can't wait to see my students whom I have missed during the evening. Heading east in the evening, I can't wait to see my husband whom I have missed during the day. And then, one day on the bridge a thought hit me that is the truest thing that I know about my life to date, and the thought was this: *Love waits for me on both sides of the river.* No matter what you have been through, what you have done or left undone, may you, too, one day know this to be the truest thing about your own life. *Love waits for you on both sides of the river.*

Bibliography

Adams, Marilyn McCord. "Truth and Reconciliation." In
Theologians in Their Own Words, edited by Derek R. Nelson,
Joshua M. Moritz, and Ted Peters, 15–33. Minneapolis, MN:
Fortress Press, 2013.

Agosin, Marjorie. *Scraps of Life Chilean Arpilleras: Chilean Women
and the Pinochet Dictatorship*. Translated by Cola Franzen.
Toronto: Zed Books, 1987.

Arendt, Hannah. *Eichmann in Jerusalem: A Report on the Banality of
Evil*. New York: Penguin, 1994.

Berg, Elizabeth. *Escaping into the Open: The Art of Writing True*.
New York: HarperCollins, 1999.

Berry, Wendell. "Manifesto: The Mad Farmer Liberation Front." In
New Collected Poems. Berekely: Counterpoint, 2012.

Bonhoeffer, Dietrich. *Letters and Papers from Prison*. Edited by
Eberhard Bethge. New York: Touchstone, 1972.

Brown, Robert McAfee. *Speaking of Christianity, Practical
Compassion, Social Justice, and Other Wonders*. Louisville, KY:
Westminster John Knox, 1997.

Brueggemann, Walter. *The Psalms and the Life of Faith*.
Minneapolis: Augsburg Fortress, 1995.

Buechner, Frederick. *Godric*. San Francisco: Harper & Row, 1980.

———. *Secrets in the Dark: A Life in Sermons*. New York: Harper One, 2006.

———. *Telling the Truth: The Gospel as Tragedy, Comedy, and Fairy Tale*. San Francisco: Harper & Row, 1977.

———. *The Alphabet of Grace*. New York: HarperCollins San Francisco, 1970.

———. *The Book of Bebb*. New York: HarperCollins, 2001.

———. *Wishful Thinking: A Seeker's ABC*. New York: Harper San Francisco, 1993.

Bussie, Jacqueline. *The Laughter of the Oppressed*. New York: T & T Clark International, 2007.

Cargas, Henry James. *Henry James Cargas in Conversation with Elie Wiesel*. New York: Paulist Press, 1976.

Chesterton, G. K. *The Paradoxes of Mr. Pond*. Los Angeles: Indo-European Publishing, 2011.

Cleave, Chris. *Little Bee*. New York: Simon & Schuster, 2008.

Day, Dorothy. *The Long Loneliness*. New York: Harper & Row, 1952.

Dillard, Annie. *Holy the Firm*. New York: Harper, 1977.

Dostoevsky, Fyodor. *The Brothers Karamazov*. Translated by Constance Garnett. New York: Macmillan, 1922.

Dunn, Stephen. "Loves." In *New and Selected Poems 1974–1994*. New York: W. W. Norton, 1994.

Endo, Shusaku. *Silence*. Translated by William Johnston. New York: Taplinger, 1969.

Fisher, Jo. *Mothers of the Disappeared*. Boston: South End Press, 1989.

Fodor, Sarah J. "Outlaw Christian: An Interview With Reynolds Price." *Christian Century* 112, no. 34 (November 22, 1995): 1128–1131.

Foer, Jonathan Safran. *Extremely Loud and Incredibly Close*. New York: Houghton Mifflin, 2005.

Fogelman, Eva. *Conscience and Courage: Rescuers of Jews During the Holocaust*. New York: Anchor, 1994.

Gibran, Kahlil. *The Prophet*. New York: Alfred A. Knopf, 1923.

Greene, Melissa Fay. *There Is No Me Without You: One Woman's Odyssey to Rescue Her Country's Children*. New York: Bloomsbury USA, 2007.

Halifax, Joan. *The Fruitful Darkness: A Journey Through Buddhist Practice and Tribal Wisdom*. New York: HarperCollins, 1993.

Hanh, Thich Nhat. *Creating True Peace: Ending Violence in Yourself, Your Family, Your Community and the World*. New York: Simon & Schuster, 2004.

Hauerwas, Stanley. *God, Medicine, and Suffering*. Grand Rapids, MI: Eerdmans, 1990.

Heard, Georgia. *Writing Toward Home: Lessons to Find Your Way*. Portsmouth, NH: Heinemann, 1995.

Hick, John. "The World as a Vale of Soul-Making." In *The Problem of Evil: Selected Readings*. Edited by Michael L. Peterson. Notre Dame, IN: University of Notre Dame Press, 1992, 215–230.

Huffington, Arianna. *Thrive: The Third Metric to Redefining Success and Creating a Life of Well-Being, Wisdom, and Wonder*. New York: Harmony Books, 2014.

Irving, John. *A Prayer For Owen Meany*. New York: Ballantine, 1989.

James, Henry. "The Art of Fiction." In *Theory of Fiction: Henry James*. Edited by James E. Miller Jr. Lincoln: University of Nebraska Press, 1972.

Juergensmeyer, Mark. *Terror in the Mind of God: The Global Rise of Religious Violence*. Berkeley: University of California Press, 2003.

Keats, John. *The Letters of John Keats: Volume 2, 1819–1821*. Edited by Hyder Edward Rollins. New York: Cambridge University Press, 1958.

King Jr., Dr. Martin Luther. "Letter from a Birmingham Jail." Martin Luther King, Jr. Research and Education Institute—Stanford University. Accessed July 25, 2015. http://okra.stanford.edu /transcription/document_images/undecided/630416–019.pdf.

Krauss, Nicole. *The History of Love*. New York: W. W. Norton & Company, 2005.

Lamott, Anne. *Bird by Bird: Some Instructions on Writing and Life*. New York: Anchor Books, 1994.

Lewis, C. S. *A Grief Observed*. New York: Harper Perennial, 1961.

———. "The Trouble With X." In *God on the Dock: Essays on Theology and Ethics*. Grand Rapids, MI: Eerdmans, 1971.

Loeb, Paul Rogat, ed. *The Impossible Will Take a Little While: A Citizen's Guide to Hope in a Time of Fear*. New York: Basic Books, 2004.

Loewen, James W. *Lies My Teacher Told Me: Everything Your American History Textbook Got Wrong*. New York: Simon & Schuster, 2007.

Luther, Martin. "Heidelberg Disputation." In *Luther's Works 31*. Philadelphia: Muhlenberg Press, 1957.

Metcalf, Linda Trichter, and Tobin Simon. *Writing the Mind Alive: The Proprioceptive Method for Finding Your Authentic Voice*. New York: Random House, 2002.

Moltmann, Jürgen. *The Source of Life: The Holy Spirit and the Theology of Life*. Translated by Margaret Kohl. Minneapolis: Augsburg Fortress, 1997.

———. *Theology of Hope: On the Ground and the Implications of a Christian Eschatology*. Minneapolis: Fortress, 1993.

Morrow, Lance. *Evil: An Investigation*. New York: Basic Books, 2003.

Mother Teresa. *Mother Teresa: Come Be My Light: The Private Writings of the Saint of Calcutta*, edited by Brian Kolodiejchuk. New York: Doubleday, 2007.

Naik, Gautam. "Major Miniaturist Makes Art that Comes With Its Own Microscope," *Wall Street Journal*, October 1, 2009, http://online.wsj.com/article/SB125426448028050665.html.

Niebuhr, Reinhold. *An Interpretation of Christian Ethics*. Louisville, KY: Westminster John Knox, 2013.

Nouwen, Henri. *Wounded Healers: Ministry in Contemporary Society*. New York: Doubleday, 1972.

———. *Theologian of Public Life*. Larry Rasmussen, ed. Minneapolis: Augsburg Fortress, 1988.

Percy, Walker. *The Second Coming*. New York: Picador, 1980.

———. *The Message in the Bottle: How Queer Man Is, How Queer Language Is, and What One Has to Do with the Other*. New York: Picador, 1954.

Reynolds, Susan Salter. "Elie Wiesel: Embracing Memory and Madness." *Los Angeles Times* (Los Angeles, CA), Feb. 22, 2009.

Richardson, Robert D. *William James: In the Maelstrom of American Modernism*. New York: Mariner, 2006.

Robinson, Marilynne. *Housekeeping*. New York: Picador, 1980.

Roth, John K. "A Theodicy of Protest." *Encountering Evil: Live Options in Theodicy*. Edited by Stephen Davis. Louisville, KY: Westminster John Knox Press, 2001, 1–20.

Rumi. *Rumi: The Book of Love: Poems of Ecstasy and Longing*. Translated by Coleman Barks. New York: HarperOne, 2005.

Schreiter, Robert J. *Reconciliation: Mission and Ministry in a Changing Social Order*. Maryknoll, New York: Orbis, 1992.

Shakespeare, William. *Hamlet*. New York: Simon & Schuster, 1992.

Shakespeare, William. *The Merchant of Venice*. Hollywood, FL: Simon and Brown, 2011.

Sher, Gail. *One Continuous Mistake: Four Noble Truths for Writers*. New York: Penguin, 1999.

Silber, Joan. *Ideas of Heaven: A Ring of Stories*. New York: W. W. Norton, 2004.

Smith, Adam. *The Wealth of Nations*. New York: Oxford, 1993.

Soelle, Dorothee. *Essential Writings*. Edited by Dianne L. Oliver. Maryknoll, New York: Orbis, 2006.

———. *The Mystery of Death*. Translated by Nancy Lukens-Rumscheidt and Martin Lukens-Rumscheidt. Minneapolis: Fortress Press, 2007.

———. *Revolutionary Patience*. Translated by Rita and Robert Kimber. Maryknoll, New York: Orbis, 1977.

Swinton, John. *Raging with Compassion: Pastoral Responses to the Problem of Evil*. Grand Rapids, MI: Eerdmans, 2007.

Taylor, Barbara Brown. *Leaving Church: A Memoir of Faith*. New York: HarperOne, 2006.

Tillich, Paul. *Love, Power and Justice: Ontological Analyses and Ethical Applications*. London: Oxford University Press, 1954.

———. *The Dynamics of Faith*. New York: Harper Perennial, 2001.

Tutu, Desmond. *No Future Without Forgiveness*. New York: Doubleday, 1999.

Voltaire. *Voltaire in His Letters*. Translated by S. G. Tallentyre. New York: G. P. Putnam's Sons, 1919.

Walker, Alice. *Possessing the Secret of Joy*. New York: Harcourt Brace, 1992.

Wallis, Jim. *God's Politics: Why the Right Gets It Wrong and the Left Doesn't Get It*. New York: HarperCollins, 2005.

Wiesel, Elie. *A Journey of Faith*. New York: Donald I. Fine, 1990.

———. *Gates of the Forest*. New York: Schocken, 1966.

———. *Night*. New York: Hill and Wang, 1985.

———. "Nobel Lecture: Hope, Despair and Memory." Presentation at the Nobel Prize Awards, December 11, 1986. http://www.nobelprize.org/nobel_prizes/peace/laureates/1986/wiesel-lecture.html.

———. "One Must Not Forget." *U.S. News & World Report*, October 27, 1986.

———. *Souls on Fire: Portraits and Legends of Hasidic Masters*. Translated by Marion Wiesel. New York: Simon & Schuster, 1972.

Wiesenthal, Simon. *The Sunflower: On the Possibilities and Limits of Forgiveness*. New York: Schocken, 1997.

Wroblewski, David. *The Story of Edgar Sawtelle*. New York: HarperCollins, 2008.

Notes

Chapter One: Tired of Dishonesty?

1. Sarah J. Fodor, "Outlaw Christian: An Interview with Reynolds Price," in *The Christian Century*, 112, November 22, 1995, http://findarticles.com/p/articles/mi_m1058/is_n34_v112 /ai_17829298/.
2. Leah helped me realize that sometimes we must see past profanity to its cause: a pain so profound, perhaps only profanity can best expose its twisted roots to those of us who have never had to suffer it.

Chapter Two: Angry at the Almighty?

1. Robert Schreiter, *Mission and Ministry in a Changing Social Order* (Maryknoll, NY: Orbis, 1992), 34. Schreiter defines "narratives of the lie" as narratives that undermine or negate the truth of one's own story and experiences.
2. Simon Wiesenthal, *The Sunflower: On the Possibilities and Limits of Forgiveness* (New York: Schocken Books, 1997), 8.
3. Alice Walker, *Possessing the Secret of Joy* (New York: Harcourt Brace, 1992), 161.
4. Quoted in Robert McAfee Brown, *Speaking of Christianity,*

Practical Compassion, Social Justice, and Other Wonders (Louisville, KY: Westminster John Knox, 1997), 74.

5. Arianna Huffington, *Thrive: The Third Metric to Redefining Success and Creating a Life of Well-Being, Wisdom, and Wonder* (New York: Harmony Books, 2014), 168.

6. I can't lie, I am still disgusted by the notion the narrative puts forward that in God's eyes, family members—i.e., human beings—are replaceable like Job's cattle.

7. Elie Wiesel, "Hope, Despair and Memory," Nobel Lecture, 1986, accessed July 20, 2014, http://www.nobelprize.org/nobel_prizes/peace/laureates/1986/wiesel-lecture.ht.

8. Elie Wiesel, *Gates of the Forest* (New York: Schocken Books, 1966), 31.

9. Dillard's story is quoted in John K. Roth, "A Theodicy of Protest," in *Encountering Evil: Live Options in Theodicy*, ed. Stephen Davis (Atlanta: John Knox Press, 1981), 20–21.

10. Ibid., 17.

11. Elie Wiesel, interview with Alvin P. Sanoff, "One Must Not Forget," *U.S. News & World Report*, October 27, 1986, 68.

12. Jürgen Moltmann, *The Source of Life: The Holy Spirit and the Theology of Life*, trans. Margaret Kohl (Minneapolis: Augsburg Fortress, 1997), 41.

Chapter Three: Doubting Your Faith?

1. Dr. Martin Luther King, Jr., "Letter from a Birmingham Jail," https://kinginstitute.stanford.edu/king-papers/documents/letter-birmingham-jail. "But though I was initially disappointed at being categorized as an extremist, as I continued to think about the matter I gradually gained a measure of satisfaction from the label."

2. Paul Tillich, *The Dynamics of Faith* (New York: Harper & Row, 1957), 18, 102.

3. C. S. Lewis, *A Grief Observed* (New York: HarperCollins, 1961), 6.

4. Alice Walker, *Possessing the Secret of Joy* (New York: Harcourt Brace, 1992), 270.

5. Voltaire, *Voltaire in His Letters*, trans. S. G. Tallentyre (New York: G. P. Putnam's Sons, 1919), 278.

6. Dietrich Bonhoeffer, *Letters and Papers from Prison*, trans. Eberhard Bethge (New York: Macmillan, 1972), 360.

7. Joan Halifax, *The Fruitful Darkness: A Journey Through Buddhist Practice and Tribal Wisdom* (New York: HarperCollins, 1993), 153.

8. Henry James Cargas, *Henry James Cargas in Conversation with Elie Wiesel* (New York: Paulist Press, 1976), 18.

9. G. K. Chesterton, *The Paradoxes of Mr. Pond* (Los Angeles: Indo-European Publishing, 2011), 42.

10. Reinhold Niebuhr, *An Interpretation of Christian Ethics* (Louisville, KY: Westminster John Knox, 2013), 117.

11. Walker Percy, *The Second Coming* (New York: Picador, 1980), 132, 190.

12. Kahlil Gibran, *The Prophet* (New York: Alfred A. Knopf, 1923), 29.

13. Quoted in Linda Trichter Metcalf and Tobin Simon, *Writing the Mind Alive: The Proprioceptive Method for Finding Your Authentic Voice* (New York: Random House, 2002), 140.

14. After all, if I might be wrong, other people might also be wrong. While we have a word to describe the belief that everyone is equally right (relativism), we have no word to describe the conviction that everyone—including myself—might be equally wrong. (Faithful skepticism?)

15. Desmond Tutu, *No Future Without Forgiveness* (New York: Doubleday, 1999), 31.

16. Frederick Buechner, *The Alphabet of Grace* (New York: HarperCollins San Francisco, 1970), 47.

17. Dietrich Bonhoeffer, *Letters and Papers from Prison*, trans. Eberhard Bethge (Macmillan, New York, 1972), 17.

18. Mother Teresa, *Mother Teresa Come Be My Light: The Private Writings of the "Saint of Calcutta"* ed. Brian Kolodiejchuk (New York: Doubleday, 2007), 187.

19. Http://anamericanatheist.org/2011/09/23/mother-teresa-was-a-fraud/, accessed 1/5/2012.

20. See Romans 1:7, 1 Corinthians 1:2, and Ephesians 2:19. In Ephesians 3:8, Paul even refers to himself as a saint, but none of his writings would suggest that label means he believes in his own perfection.

21. Nicole Krauss, *The History of Love* (New York: W. W. Norton & Company, 2005), 168.

22. Elie Wiesel, *A Journey of Faith* (New York: Donald I. Fine, Inc., 1990), 2.

23. Elie Wiesel, *Night* (New York: Hill and Wang, 1985), 65.

24. *Souls on Fire: Portraits and Legends of Hasidic Masters*, trans. Marion Wiesel (New York: Random House, 1972), 111.

25. Frederick Buechner, *Telling the Truth: The Gospel as Tragedy, Comedy and Fairytale* (San Francisco: Harper & Row, 1977), 56.

26. Walter Brueggemann, *The Psalms and the Life of Faith* (Minneapolis: Augsburg Fortress, 1995), 84.

27. John Swinton, *Raging with Compassion: Pastoral Responses to the Problem of Evil* (Grand Rapids, MI: Wm. B. Eerdmans, 2007), 92–93.

Chapter Four: Sick of Hearing "God Has a Plan"?

1. William Shakespeare, *Hamlet* (New York: Simon & Schuster, 1992), 151.

2. Dorothee Soelle, *The Mystery of Death*, trans. Nancy Lukens-Rumscheidt and Martin Lukens-Rumscheidt (Minneapolis: Fortress Press, 2007), 82.

3. Mark Juergensmeyer, *Terror in the Mind of God: The Global Rise of Religious Violence* (Berkeley: University of California Press, 2003).

4. Martin Luther, "Heidelberg Disputation," *Luther's Works* 31 (Philadelphia: Muhlenberg Press, 1957), 53. "A theology of glory calls evil good and good evil. A theology of the cross calls the thing what it actually is."

5. Lance Morrow, *Evil: An Investigation* (New York: Basic Books, 2003), 39.

6. Martin Luther, *Luther's Works* 28 (Philadelphia: Muhlenberg Press, 1957), 245.

7. C. S. Lewis, "The Trouble With X," in *God in the Dock: Essays on Theology and Ethics* (Grand Rapids, MI: Eerdmans, 1971), 151–55.

8. Reinhold Niebuhr, *The Irony of American History* (Chicago: University of Chicago Press, 1952), 63.

9. John Hick, "The World as a Vale of Soul-Making," in *The Problem of Evil: Selected Readings*, Michael L. Peterson, ed. (Notre Dame, IN: University of Notre Dame Press, 1992), 215–30.

10. *The Letters of John Keats*, 1814–1821, ed. Hyder Rollins, vol. 2 (Cambridge, MA: Harvard UP, 1958), 101–102.

11. Marilynne Robinson, *Housekeeping* (New York: Picador, 1980), 92.

12. Walker Percy, *The Message in the Bottle: How Queer Man Is, How Queer Language Is, and What One Has to Do with the Other* (New York: Picador, 1954), 116.

13. David Wroblewski, *The Story of Edgar Sawtelle* (New York: HarperCollins, 2008), 439.

14. Frederick Buechner, *The Book of Bebb* (New York: HarperCollins, 2001), 94.

15. Paul Tillich famously defines salvation as accepting ourselves as accepted.

16. Hannah Arendt, *Eichmann in Jerusalem: A Report on the Banality of Evil* (New York: Penguin, 1994), 287.

17. Shusaku Endo, *Silence*, trans. William Johnston (New York: Taplinger, 1969), 86.

Chapter Five: Scared to Tell Your Real Story?

1. Paul Tillich, *Love, Power and Justice: Ontological Analyses and Ethical Applications* (London: Oxford UP, 1954), 84.

2. Joan Silber, *Ideas of Heaven: A Ring of Stories* (New York: W. W. Norton, 2004), 121.

3. Anne Lamott, *Bird by Bird: Some Instructions on Writing and Life* (New York: Anchor Books, 1994), 22.

4. Elizabeth Berg, *Escaping Into the Open: The Art of Writing True* (New York: HarperCollins, 1999), 118.

5. Jonathan Safran Foer, *Extremely Loud and Incredibly Close* (New York: Houghton Mifflin, 2005), 76.

6. Wiesel, *Gates of the Forest*, 27.

7. See "Kisa-Gotami," http://www.clear-vision.org/schools/Teachers/teacher-info/Buddhist-stories/Kisa-Gotami.aspx. Last accessed August 29, 2015.

8. Quoted in Robert McAffee Brown, *Liberation Theology: An Introductory Guide* (Louisville, KY: Westminster John Knox, 1993), 107.

9. Martin Luther, "The Heidelberg Disputation," in *Martin Luther's Basic Theological Writings*, edited by Timothy F. Lull (Minneapolis: Fortress Press, 1989), 30–44. Simon Wiesenthal, *The Sunflower: On the Possibilities and Limits of Forgiveness* (New York: Schocken Books, 1997), 8

10. Chris Cleave, *Little Bee* (New York: Simon & Schuster, 2008), 9.

11. Frederick Buechner, *Secrets in the Dark: A Life in Sermons* (New York: HarperOne, 2006), 205–20.

12. Buechner, *Book of Bebb*, 352.

13. Rumi, Rumi: *The Book of Love: Poems of Ecstasy and Longing*, trans. Coleman Barks (New York: HarperOne, 2005), 52.

14. See Henri Nouwen, *Wounded Healers: Ministry in Contemporary Society* (New York: Doubleday, 1972).

15. Derek R. Nelson, Joshua M. Moritz, and Ted Peters, eds., *Theologians in Their Own Words* (Minneapolis, MN: Fortress Press, 2013), 24.

16. Dorothy Day, *The Long Loneliness* (New York: Harper & Row, 1952), 243.

17. Soelle, *The Mystery of Death*, 114.

18. Melissa Faye Greene, *There Is No Me Without You: One Woman's Odyssey to Rescue Her Country's Children* (New York: Bloomsbury, 2007), 238.

19. Thich Nhat Hanh, *Creating True Peace: Ending Violence in Yourself, Your Family, Your Community and the World* (New York: Simon & Schuster, 2004), 176–177.

20. *Lars and the Real Girl*, directed by Craig Gillespie (2007; MGM Home Entertainment, 2008), DVD.
21. To read more about the practice of shiva, check out http://www .myjewishlearning.com/life/Life_Events/Death_and_Mourning /Burial_and_Mourning/Shiva.shtml.
22. Soelle, *Mystery of Death*, 78.

Chapter Six: Longing for Hope?

1. Susan Salter Reynolds, "Elie Wiesel: Embracing Memory and Madness," *Los Angles Times* (Los Angeles, CA), Feb. 22, 2009.
2. Vern Huffman, "Stories from the Cha Cha Cha," Paul Rogat Loeb, ed., *The Impossible Will Take a Little While: A Citizen's Guide to Hope in a Time of Fear* (New York: Basic Books, 2004), 161–62.
3. Susan Griffin, "To Love the Marigold," *The Impossible Will Take a Little While: A Citizen's Guide to Hope in a Time of Fear*, ed. Paul Rogat Loeb (New York: Basic Books, 2004), 137.
4. Jo Fisher, *Mothers of the Disappeared* (Boston: South End Press, 1989), 28.
5. Ibid., 60–62.
6. Ibid., 79.
7. Ibid., 156–57.
8. Marjorie Agosin, *Scraps of Life Chilean Arpilleras: Chilean Women and the Pinochet Dictatorship*, trans. Cola Franzen (Toronto: Zed Books, 1987), 53.
9. Ibid., 13.
10. Ibid., 83.
11. Ibid., 12.
12. See http://www.youtube.com/watch?v=SQzu4R6LRps.
13. Leah Green, "Just Listen," *Yes!*, November 5, 2001, http://www .yesmagazine.org/issues/can-love-save-the-world/just-listen.
14. Greene, *There is No Me Without You*, 55.
15. Ibid., 94.

16. Ibid., Epilogue (n.p.).

17. Eva Fogelman, *Conscience and Courage: Rescuers of Jews During the Holocaust* (New York: Anchor, 1994), 70.

18. Ibid.,106.

19. Jim Wallis, *God's Politics: A New Vision for Faith and Politics in America* (New York: Harper San Francisco, 2005), xxii.

20. Quoted in Dorothee Soelle, *Essential Writings* (Maryknoll, NY: Orbis, 2006), 73.

21. Quoted in Jürgen Moltmann, *A Theology of Hope: On the Ground and Implications of a Christian Eschatology* (Minneapolis: Fortress, 1993), 20.

22. Jim Wallis, "Faith Works," *The Impossible Will Take a Little While: A Citizen's Guide to Hope in a Time of Fear*, ed. Paul Rogat Loeb (New York: Basic Books, 2004), 203.

23. Statistic is from the latest AFL-CIO Report, http://www.aflcio .org/Corporate-Watch/Paywatch-2015.

24. Statistics are from the U.N. Development Report 2006–2007.

25. Fyodor Dostoevsky, *The Brothers Karamazov*, trans. Constance Garnett, (New York: Macmillan, 1922), 55.

26. Stephen Dunn, *New and Selected Poems: 1974–1994* (New York: W. W. Norton and Company, 1994), 276–77.

27. See Gail Sher, *One Continuous Mistake: Four Noble Truths for Writers* (New York: Penguin, 1999).

28. See Georgia Heard, *Writing Toward Home: Lessons to Find Your Way* (Portsmouth, NH: Heinemann, 1995).

29. Reprinted with permission of the author. Both the author and I want to thank the poet Scott Owens, whose daughter coined the word *effluctress*.

30. Henry James, "The Art of Fiction," *Theory of Fiction: Henry James*, ed. James E. Miller, Jr. (Lincoln: University of Nebraska Press, 1972), 35.

31. See "Major Miniaturist Makes Art That Comes with Its Own Microscope," http://online.wsj.com/article/SB125426448028050665 .html.

32. William Shakespeare, *The Merchant of Venice* (Hollywood, FL: Simon and Brown, 2011), 113.
33. Walker, *Possessing the Secret Joy*, 279.
34. Frederick Buechner, *Wishful Thinking: A Seeker's ABC* (New York: HarperOne, 1993).

Acknowledgments

In life we keep coming back in gratitude to the same cluster of people who have always been there for us and give our lives purpose and hope. For me, those cherished people in my life are my loving husband, my compassionate mother, and my amazing students; without them, *Outlaw Christian* could never have been born. In the course of writing this book, I added two more people to this list: my agent Greg Daniel and my publisher Webster Younce. Their faith in me and my work has changed the course of my life and helped me own my vocation as an author. Thank you to the entire team at Nelson Books/HarperCollins Christian Publishing for all your support of this manuscript.

My heart is filled with gratitude for all the dear friends who walked alongside me as I wrote this book, especially Tony Abbott, Helen Beth Kuhens, Caryn Riswold, Amy Watkin, Michael Larson, Susan O'Shaugnessy, Caroline Watkins, Julia Jones, Tom Schlotterback, Ann Younker, Cheryl Peterson, Heather Lowe, Bryce Williams, Pete and Libby Slade, Karen and Mary Andersen, Tim Beagley, Jill Hunter Dale, and Mary-Helen,

Ali and Naomi Ülkü. I want to give a huge shout-out of love and appreciation to my former students: solidarity sisters Sarah McIlvried, Carolyn May, Abbie Carver, and Katie Grooms; and first-draft readers Becki Kidder, Jordan Trumble, Julie Adams, and Bret Wilson. Special thanks also goes out to the Evangelical Lutheran Church in America for nurturing me into a theologian; Gil Harari and Steve Fisher for their help along the way; all my friends at the Kona Tiki Hotel for never judging me for spending my vacation writing; and my 2015 Modern Christian Thought students for being marvelous readers and people who inspire me. And finally, I want to thank Concordia College for giving me the opportunity every day to facilitate conversations about faith and life and to learn from students and colleagues. *There is no me without you.*

About the Author

Jacqueline Bussie is an author, professor, theologian, public speaker, and student of life in all its messy beauty. Her first book, *The Laughter of the Oppressed* (2007), won the national Trinity Prize. An active leader in the Evangelical Lutheran Church in America, Jacqueline teaches religion and theology classes at Concordia College in Moorhead, Minnesota, where she also serves as the director of the forum on faith and life. Jacqueline's favorite classes to teach include The Problem of Evil, Modern Christian Thought, Religion and Literature, Faith in Dialogue, and Compassion and Hope. Every day she is amazed and grateful that she actually gets paid to do the three things she loves most: 1) interact with incredible students, 2) write, and 3) try to make the world a more compassionate place.

In her free time, Jacqueline loves to read books, ride in the front car of roller coasters, take ballroom dance classes with her husband, and travel to any place she has never been before. She is a huge fan of long walks, laughter, the band Bon Iver, the smell of honeysuckle on a hot day, and her husband's fantastic fajitas. Her favorite place to write is next to any body of water. Though Jacqueline hails from Florida, she now lives in Fargo, North Dakota—which is all the proof she needs that God's sense of humor is alive and well.